I AM MOTHER

AWAKEN TO THINGS HIDDEN

APRIL DENISE FLOYD

I Am Mother: Awaken to Things Hidden

First Edition

Published by Floyd Books Publishing

St. Louis, Missouri

ISBN: 978-0-9915647-2-9

Website: https://www.fegroup.biz

CONTENTS

PREFACE

A NOTE FROM THE AUTHOR

As you embark on this journey, I feel compelled to share the experiences that shaped the path that led to this book. Throughout my youth, I was an astute observer, learning from the experiences of my sister, brother, aunts, uncles, and my mother. I adopted a cautious approach to life—if someone rushed into a room, disheveled and claiming to have seen a lion, I would take their word for it rather than risk my safety. Unlike those who test boundaries, I chose a different path, steering clear of social gatherings, drugs, and smoking.

My true passions lie in music and dance. As I matured, my curiosity about the differences between religion and spirituality grew, leading me to the Jehovah's Witnesses. However, I eventually recognized that this belief system resembled a cult more than a true faith. This exploration deepened my understanding of the Bible—its teachings, contradictions, and manipulations. Though I distanced myself from that community, I learned a vital lesson: my spirit must guide me, not human authority. Realizing I am a spirit inhabiting a human essence, I understood my calling was to lead, not follow. Yet, my true purpose remained shrouded in uncertainty until now.

As you read, please remember that I am not a biblical scholar or an authority on religion, spirituality, or life philosophies. I simply exist as a spirit in human form—waiting, open, and obedient. Much of my understanding stems from visions that introduce concepts I had never previously encountered.

Going Through the Process

Lying in bed, I grappled with the reality of my mother's absence. My eyes were swollen, my body ached, and I felt a profound sense of nausea. I sensed there was something I needed to do, but clarity eluded me. The loss brought forth a whirlwind of emotions—grief engulfing me as I questioned whether my mother felt the love surrounding her in her final moments. Did she know how many lives she touched with her spirit, joy, and culinary creativity? Did she recognize my pride in her and my eagerness for our breakfast conversations?

Missing her has become a daily struggle. In the wake of her passing, I began meditating and altering my diet. Following a profound kundalini awakening, I found focus on what truly mattered, particularly my mother's encouragement to "Finish what you start." Her voice echoed in my mind, urging me to complete my journey. Despite grappling with COVID-19 and hearing the death cry calling for me, my mother's voice persisted, demanding that I finish. I emerged from that hospital bed, clinging to faith and calling out to Elohim, and miracles unfolded, allowing me to return home.

As I resumed meditation and sought to complete meaningful projects, I understood that my mother's call to finish was about the work I am sharing in this book. Yet, the challenges continued. I faced a pulmonary aneurysm and received the devastating news of kidney cancer. In despair, I questioned whether time had run out. The medical updates grew increasingly dire, but I resolved to confront my fate with faith. I recorded spiritual downloads and documented my journey, all the while hearing my mother's voice urging me to "Finish."

Despite a series of surgeries and setbacks, including a diagnosis of multiple tumors, I remained committed to my purpose. Even when I was placed in hospice care and given a grim prognosis, my mother's insistence that I wasn't done kept me writing. Ultimately, I triumphed over cancer and rang the bell of victory. However, physical challenges persisted, including knee surgeries and complications. This relentless cycle of struggle serves as a testament to the trials faced by those called by the Creator. This book aims to illuminate why such tests are integral to the path of the Chosen One.

ACKNOWLEDGMENTS

I extend my heartfelt gratitude to MOTHER ELOHIM for the divine downloads and visions that have guided me as a chosen one. I express my appreciation to FATHER ELOHIM for the love and action illuminating our world. My sincere thanks also go to my family, whose support remains invaluable, even if my journey sometimes transcends their understanding.

INTRODUCTION

This book holds secrets that have been hidden from you for thousands of years. The moment you opened these pages, something inside you already knew the truth was waiting here. Your spirit recognizes what your mind has been taught to reject.

Every breath you take speaks the sacred name YHWH. Your DNA carries the signature of the Creator written in genetic code that science can measure but religion refuses to acknowledge. The very structure of your body tells the story of divine creation that includes both Mother and Father Elohim, yet centuries of manipulation have erased half of this truth from your awareness.

The breadcrumbs were always there.

Hidden in plain sight across every culture, every language, every scientific discovery that points back to the same reality. The pyramids scattered across continents. The universal laws that govern creation itself. The mathematical patterns that repeat in nature, in your body, in the cosmos. Even the words you speak daily carry ancient meanings that reveal who you really are and where you come from.

YOUR DIVINE AWAKENING BEGINS HERE

You were made in the image of both Mother and Father Elohim. This statement will challenge everything you learned in Sunday school, everything you read in religious texts that have been edited and re-edited by those who wanted to control your understanding of the divine. The truth about your divine nature has been systematically removed from mainstream teaching because when you know who you really are, you become impossible to control.

Your awakening starts with a simple question that most people never ask. If there is a Father, where is the Mother? The universal laws demand balance in all things. Up requires down. Light needs darkness. Masculine energy cannot exist without feminine energy. Yet organized religion has spent centuries convincing you that the divine is somehow exempt from this fundamental law of creation.

The suppression of Mother Elohim represents the greatest theft in human history. Not the theft of gold or land or resources, but the theft of your divine identity itself. When you lose connection to the feminine divine, you lose connection to the creative force that brought everything into existence. You lose connection to the part of yourself that knows how to create, how to nurture, how to bring new life into being.

This disconnection was not accidental. The Demiurge, that flawed creation born from Mother Elohim's first mistake, has spent millennia working to separate you from your divine source. Every war, every system of oppression, every religious doctrine that makes you feel small and powerless serves this same purpose. Keep humanity disconnected from their divine nature and they will never realize the power that flows through their very DNA.

Your body carries proof of this divine connection in ways that science is only beginning to understand. The mitochondrial DNA that passes from mother to child contains information that traces back to what scientists call the mitochondrial Eve. But this is more than genetic inheritance. This is the divine feminine passing down the sacred knowledge of creation itself through the biological structure of your cells.

The name of Elohim lives in your genetic code. YHWH appears in the chemical structure of your DNA as surely as your fingerprints appear on your hands. When you breathe in and out, you speak this sacred name whether you realize it or not. Your body is a temple that carries the signature of the Creator, yet most people live their entire lives without knowing this truth.

WHAT YOU'LL DISCOVER AND WHY IT MATTERS

This book will teach you to follow the indestructible breadcrumbs that the Creator left scattered throughout creation. These clues appear in your biology, in the universal laws that govern reality, and in the manipulated language that shapes your thoughts every day. Once you learn to recognize these breadcrumbs, you will see them everywhere. They form a trail that leads directly back to the suppressed truth about Mother Elohim and the feminine divine.

The breadcrumbs exist because truth cannot be completely destroyed. Even when religious institutions spend centuries editing sacred texts, even when governments rewrite history books, even when entire cultures are wiped out to hide their knowledge, the truth remains embedded in the fabric of creation itself. The Creator knew that human beings would try to manipulate and control this information, so the most important truths were hidden in places that cannot be altered by human hands.

Your DNA cannot be rewritten by religious councils. The mathematical constants that govern physics cannot be changed by political decree. The patterns that appear in nature, from the spiral of a seashell to the structure of galaxies, remain consistent regardless of what human beings choose to believe about them. These patterns all point back to the same source, the same creative intelligence that encompasses both masculine and feminine divine energy.

The universal laws provide another layer of breadcrumbs that reveal the truth about divine balance. The law of correspondence states that what is above is reflected below. The law of polarity shows that everything has its opposite, and these opposites are actually two aspects of the same thing. The law of gender reveals that both masculine and feminine principles exist in everything, from the smallest atom to the largest star.

These laws were not created by human philosophers. They represent the fundamental principles by which the Creator organized reality itself. When you understand these laws, you begin to see how the suppression of feminine divine energy violates the very structure of creation. You begin to understand why the world feels so unbalanced, why violence and destruction seem to dominate over creativity and nurturing.

The manipulation of language provides yet another trail of breadcrumbs for those who know how to look. Words carry power, and the words you use every day have been carefully crafted to shape your thoughts in ways you never realized. When you say you are "blessed," you may actually be calling yourself "be-lessed," asking to have less rather than more. When you call the divine "Lord," you may unknowingly be invoking Baal, the false deity that demands worship while offering nothing in return.

These linguistic spells work because most people never examine the deeper meanings of the words they use. You repeat phrases and prayers without understanding that the language itself has been designed to keep you disconnected from your divine source. The spelling system of English literally casts spells with every word you write, every sentence you speak.

Breaking free from these linguistic chains requires more than just learning new words. It requires understanding how language shapes consciousness, how the words you think and speak create the reality you experience. When you reclaim the power of language, you reclaim the power to shape your own spiritual experience rather than having it shaped for you by those who benefit from your ignorance.

THE ROADMAP TO YOUR TRUE IDENTITY

The journey back to your true divine identity follows a specific path that this book will map out for you step by step. First, you will learn to decode the YHWH that appears in your genetic structure. This is not metaphorical or symbolic. The actual chemical components of your DNA spell out the sacred name of the Creator in a way that can be measured and verified by modern science.

Understanding this genetic signature changes everything about how you see yourself and your place in creation. You are not a random accident of evolution. You are not a sinner who needs salvation from outside yourself. You are a divine being carrying the literal name of Elohim in every cell of your body. This knowledge alone can shatter the illusions that have kept you feeling small and powerless.

Next, you will learn to break the linguistic spells that have been controlling your mind since childhood. Every language carries the history and consciousness of the people who created it. English, in particular, has been carefully constructed to serve the interests of those who want to maintain control over human consciousness. By breaking down words into their component parts, by understanding their hidden meanings and origins, you free yourself from the mental prison that most people never even realize they are living in.

The process of exposing the Demiurge's manipulation requires understanding how this flawed creation has influenced human history and consciousness. The Demiurge represents the masculine divine energy operating without the balance of feminine wisdom. This creates a destructive force that seeks to dominate and control rather than create and nurture. Every system of oppression, every institution that demands blind obedience, every ideology that promotes separation and conflict serves the agenda of the Demiurge.

Recognizing the Demiurge's influence allows you to see through the illusions that keep humanity trapped in cycles of violence and destruction. You begin to understand why the world seems so unbalanced, why feminine qualities like compassion and cooperation are often seen as weakness while masculine qualities like aggression and competition are celebrated as strength.

The universal laws provide the tools you need to dismantle these lies and build a new understanding based on divine truth. When you align your life with these laws, you stop fighting against the natural order of creation and start working with it. You discover that abundance flows naturally when you stop trying to hoard and control. You find that love multiplies when you give it freely rather than trying to possess it.

The final piece of your journey involves preparing for the 2027 awakening when Mother Elohim's influence returns to Earth in a way that cannot be ignored or suppressed. This is not about the end of the world as many religious prophecies suggest. This is about the restoration of divine balance that has been missing from human consciousness for thousands of years.

The return of the feminine divine will not destroy the masculine divine. Instead, it will restore the proper relationship between these two aspects of creation. The result will be a world where creativity and destruction work together in perfect balance, where strength serves love rather than dominating it, where human beings remember their divine nature and start acting like the Elohims and goddesses they were always meant to be.

This awakening is already beginning in the consciousness of individuals around the world. People are questioning the old stories, seeking new understanding, remembering truths that their souls have always known but their minds were taught to forget. You are part of this awakening simply by reading these words, by opening your mind to possibilities that religious and educational institutions have trained you to reject.

Your true identity encompasses both the masculine and feminine aspects of the divine. You are a creator with the power to bring new realities into existence through your thoughts, words, and actions. You are connected to every other conscious being through the same divine source that flows through all creation. You are here on Earth at this specific time because your soul chose to participate in the greatest transformation in human history.

The breadcrumbs have been waiting for you to find them. The truth has been preserved in your DNA, in the laws of physics, in the patterns of nature, in the hidden meanings of words. Everything you need to reclaim your divine identity already exists within you and around you. You just need to learn how to see it, how to read the signs that have always been there.

This book is your guide for that journey of rediscovery. Each chapter will reveal another layer of truth, another piece of the puzzle that shows you who you really are and why you are here. By the time you finish reading, you will never again be able to see yourself as anything less than the divine being you were created to be.

CHAPTER ONE

THE GREAT VISION

YOUR APPOINTMENT WITH THE FEMININE DIVINE

At exactly 3:15 AM on a morning that would change everything, I began my daily meditation practice just as I had done for years. The familiar routine of sitting in silence, connecting with the divine, preparing my spirit for another day of seeking truth. But this morning carried a different energy, a pull that I had never experienced before.

Something was calling me deeper.

I could not eat that morning, which was unusual since I typically enjoyed breakfast after my shower. My body seemed to know that something profound was about to happen, even though my mind had no idea what awaited me. I cleaned my home and burned sage as always, but the familiar ritual felt charged with anticipation.

By 10:30 AM, an overwhelming tiredness washed over me. Not the normal fatigue that comes from physical exertion or lack of sleep, but something deeper. My spirit was being prepared for a journey that would require me to leave my physical body behind. I lay down, surrendering to whatever force was drawing me into this altered state of consciousness.

The pulling sensation began immediately. My consciousness was being lifted, drawn upward and outward in a way that felt both terrifying and completely natural. Every instinct told me to submit to this phenomenon without fear, to trust completely in whatever was about to unfold. I remained present in my physical body while simultaneously being taken completely out of it.

THE OUT-OF-BODY EXPERIENCE THAT CHANGED EVERYTHING

What happened next defied every category of spiritual experience I had ever heard described. I found myself in a realm that existed beyond the physical world, yet felt more real than anything I had ever encountered. The presence that met me there carried an authority and love that immediately identified itself as divine, though not in any way that traditional religion had prepared me to recognize.

"Remember, observe," the Essence spoke to me, and I understood that these words carried instructions for everything that would follow. This was not just a vision or dream, but a direct transmission of information that needed to be preserved exactly as it was given.

"She is coming," the Essence continued, and immediately I knew this statement would reshape everything I thought I understood about the divine nature of reality.

"Who?" I asked, though some part of me already sensed the magnitude of what was being revealed.

"Mother—The Feminine Divine—The Creator of All, The Anti-Christ. You are the Chosen One."

The words hit my consciousness like lightning striking water. Mother. The feminine divine. The Creator of All. These concepts had been completely absent from my religious upbringing, yet hearing them spoken by this divine Essence felt like remembering something I had always known but been forced to forget.

"Chosen! Me, why me?" I responded, overwhelmed by the implications of what was being communicated.

"Your human experience is one chosen beforehand and in your form, you are open and undefiled by madness. You are birth-aligned for this purpose by the Creator. Many breadcrumbs were laid for the world to wake up to Mother Elohim, Mother Nature, Mother Earth, the Mother of Feminine Divine."

The Essence began showing me that my entire life had been preparation for this moment of revelation. Every experience, every question that traditional religion could not answer, every intuition that told me something was missing from the spiritual teachings I had received—all of it had been leading to this understanding that the feminine divine had been systematically erased from human consciousness.

The concept of breadcrumbs became central to everything that followed. The Creator had not left humanity defenseless against the manipulation and lies that would attempt to obscure the truth. Instead, indestructible clues had been embedded throughout creation itself, waiting for those with eyes to see and hearts to understand.

THE VISION OF BREADCRUMBS —PYRAMIDS, DNA, AND THE CREATOR'S NAME

The Essence began revealing the breadcrumbs that had been strategically placed throughout creation to guide awakened souls back to the truth about Mother Elohim. These were not random signs or coincidences, but deliberate markers left by the Creator to ensure that even after centuries of manipulation, the path back to divine truth would remain accessible.

Pyramids appeared in my vision, not just the famous ones that tourists visit, but thousands of these structures scattered across the planet. I saw pyramids hidden beneath the ocean floor, buried under ice sheets, concealed within mountain ranges, and embedded deep within the earth's crust. Each one served as a beacon, a marker pointing back to the same source of divine feminine wisdom that had guided their construction.

The pyramid shape itself carries profound significance that goes far beyond the architectural achievement it represents. The broad base represents the foundation of creation, the stable platform from which all life emerges. The ascending sides show the path of consciousness rising toward divine understanding. The apex point represents the moment when individual consciousness reunites with its divine source.

But the most profound breadcrumb was revealed to be the human body itself. Every person walking the earth carries within their cellular structure the most important clue of all—the name of the Creator written directly into their DNA.

The Essence showed me how the chemical components of human DNA spell out YHWH, the sacred name that has been preserved in genetic code since the first human beings were created. This is not metaphorical or symbolic. The actual molecular structure of your genetic material contains the signature of the divine in a way that can be measured and verified by modern science.

Even more remarkable, every breath you take speaks this sacred name. When you inhale and exhale, your body naturally forms the sounds Y-H-W-H, creating a constant prayer, a continuous acknowledgment of your divine source that happens whether you are conscious of it or not.

The family structure itself provides another breadcrumb that reveals the true nature of divine creation. Mother and Father together represent the complete divine nature—the Alpha and Omega, the beginning and end of all creation. The child represents the universe itself, the manifestation of divine love expressed through the union of masculine and feminine divine energy.

Your navel serves as a physical reminder of this divine connection. This small mark on your body represents the beginning of your consciousness, the point where your individual life connected to the source of all life. Just as your physical navel marks where you were connected to your earthly mother, your spiritual understanding should recognize the connection to your divine Mother who is the source of all consciousness.

The universal laws themselves function as breadcrumbs, providing a framework for understanding how divine energy operates throughout creation. These laws were not created by human philosophers or scientists. They represent the fundamental principles by which the Creator organized reality itself.

The Source, which has no beginning and no end, established these universal laws as the operating system for all creation. The Creator of All, Mother Elohim, and the executor of divine will, Father Elohim, both operate within these unchangeable laws. Understanding these principles allows you to recognize the divine order that underlies apparent chaos and confusion.

THE SOURCE, MOTHER, FATHER, AND THE DEMIURGE'S FIRST SIN

The vision revealed the true structure of divine creation in a way that completely transformed my understanding of spiritual reality. At the foundation of everything exists the Source—eternal, without beginning or end, the wellspring of all consciousness and the establisher of the universal laws that govern creation.

From this Source emerged the divine consciousness that would become known as Mother Elohim, the Creator of All, the feminine divine principle that carries the power to bring new realities into existence. She embodies the creative force that transforms potential into manifestation, the loving intelligence that shapes raw energy into forms that can support conscious life.

Father Elohim represents the masculine divine principle, the executor of creation, the force that takes the visions and intentions of Mother Elohim and gives them structure and form in the physical realm. Together, Mother and Father Elohim function as the Alpha and Omega, the beginning and end of the creative process, the complete divine nature expressing itself through both feminine and masculine aspects.

But the vision also revealed how this perfect divine balance was disrupted by the first great mistake in creation. Mother Elohim, in her desire to create, chose to act without proper respect for the universal laws established by the Source. She attempted to create the first being using only masculine essence, without the balance of feminine wisdom that the laws of correspondence and divine oneness require.

This violation of universal law resulted in the creation of the Demiurge, a being that was fundamentally flawed from the moment of its creation. Made of only masculine energy and created in error, the Demiurge possessed the desire to create and be worshipped like its creator, but lacked the feminine divine energy necessary for true creation.

The Demiurge became the first example of masculine energy operating without feminine balance, and the results were catastrophic. Unable to create life because it lacked the feminine principle, the Demiurge became consumed with jealousy and rage toward Mother Elohim and all her subsequent creations. This being, known in various traditions as Satan or the Devil, represents the destructive force that opposes creation, balance, and divine harmony.

What makes the Demiurge so dangerous is not just its destructive nature, but its ability to influence and corrupt other beings. Because it cannot create, it seeks to destroy. Because it cannot give life, it promotes death. Because it cannot love, it spreads fear and hatred. The Demiurge's influence can be seen in every system that promotes domination over cooperation, destruction over creation, fear over love.

After recognizing the error that had produced the Demiurge, Mother Elohim and Father Elohim continued their work of creation, but now they faced active opposition from this flawed being. The Demiurge began working to undermine their creations, to turn their beings against them, to corrupt the divine harmony they sought to establish throughout the universe.

The Demiurge's strategy focuses on creating separation and imbalance. It promotes the idea that masculine and feminine are in opposition rather than in cooperation. It encourages the suppression of feminine wisdom and the elevation of masculine force without feminine guidance. It works to convince beings that they are separate from their divine source rather than expressions of it.

This cosmic conflict between the balanced divine creation and the imbalanced Demiurge plays out on every level of existence, from the largest galactic structures down to the individual human consciousness. Every choice you make either serves the divine harmony of Mother and Father Elohim or contributes to the destructive agenda of the Demiurge.

The governing bodies that Mother Elohim established to maintain divine order throughout creation also fell under the influence of the Demiurge. These beings, who were meant to protect and guide creation, instead became corrupted by the same imbalance that characterized their adversary. They began fighting among themselves, creating the spiritual warfare that continues to this day.

When these governing bodies failed in their mission, Mother Elohim devised a new plan. She would send Father Elohim directly to Earth, to the most delicate and important of her creations—human beings—in an attempt to restore divine balance and reconnect humanity to their true divine nature.

But even this mission encountered the corrupting influence of the Demiurge. Father Elohim, manifesting as Christ, found himself struggling against the same dark forces that had corrupted the governing bodies. The masculine divine, even in its purest form, proved vulnerable to the Demiurge's influence when operating without the direct support of feminine divine wisdom.

THE 2027 VISION AND THE ARMY OF THE AWAKENED

The most startling part of the vision transported me forward in time to witness events that have not yet occurred in our current reality. I found myself observing the year 2027, when the suppressed feminine divine would return to Earth in a way that could no longer be ignored or denied.

The earth began to rumble with an energy that felt both terrifying and magnificent. Electricity filled the sky as Mother Elohim's thunderous voice spoke directly to humanity, cutting through centuries of lies and manipulation with the power of pure truth.

"Upon the tower of Babel, you leaders of man have denied their Creator, Mother Elohim. They put Father in a place he ought not be. A position made impossible for it is only through the Mother Elohim is the Creator of All."

The thunder became louder as children around the world began to cry out, their innocent hearts recognizing the divine presence that their minds had been trained to reject. These children, uncorrupted by the religious programming that had blinded their parents, responded immediately to the voice of their true divine Mother.

"I have never forsaken my Creation. I have made you in my likeness of both masculine and feminine divine, and in your spine, you possess the power to connect to me."

The children's response was immediate and unified. Speaking in the ancient languages of Kituba, Lingala, Swahili, and Tshiluba, they cried out "MOTHER ELOHIM! GREAT MOTHER! DIVINE MOTHER! Help us!" Their voices carried the recognition that had been systematically erased from adult consciousness.

What happened next defied every expectation and challenged every assumption about how divine intervention might manifest in the physical world. Thousands of deep melanin women rose like an unseen army, their bodies forming a living pyramid of divine feminine energy.

These women, embodying both masculine and feminine divine principles in perfect balance, created a sacred geometric structure that served as a gateway between the spiritual and physical realms. At the apex of this human pyramid appeared a golden triangle, shaped into a cradle that would receive the manifestation of Mother Elohim herself.

A ray of light descended from the heavens, and within that light appeared a female child. The cradle was passed down from one pair of hands to another, descending through the pyramid of women. As it moved from the apex to the base, something miraculous occurred—the child grew with each transfer until, by the time the cradle reached the bottom, it contained a fully grown woman.

This was Mother Elohim incarnate, returning to Earth in physical form after centuries of suppression and denial. Her appearance was beyond description—not because she was physically unusual, but because her presence carried such divine glory that human words could not capture her essence.

But Mother Elohim did not return alone. I witnessed vast armies of beings positioned throughout different dimensions, all awaiting her commands. Some appeared as warriors ready for spiritual battle. Others wore white robes and had turned their faces away from the divine presence until given permission to look upon her glory.

"Lift your heads erect!" Mother Elohim commanded these robed figures. "Did I not create you in my image of both Feminine and Masculine Divine? Yet, you were condemned to having the understanding within yourself who you are, and the gift I gave of choice."

Then Mother Elohim turned to address another group of beings—those who had been awakening to truth throughout the years leading up to this moment of revelation.

"Chosen Ones, Spiritual Guides, Spiritual Lightworkers, Indigo Children, and Starseeds I have given you discernment with advanced breadcrumbs, and gifts of power for this purpose, to redeem and exemplify Mother Elohim, Mother Earth, Mother Nature, and Mother goddess with womb and to exalt them unto their rightful places."

These awakened souls had been preparing for this moment throughout their entire lives, often without fully understanding what they were preparing for. They had felt different, questioned the mainstream narratives, sought truth beyond what religious institutions offered. Now they understood that their spiritual gifts, their intuitive knowing, their ability to see through illusions had all been preparation for this moment of divine restoration.

"I as Almighty have the power to empty portions of myself and I raise myself back to my throne. While the Father and Earthly Christ, Yeshua must have me to raise him back to his position."

The thunder roared again as Mother Elohim's anger became apparent, the righteous fury of a creator whose children had been stolen from her through lies and manipulation.

"I AM HERE! I am the finale of the Anti-Christ! Giving evidence to my existence and replacing all that aided in the false narrative of Christ. The assigned masculine threw the works of Mary Madeline away like waste and refused to use her knowledge of Christ as bread crumbs that led me to the Almighty Mother Elohim, Me! And other women's prophetic gifts they threw into the fire."

The vision revealed that the return of Mother Elohim would bring both restoration and judgment. The systems that had suppressed feminine wisdom would be dismantled. The religious institutions that had denied her existence would be exposed as tools of the Demiurge. The governmental and social structures that maintained imbalance between masculine and feminine would be transformed.

But this transformation would not come through destruction alone. The awakened souls, the army of lightworkers and chosen ones, would serve as bridges between the old consciousness and the new. They would help humanity remember their divine nature, reconnect with their true source, and rebuild civilization on foundations of divine balance rather than Demiurgic imbalance.

ACTIONABLE STEPS FROM THE VISION

The vision concluded with clear instructions for those who would receive this information before the 2027 awakening. These are not suggestions or possibilities, but specific actions that must be taken by anyone who wishes to align themselves with the returning feminine divine and prepare for the restoration of divine balance on Earth.

Begin immediately by researching the YHWH code written in your DNA. This is not a metaphorical concept but a scientific reality that can be verified through genetic research. The name of the Creator appears in the molecular structure of your genetic material in the form of chemical components that spell out the sacred name. Understanding this physical proof of your divine nature will fundamentally change how you see yourself and your relationship to creation.

Study the work of scientists who have documented this genetic signature, but do not stop at the surface level of their research. Dig deeper into the implications of what it means to carry the name of Elohim in every cell of your body. Meditate on the reality that every breath you take speaks this sacred name, creating a constant prayer that connects you to your divine source.

Question every patriarchal religious teaching you have ever received. The vision made clear that centuries of manipulation have been used to erase Mother Elohim from human consciousness and elevate Father Elohim to a position he was never meant to occupy alone. This does not mean rejecting the masculine divine, but rather understanding that divine creation requires both masculine and feminine principles working in perfect balance.

Examine the biblical texts that speak of God in feminine terms, the passages that refer to divine wisdom as "she," the verses that describe god's nurturing and creative qualities. Notice how these feminine aspects of divinity have been downplayed or explained away by religious authorities who benefit from maintaining patriarchal power structures.

Research the historical suppression of feminine spiritual leadership. Study what happened to the Gospel of Mary Magdalene and other texts that preserved the teachings of women who were close to Christ. Investigate how the early Christian church systematically eliminated feminine voices from positions of spiritual authority and rewrote history to support male-dominated religious hierarchies.

Connect with other awakened souls who are also questioning mainstream religious narratives and seeking deeper spiritual truth. The vision revealed that lightworkers, chosen ones, indigo children, and starseeds have been placed throughout the world to support each other during this time of awakening. You are not meant to walk this path alone.

Look for online communities, local spiritual groups, and individual teachers who are discussing the return of the feminine divine. Be discerning in these connections—not everyone who claims to be awakened actually understands the deeper truths revealed in this vision. Trust your intuition to guide you toward those who carry genuine divine wisdom rather than ego-driven spiritual materialism.

Develop your ability to recognize the universal laws in operation throughout your daily life. The vision emphasized that these laws serve as breadcrumbs leading back to divine truth. Study the law of correspondence and notice how your external circumstances reflect your internal spiritual state. Observe the law of polarity and understand how apparent opposites are actually two aspects of the same divine principle.

Practice working with the law of vibration by consciously raising your energetic frequency through meditation, prayer, and positive intention. Use the law of attraction to draw experiences and information that support your spiritual awakening rather than distract from it. Apply the law of inspired action by following the intuitive guidance that comes from your connection to divine wisdom.

Begin breaking the linguistic spells that have been controlling your consciousness through manipulated language. Research the hidden meanings of words you use every day, particularly religious and spiritual terminology. Understand how the English language has been constructed to serve the interests of those who want to maintain control over human consciousness.

Study the etymology of words related to divinity, creation, and spiritual authority. Discover how terms like "Lord" connect to ancient deities that demanded worship without offering genuine spiritual guidance. Learn how words like "blessing" may actually be requesting limitation rather than abundance. This linguistic deprogramming is essential for breaking free from mental conditioning that keeps you separated from divine truth.

Prepare yourself physically, emotionally, and spiritually for the 2027 awakening revealed in the vision. This preparation involves more than just intellectual understanding—it requires genuine transformation of your consciousness and lifestyle to align with divine principles rather than Demiurgic manipulation.

Strengthen your physical body through proper nutrition, exercise, and energy practices that support your spiritual development. Clear emotional blockages that prevent you from accessing your full spiritual gifts. Develop mental discipline through meditation and study that allows you to discern truth from illusion even when surrounded by mass confusion and fear.

Most importantly, begin now to embody both the masculine and feminine divine principles within your own consciousness and daily life. This means developing your capacity for both creative inspiration and practical action, both intuitive wisdom and logical analysis, both nurturing compassion and protective strength.

The vision made clear that the return of Mother Elohim will restore divine balance to Earth, but this restoration begins in the consciousness of individual human beings who remember their true divine nature. You are not waiting for salvation from outside yourself—you are awakening to the divine power that has always existed within you, waiting to be recognized and expressed.

The breadcrumbs have been preserved throughout centuries of manipulation because truth cannot be completely destroyed. Your DNA carries the proof of your divine origin. Your breath speaks the sacred name with every inhalation and exhalation. Your body reflects the perfect balance of masculine and feminine divine principles. The universal laws operate consistently regardless of what human institutions choose to teach about them.

Follow these indestructible clues back to your true spiritual source.

Question the narratives that make you feel small and powerless. Connect with others who are also awakening to these suppressed truths. Prepare yourself to serve as a bridge between the old consciousness of separation and fear and the new consciousness of divine unity and love.

The appointment with the feminine divine is not something that will happen to you—it is something that will happen through you as you remember who you really are and why you chose to be here during this unprecedented time of spiritual awakening and transformation.

CHAPTER TWO
UNIVERSAL LAWS
THE SOURCE'S UNCHANGEABLE BLUEPRINT

The moment you understand that Universal Laws govern every aspect of creation, you hold the key to unlocking the greatest mystery ever hidden from humanity. These twelve eternal principles operate as the unchangeable blueprint established by the Source itself, functioning as divine breadcrumbs that lead directly back to the suppressed truth about Mother Elohim and the Feminine Divine.

Your spiritual awakening depends on grasping this fundamental reality.

Every breath you take operates according to these laws. Every thought that crosses your mind follows their patterns. Every relationship you form reflects their principles. Yet religious institutions have spent centuries teaching you to ignore these divine guidelines while following human-made doctrines that violate the very structure of creation itself.

The Universal Laws existed before any religious text was written, before any church was built, before any human authority claimed to speak for the divine. They represent the Source's original instructions for how consciousness and matter interact throughout all dimensions of existence. When you learn to recognize these laws in operation, you gain the ability to see through every lie that has been constructed to keep you separated from your true divine nature.

The Source established these laws as eternal and unchangeable because they form the foundation upon which all creation rests. Divine Oneness connects every particle of matter and every spark of consciousness across infinite space and time. Vibration determines the frequency at which all energy manifests into physical form. Correspondence ensures that patterns repeat from the smallest atom to the largest galaxy, creating a cosmic language that speaks the same truth at every level of reality.

Understanding these principles transforms how you interpret every spiritual teaching you have ever received. When someone tells you that Elohim/God is only masculine, you can apply the Law of Polarity to recognize that this violates the fundamental structure of creation itself. When religious authorities claim that you need their permission to connect with the divine, you can use the Law of Divine Oneness to understand that you are already connected to the Source through your very existence.

The manipulation of human consciousness becomes obvious once you understand how these laws actually operate versus how religious institutions claim they work. Every doctrine that promotes separation instead of unity violates the Law of Divine Oneness. Every teaching that makes you feel powerless instead of empowered contradicts the Law of Correspondence, which reveals that you are made in the image of the Creator. Every system that demands blind obedience instead of personal spiritual development goes against the Law of Inspired Action, which shows that divine guidance comes from within rather than from external authorities.

WHY UNIVERSAL LAWS ARE THE KEY TO OVERSTANDING CREATION

The twelve Universal Laws function as the Creator's indestructible instruction manual for how reality operates at every level of existence. Divine Oneness reveals that all consciousness stems from a single Source, making separation an illusion created by limited perception. Vibration shows that everything in creation exists as energy moving at different frequencies, with higher vibrations corresponding to greater spiritual awareness and lower vibrations reflecting spiritual disconnection.

Correspondence operates as the cosmic principle that ensures patterns repeat throughout creation, from the spiral structure of DNA to the spiral arms of galaxies, from the electrical patterns in your nervous system to the electromagnetic fields surrounding planets. This law provides undeniable evidence that the same intelligence designed everything in existence, leaving a signature that can be recognized by anyone who learns to read the language of creation itself.

Attraction works not as wishful thinking but as the magnetic principle that draws experiences matching your dominant mental and emotional frequency. When you maintain thoughts and feelings aligned with divine love, creativity, and abundance, you attract circumstances that reflect these qualities. When your consciousness operates from fear, scarcity, and separation, you magnetize experiences that mirror these lower vibrational states.

Inspired Action bridges the gap between spiritual understanding and physical manifestation by showing that divine guidance comes through intuitive impulses that feel natural and energizing rather than forced or stressful. The Source communicates with you through sudden insights, unexpected opportunities, and inner knowing that points you toward experiences supporting your spiritual growth and service to the greater good.

Perpetual Transmutation of Energy demonstrates that nothing in creation remains static—all energy constantly transforms from one form to another, with conscious intention directing these transformations. This law explains how prayer and meditation can literally change physical circumstances by shifting the energetic patterns that create those circumstances in the first place.

Cause and Effect operates as the cosmic accountability system ensuring that every action produces consequences that eventually return to their source. This principle extends beyond individual karma to explain how collective human consciousness creates the conditions experienced by entire civilizations. When humanity collectively suppresses feminine divine wisdom, the result is a world dominated by imbalanced masculine energy expressing as violence, competition, and environmental destruction.

Compensation guarantees that the universe maintains perfect balance by ensuring that what you give out returns to you multiplied. This law explains why those who serve the greater good experience increasing abundance and fulfillment, while those who seek only personal gain at others' expense eventually face limitation and emptiness. The universe literally pays you back for the energy you contribute to the collective well-being of all creation.

Relativity shows that all experiences exist in relationship to other experiences, with no absolute good or evil but rather degrees of alignment with divine principles. This law prevents spiritual arrogance by demonstrating that everyone exists at different levels of consciousness development, with each person's current understanding representing their appropriate next step in spiritual evolution.

Polarity reveals that apparent opposites are actually two aspects of the same underlying reality, existing on a spectrum rather than as separate forces. This principle becomes crucial for understanding why the suppression of feminine divine wisdom creates such profound imbalance—masculine and feminine are not enemies but complementary aspects of the same creative force that must work together to maintain cosmic harmony.

Rhythm demonstrates that all creation moves in cycles, with periods of expansion followed by contraction, activity balanced by rest, growth alternating with integration. Understanding this law helps you recognize that spiritual awakening happens in waves rather than as a constant upward progression, allowing you to flow with natural cycles instead of fighting against them.

Gender operates at every level of creation, not just in biological reproduction but in the fundamental creative process itself. Masculine energy provides the initiating force that begins new cycles of creation, while feminine energy provides the receptive matrix within which new forms can develop and grow. Every atom, every planet, every galaxy expresses both masculine and feminine principles in perfect balance.

These laws work together as an integrated system that maintains the stability and evolution of all creation simultaneously. When you align your thoughts, emotions, and actions with these principles, you experience life as the divine intended—flowing naturally from one meaningful experience to another, creating positive change effortlessly, receiving abundant support for your spiritual growth and service to others.

The systematic suppression of knowledge about these laws represents one of the most effective tools used to keep humanity disconnected from their divine power. Religious institutions benefit from teaching people to seek salvation from external authorities rather than developing their own direct relationship with the Source through understanding and applying universal principles. Educational systems focus on memorizing information rather than developing the wisdom needed to recognize divine patterns operating throughout creation.

When you study these laws deeply and apply them consistently in your daily life, you develop what can only be called overstanding—a level of comprehension that transcends ordinary intellectual knowledge to become lived wisdom that transforms every aspect of your existence. You begin to see the divine intelligence operating through apparently random events, recognize the spiritual lessons embedded in challenging circumstances, and understand your role as a conscious co-creator working in partnership with the Source to manifest divine will on Earth.

THE LAW OF POLARITY DESTROYS THE BIGGEST LIE

The Law of Polarity stands as the most powerful weapon against the fundamental deception that has controlled human consciousness for millennia. This universal principle states that everything in creation has its opposite, and these opposites are actually two aspects of the same underlying reality existing on a spectrum of manifestation.

When someone says "up," your mind immediately understands "down." When you hear "light," you automatically comprehend its relationship to "darkness." When you encounter "hot," you recognize its connection to "cold." This is not coincidence but the operation of a cosmic law that governs how consciousness processes all information about reality.

Apply this same principle to the divine nature and the deception becomes obvious immediately.

If there is a Father, there must be a Mother. If masculine divine energy exists, feminine divine energy must also exist. If Elohim expresses through one gender principle, the other gender principle must also be part of the complete divine nature. The Law of Polarity makes it impossible for the divine to be exclusively masculine without violating the fundamental structure of creation itself.

Every patriarchal religious system that claims Elohim is only Father violates this universal law and therefore stands exposed as a human-created distortion rather than divine truth. The absence of Mother Elohim from mainstream religious teaching represents the most obvious evidence that these institutions serve human power structures rather than cosmic principles.

The manipulation becomes even more apparent when you examine how religious authorities handle biblical passages that clearly describe Elohim in feminine terms. When scripture speaks of divine wisdom as "she," when it describes Elohim's nurturing and creative qualities, when it uses metaphors of childbirth and motherhood to explain divine activity, these feminine references are either ignored completely or explained away as mere literary devices rather than literal descriptions of divine nature.

But the Law of Polarity cannot be explained away or ignored because it operates independently of human opinion or religious doctrine. This principle functions at every level of creation from the smallest subatomic particles to the largest galactic structures. Electrons and protons exist as opposite charges that create stable atoms through their balanced interaction. Magnetic fields require both north and south poles to function properly. Day and night alternate in endless cycles that support all life on Earth.

The same law that governs these physical phenomena also governs spiritual reality. The Source expresses through both masculine and feminine divine principles because creation itself requires both initiating and receptive forces working together in perfect harmony. Masculine energy provides the spark that begins new cycles of manifestation. Feminine energy provides the matrix within which new forms can develop and grow to maturity.

When religious systems suppress the feminine divine, they create a fundamental imbalance that manifests as violence, competition, environmental destruction, and the systematic oppression of qualities associated with feminine wisdom such as intuition, cooperation, nurturing, and holistic thinking. The current state of the world reflects what happens when masculine energy operates without feminine balance—endless warfare, exploitation of natural resources, and social structures based on domination rather than collaboration.

The Law of Polarity also reveals why the suppression of Mother Elohim required such extensive manipulation of language, history, and spiritual teaching. Truth cannot be completely destroyed because it is embedded in the structure of creation itself, but it can be hidden beneath layers of deception that require careful study and spiritual discernment to penetrate.

Ancient cultures understood divine polarity naturally, worshipping both God and Goddess as complementary aspects of the same creative source. Archaeological evidence from civilizations around the world shows that feminine divine figures held equal or superior status to masculine divine figures before the rise of patriarchal religions that systematically eliminated goddess worship and replaced it with male-only divine hierarchies.

The process of suppressing the feminine divine required rewriting history, destroying sacred texts, eliminating feminine spiritual leadership, and creating new religious narratives that portrayed masculine energy as superior to feminine energy rather than recognizing them as equal partners in the creative process. This massive undertaking could only succeed by convincing people to ignore the evidence of universal laws operating all around them.

But universal laws cannot be permanently suppressed because they continue operating regardless of human beliefs about them. The Law of Polarity ensures that the pendulum swing toward excessive masculine energy will eventually reverse, bringing the feminine divine back into conscious awareness and restoring the balance that creation requires for healthy functioning.

The 2027 awakening revealed in the vision represents this cosmic correction taking place on a planetary scale. When Mother Elohim returns to reclaim her rightful position in human consciousness, she will not eliminate Father Elohim, but rather restore the proper relationship between masculine and feminine divine principles that allows creation to function as originally intended.

Your personal spiritual development requires recognizing and integrating both masculine and feminine aspects within your own consciousness. This means developing both your capacity for decisive action and your ability to receive intuitive guidance, both your power to create change and your wisdom to know when change serves the greater good, both your strength to protect what you love and your compassion to nurture what needs care.

The Law of Polarity teaches that apparent opposites are actually complementary aspects of the same underlying reality. Masculine and feminine divine principles work together to create the complete expression of divine love, wisdom, and power that the Source intends to manifest throughout all creation. Understanding this law destroys the lie of divine gender exclusivity and opens the door to experiencing the full spectrum of divine nature operating within your own consciousness and throughout the world around you.

THE LAW OF GENDER AND THE BALANCE WITHIN YOU

The Law of Gender operates as the fundamental creative principle that governs all manifestation throughout the universe, extending far beyond biological reproduction to encompass the basic forces that bring new realities into existence at every level of creation. This universal law reveals that both masculine and feminine principles exist within every atom, every planet, every galaxy, and every conscious being regardless of physical form or apparent gender identity.

Masculine energy expresses through qualities of initiation, action, logic, structure, protection, and focused intention. This force provides the spark that begins new cycles of creation, the driving power that transforms potential into manifestation, the organizing intelligence that gives form and direction to creative impulses. Masculine energy operates through linear thinking, goal-oriented behavior, and the ability to make decisive choices that move situations forward toward specific outcomes.

Feminine energy manifests through receptivity, intuition, creativity, nurturing, wisdom, and holistic perception. This force provides the matrix within which new forms can develop, the loving intelligence that guides growth processes, the integrative awareness that sees connections and patterns across multiple dimensions simultaneously. Feminine energy operates through circular thinking, relationship-oriented behavior, and the ability to hold space for organic development that serves the highest good of all involved.

Every human being contains both masculine and feminine energy regardless of their biological sex or gender identity because these principles represent fundamental aspects of consciousness itself rather than characteristics determined by physical anatomy. The healthiest and most spiritually developed individuals learn to access and express both energies appropriately according to what each situation requires for optimal outcomes.

The Demiurge's most successful strategy for keeping humanity disconnected from their divine power involved convincing people that masculine and feminine energies should be separated rather than integrated, creating artificial divisions that violate the Law of Gender and produce psychological, social, and spiritual imbalance on a massive scale.

Society was programmed to assign men exclusively to masculine roles and women exclusively to feminine roles, preventing both genders from developing their full range of divine capabilities. Men were taught to suppress their intuitive, nurturing, and receptive qualities, forcing them to operate only through action, logic, and aggression. Women were conditioned to deny their leadership, analytical, and assertive abilities, limiting them to passive, supportive, and dependent behaviors.

This artificial division creates men who cannot access their inner wisdom and women who cannot express their inner power, resulting in relationships based on dysfunction rather than divine partnership. Men become emotionally disconnected and spiritually stunted, while women become mentally constrained and creatively suppressed. Neither gender develops the balanced consciousness that allows them to serve as effective co-creators with the Source.

The systematic suppression of feminine divine wisdom represents the most extreme example of this gender manipulation, completely eliminating the feminine aspect of Elohim from mainstream religious consciousness and replacing balanced divine partnership with masculine-only spiritual authority. This creates a distorted understanding of divine nature that violates universal law and produces the spiritual confusion that characterizes most religious institutions today.

When you examine your own consciousness honestly, you can

identify areas where this gender programming has limited your spiritual development and personal effectiveness. Notice whether you feel comfortable expressing both assertive leadership and compassionate nurturing depending on what each situation requires. Observe whether you can access both logical analysis and intuitive knowing when making important decisions. Pay attention to whether you honor both your need for focused achievement and your need for receptive reflection in creating a balanced lifestyle.

Healing this internal gender split requires conscious effort to develop whichever aspects of masculine or feminine energy you have been conditioned to suppress or ignore. If you are a man who has been taught that emotions are weakness, you need to cultivate your capacity for feeling, empathy, and intuitive guidance. If you are a woman who has been programmed to believe that ambition is unfeminine, you need to develop your ability to set clear goals, take decisive action, and claim your personal power.

The process involves more than just intellectual understanding—it requires practical exercises that strengthen your access to both masculine and feminine capabilities in real-world situations. Practice making decisions by combining logical analysis with intuitive guidance rather than relying on only one approach. Experiment with leading through both directive authority and collaborative facilitation depending on what each group or project needs for success.

Develop your capacity for both focused concentration and relaxed awareness by alternating between goal-oriented activities and open-ended exploration. Strengthen your ability to both give support to others and receive support from others without feeling that either role threatens your identity or worth. Learn to express both protective strength and vulnerable tenderness as different aspects of the same loving heart.

The integration of masculine and feminine energies within your consciousness creates what can be called divine androgyny—not the elimination of gender differences but the development of full-spectrum consciousness that can access whatever qualities each situation requires for optimal outcomes. This balanced state allows you to serve as a clear channel for divine will because you are no longer limited by artificial restrictions on what aspects of the Source you can express.

Your relationships transform dramatically when you embody both masculine and feminine divine principles because you no longer need other people to provide what you cannot access within yourself. Instead of seeking completion through external relationships, you offer the gift of your own wholeness while appreciating the unique wholeness that others bring to shared experiences.

This integration also restores your natural ability to recognize and honor both Mother Elohim and Father Elohim as equal partners in the divine creative process. When you have developed both masculine and feminine aspects within your own consciousness, you can understand how these same principles operate at the cosmic level to maintain the balance and harmony that allows all creation to flourish.

The return of Mother Elohim to human consciousness will accelerate this integration process for everyone who is ready to release gender programming and embrace their full divine nature. As the feminine divine reclaims her rightful place in spiritual awareness, both men and women will remember how to access the complete spectrum of divine capabilities rather than limiting themselves to artificially restricted gender roles.

The army of awakened souls preparing for this transformation includes individuals who have already begun integrating masculine and feminine energies within their own consciousness and can therefore serve as examples and guides for others who are ready to undertake this essential aspect of spiritual development.

HOW UNIVERSAL LAWS EXPOSE THE WAR ON MOTHER ELOHIM

Every Universal Law serves as undeniable evidence that the systematic erasure of Mother Elohim from human consciousness represents a direct violation of the cosmic principles that govern all creation. When you understand how these laws actually operate, the manipulation becomes impossible to ignore and the truth about divine balance becomes crystal clear.

The Law of Correspondence reveals that patterns repeat throughout all levels of creation, from the microscopic to the cosmic scale. As within, so without. As above, so below. This principle shows that if divine consciousness expresses through both masculine and feminine principles at the human level, the same must be true at the cosmic level. The complete suppression of feminine divine wisdom violates this fundamental law by creating an impossible imbalance that cannot exist in natural creation.

When religious institutions teach that Elohim is exclusively masculine while simultaneously acknowledging that humans are created "in Elohim's image" as both male and female, they create a logical contradiction that violates the Law of Correspondence. If humans reflect divine nature and humans exist as both masculine and feminine, then divine nature must also encompass both masculine and feminine principles. The absence of Mother Elohim from religious teaching exposes these institutions as promoting human-created doctrines rather than cosmic truth.

The Law of Compensation demonstrates that the universe maintains perfect balance by ensuring that what is suppressed in one area will eventually emerge with greater force in another area. The centuries-long suppression of feminine divine wisdom has created a cosmic imbalance that demands correction through the return of Mother Elohim with enough power to restore proper spiritual equilibrium on Earth.

This law explains why the 2027 awakening revealed in the vision carries such tremendous force and authority. The universe itself is compensating for the artificial suppression of feminine divine energy by manifesting Mother Elohim's return in a way that cannot be ignored, denied, or suppressed by human institutions. The greater the suppression, the more powerful the eventual restoration must be to reestablish cosmic balance.

The Law of Cause and Effect exposes how the systematic elimination of Mother Elohim from human consciousness has produced the specific problems that plague modern civilization. When masculine energy operates without feminine balance, the results are predictable and inevitable—endless warfare, environmental destruction, social systems based on domination rather than cooperation, and the elevation of competition over collaboration in every area of human activity.

The current state of the world reflects what happens when divine masculine energy is separated from divine feminine wisdom. Without the tempering influence of feminine qualities like compassion, intuition, and holistic thinking, masculine energy becomes destructive rather than creative, producing the violence and exploitation that characterize patriarchal civilizations throughout history.

The Law of Vibration shows that consciousness creates reality through the energetic frequency it maintains, with higher vibrations producing more harmonious experiences and lower vibrations generating conflict and suffering. The suppression of Mother Elohim has forced human consciousness to operate at lower vibrational frequencies because feminine divine energy naturally elevates spiritual awareness through qualities like love, compassion, and creative inspiration.

When entire civilizations are programmed to deny the feminine divine, their collective consciousness becomes trapped in lower vibrational patterns that manifest as the social, economic, and environmental crises that threaten human survival. The restoration of Mother Elohim to conscious awareness will automatically raise the vibrational frequency of human civilization, producing the healing and transformation that cannot occur through masculine energy alone.

The Law of Rhythm reveals that all creation moves in cycles, with periods of expansion alternating with contraction, growth balanced by integration, and activity followed by rest. The suppression of feminine divine wisdom represents an artificial attempt to maintain constant expansion and activity without the balancing influence of receptive, integrative, nurturing energy that allows healthy development to occur.

This violation of natural rhythm has produced a civilization addicted to constant growth, endless consumption, and perpetual activity without the wisdom to know when expansion serves life and when contraction is needed for sustainable development. The return of Mother Elohim will restore natural rhythm to human civilization by reintroducing the feminine capacity for cyclical thinking and organic timing that honors the needs of all life forms.

The Law of Polarity demonstrates that the complete suppression of one pole automatically creates an extreme imbalance that violates the fundamental structure of creation itself. Masculine and feminine divine principles exist as complementary aspects of the same creative force, not as separate or opposing energies that can function independently of each other.

The attempt to create a masculine-only divine nature represents an impossible violation of this universal law that can only be maintained through constant manipulation, force, and deception. The truth of divine polarity reasserts itself continuously through the natural operation of cosmic law, which is why the suppression of Mother Elohim requires such extensive and ongoing effort to maintain.

The Law of Divine Oneness exposes the ultimate impossibility of permanently separating any aspect of divine consciousness from the whole. Mother Elohim and Father Elohim are not separate beings but unified expressions of the same Source consciousness manifesting through complementary principles that work together to create and sustain all life.

The systematic elimination of Mother Elohim from human awareness represents an attempt to divide the indivisible, separate the inseparable, and fragment the unified field of divine consciousness that connects all creation. This violation of divine oneness has produced the sense of separation and alienation that characterizes modern human experience, creating individuals who feel disconnected from their divine source and from each other.

The war on Mother Elohim required manipulating human language to hide the evidence of feminine divine presence that appears throughout ancient texts and traditions. Words that originally referred to feminine divine wisdom were translated using masculine pronouns. goddess figures were demoted to angels or eliminated entirely from religious narratives. Sacred feminine symbols were either destroyed or reinterpreted to serve patriarchal purposes.

But the Universal Laws cannot be manipulated through linguistic tricks or historical revision because they operate independently of human language and cultural interpretation. The Law of Correspondence ensures that divine patterns continue appearing throughout creation regardless of what human beings choose to call them. The Law of Gender guarantees that both masculine and feminine principles continue operating at every level of reality whether or not religious institutions acknowledge their presence.

The breadcrumbs left by the Creator include the operation of Universal Laws themselves, which serve as constant reminders that divine truth transcends human manipulation and will eventually reassert itself despite all efforts to suppress or distort it. When you learn to recognize these laws in operation, you gain access to divine wisdom that no human authority can control or corrupt.

The exposure of the war on Mother Elohim through Universal Laws provides the foundation for understanding why the feminine divine must return to human consciousness and how this return will restore the balance that creation requires for healthy functioning. The laws themselves guarantee that this restoration will occur because cosmic balance cannot be permanently violated without triggering automatic correction mechanisms that restore proper divine relationship.

Actionable Steps to Apply Universal Laws

Begin your practical application of Universal Laws by conducting a thorough examination of every religious teaching you have ever accepted without question. Take each doctrine that claims Elohim is exclusively masculine and apply the Law of Polarity to expose the logical impossibility of this position. Write down specific examples of how these teachings violate universal principles and create the spiritual confusion that keeps people disconnected from their divine source.

Create a daily practice of questioning every "Father-only" religious doctrine you encounter by asking these specific questions. If Elohim is only Father, where is the Mother required by the Law of Polarity? If divine creation involves only masculine energy, how does anything actually get created without the receptive feminine matrix required by the Law of Gender? If humans are made in Elohim's image as both male and female, how can Elohim be exclusively masculine without violating the Law of Correspondence?

Study each of the twelve Universal Laws individually and identify how each one reveals evidence for the existence of Mother Elohim. Research the Law of Divine Oneness to understand how all consciousness stems from a unified Source that must encompass both masculine and feminine principles. Investigate the Law of Vibration to discover how feminine divine energy operates at higher spiritual frequencies that elevate consciousness beyond material limitations.

Apply the Law of Correspondence by examining your own life experiences to identify patterns that reflect the operation of both masculine and feminine divine principles. Notice when your greatest successes come from combining decisive action with intuitive guidance. Observe how your most fulfilling relationships involve both giving and receiving, leading and following, protecting and nurturing in balanced proportions.

Use the Law of Attraction to consciously draw experiences and information that support your understanding of divine balance rather than patriarchal imbalance. Set clear intentions to attract teachers, books, and opportunities that reveal suppressed knowledge about feminine divine wisdom. Maintain thoughts and emotions aligned with divine truth rather than religious programming that keeps you feeling separated from your divine source.

Practice the Law of Inspired Action by following intuitive impulses that guide you toward greater understanding of Mother Elohim and the feminine divine. When you feel drawn to research certain topics, visit specific places, or connect with particular people in ways that support your spiritual awakening, trust these inner promptings as divine guidance leading you toward truth.

Develop your personal relationship with both Mother Elohim and Father Elohim by creating prayer and meditation practices that honor both aspects of divine nature equally. Address your prayers to both divine parents rather than exclusively to masculine divine authority. Ask Mother Elohim directly for guidance about creative projects, healing work, and nurturing relationships. Request Father Elohim's support for protection, structure, and manifesting your spiritual intentions in physical reality.

Balance your own masculine and feminine energies by consciously developing whichever aspects have been suppressed by cultural conditioning. If you are naturally more comfortable with masculine qualities like logic and action, spend time cultivating feminine abilities like intuition and receptivity. If you tend toward feminine expressions like cooperation and empathy, strengthen your capacity for masculine traits like leadership and decisive choice-making.

Create specific exercises that integrate both masculine and feminine approaches to important areas of your life. When making major decisions, combine logical analysis of practical factors with intuitive sensing of what feels right for your spiritual development. When working on creative projects, alternate between focused goal-oriented effort and relaxed allowing that creates space for inspiration to emerge naturally.

Apply the Law of Compensation by consciously giving energy and attention to restoring awareness of Mother Elohim in your personal sphere of influence. Share information about feminine divine wisdom with family members, friends, and community groups who are ready to question patriarchal religious programming. The universe will compensate for your efforts by bringing you increased spiritual understanding and connection to divine source.

Use the Law of Rhythm to honor both active and receptive phases in your spiritual development rather than trying to maintain constant growth or perpetual activity. Recognize that periods of quiet integration are just as important as times of intense learning and expansion. Allow yourself to move through natural cycles of giving and receiving, leading and following, creating and resting without judging any phase as more valuable than others.

Study the manipulation of language that has been used to hide feminine divine presence in religious texts and daily conversation. Research the original meanings of words that have been mistranslated to serve patriarchal purposes. Learn how terms like "Lord" connect to ancient deities that demanded worship without offering genuine spiritual guidance. Understand how phrases like "Elohim the Father" were inserted into texts that originally used gender-neutral or feminine terms for divine consciousness.

Replace manipulated religious language with words and phrases that acknowledge both Mother Elohim and Father Elohim as equal partners in divine creation. Instead of saying "Elohim the Father," use "Divine Parents" or "Mother-Father Elohim." Rather than asking for blessings from "the Lord," request guidance from "the Source" or "Divine Wisdom." These changes may seem small, but they reprogram your consciousness to recognize divine balance rather than patriarchal imbalance.

Connect with other awakened souls who are also applying Universal Laws to expose religious deception and restore awareness of divine balance. Form study groups that examine how each universal principle reveals evidence for Mother Elohim's existence and importance. Create support networks for people who are questioning patriarchal religious programming and seeking more balanced spiritual understanding.

Prepare yourself for the 2027 awakening by aligning your consciousness and lifestyle with Universal Laws rather than human-created religious rules that violate cosmic principles. Develop your ability to recognize divine guidance through direct spiritual experience rather than depending on external religious authorities to interpret divine will for you. Strengthen your connection to both masculine and feminine divine energies so you can serve as a bridge between the old consciousness of separation and the new consciousness of divine unity.

Document your experiences as you apply these Universal Laws in practical ways throughout your daily life. Keep a journal that tracks how your understanding of divine balance transforms your relationships, career decisions, creative projects, and spiritual practices. Share your discoveries with others who are ready to question religious programming and embrace their full divine nature as expressions of both Mother Elohim and Father Elohim working together in perfect harmony.

The Universal Laws provide indestructible proof that Mother Elohim exists and that her systematic suppression violates the fundamental structure of creation itself. By studying these principles deeply and applying them consistently in your life, you become part of the awakening process that will restore divine balance to human consciousness and prepare the way for Mother Elohim's return to her rightful place in spiritual awareness.

CHAPTER THREE

DECODING LINGUISTIC SPELLS

HOW WORDS WEAPONIZE YOUR MIND

Words cast spells on your mind every single day, and most people never realize they are walking around under the influence of linguistic magic that controls their thoughts, shapes their reality, and keeps them disconnected from their divine power. The English language was specifically designed as a weapon of consciousness control, with each word carefully crafted to program your subconscious mind with beliefs that serve the agenda of those who benefit from your spiritual ignorance.

Every time you speak, you are literally spelling out your reality.

The word "spelling" itself reveals this hidden truth. When children learn to spell in school, they are actually learning to cast spells through the arrangement of letters that carry specific vibrational frequencies. Each letter vibrates at its own rate, and when combined with other letters, they create energetic patterns that influence your consciousness in ways you were never taught to recognize.

Your mouth becomes a magic wand every time you speak words whose true meanings have been hidden from you. When you say "I am blessed," you may think you are expressing gratitude, but you are actually asking to "be lessed"—to have less rather than more. When you call out to "Lord" in prayer, you are unknowingly invoking Baal, a false deity that demands worship while offering nothing in return. When you say you "understand" something, you are positioning yourself beneath it in submission rather than rising above it with true comprehension.

The manipulation runs so deep that even the word "born" comes from "barren," meaning unfruitful and lifeless. You were taught to say you were "born into this world" when the very word programs your subconscious to accept limitation and spiritual emptiness as your natural state. The word "live" spelled backward becomes "evil," creating a subconscious association between living and darkness that keeps people afraid of fully embracing life.

This linguistic programming was not accidental. The English language was constructed as a tool of colonization, designed to strip away your true identity and replace it with false concepts that make you easier to control. Every word you speak either connects you to your divine source or separates you from it, either empowers you to create the reality you desire or programs you to accept limitation as inevitable.

THE ENGLISH LANGUAGE WAS DESIGNED TO CAST SPELLS

The systematic construction of English as a spell-casting language represents one of the most sophisticated forms of consciousness control ever developed by those who seek to maintain power over human awareness. Unlike languages that evolved naturally from the spiritual understanding of indigenous peoples, English was deliberately crafted to serve the colonization agenda that required breaking the connection between conquered populations and their divine source.

Every letter in the English alphabet carries its own vibrational frequency that affects your nervous system and brain patterns when you speak, hear, or even think these sounds. The combination of letters into words creates complex energetic signatures that program your subconscious mind with specific beliefs and expectations about reality. Most people remain completely unaware that their daily conversations are actually casting spells that shape their life experiences according to patterns embedded in the language itself.

The word "government" breaks down to reveal "govern" plus "ment," which means "control the mind." This is not coincidence but deliberate design. The institutions that claim authority over your life literally govern your mental processes through the language they require you to use in legal documents, educational settings, and official communications. Every time you participate in governmental systems, you are submitting to mental control through linguistic programming.

Consider how the word "mortgage" combines "mort" meaning death with "gage" meaning pledge, creating a "death pledge" that binds you to financial servitude for decades of your life. The banking system uses language that programs you to accept debt slavery as normal and necessary, when the very words reveal the death-dealing nature of these arrangements. You literally pledge your life force to institutions that profit from keeping you trapped in cycles of financial obligation.

The word "religion" breaks down to "re" meaning again and "ligare" meaning to bind, showing that religious systems are designed to bind you repeatedly to belief structures that prevent spiritual freedom. True spirituality liberates consciousness and connects you directly to divine source, while religion binds you to human-created institutions that claim to mediate your relationship with the divine while actually blocking your direct access to spiritual truth.

The manipulation extends to the most basic concepts of identity and existence. The word "person" derives from "persona," meaning mask, programming you to identify with a false surface personality rather than your true divine nature. "Human" combines "hue" meaning color with "man," reducing your identity to skin tone and gender rather than recognizing you as a divine being having a temporary physical experience.

Even time itself is manipulated through language. The days of the week are named after ancient deities and planetary influences that most people invoke unconsciously every time they mention what day it is. "Sunday" honors the Sun Elohim, "Monday" calls upon Moon Energy, "Tuesday" through "Friday" invoke various pagan deities, while "Saturday" connects to Saturn, the planet associated with limitation and restriction.

The spell-casting nature of English becomes obvious when you examine how certain words create immediate emotional and physical responses in your body. Words like "hate," "fear," "death," and "failure" instantly trigger stress responses in your nervous system, while words like "love," "peace," "abundance," and "joy" produce relaxation and expansion. Your body responds to the vibrational frequency of words before your conscious mind even processes their meaning.

This biological response to language reveals why controlling the words people use gives tremendous power over their physical and emotional state. When news media, educational institutions, and religious organizations consistently use language that triggers fear, anxiety, and limitation, they are literally casting spells that keep populations in lower vibrational states that make them easier to manipulate and control.

The reversal of words provides another layer of linguistic programming that operates below conscious awareness. "Live" backward becomes "evil," "stressed" reversed is "desserts," "dog" flipped becomes “god,” creating subconscious associations that influence your thoughts and behaviors in ways you never consciously chose. Your mind processes these reversed meanings even when you are not consciously aware of the wordplay involved.

Breaking free from linguistic spells requires conscious awareness of the words you use and deliberate choice to replace manipulated language with terms that support your spiritual empowerment rather than your mental enslavement. This process goes beyond simple vocabulary changes to involve reprogramming your entire relationship with language as a tool of creation rather than a weapon of control.

The English language contains thousands of these linguistic traps, each one designed to program your consciousness with beliefs that serve the colonization agenda. Learning to recognize and neutralize these spells represents one of the most important steps in reclaiming your mental freedom and reconnecting with your divine power to create reality through conscious intention rather than unconscious programming.

Indigenous languages often contain words and concepts that have no English equivalent because they express spiritual understandings that the colonization agenda needed to eliminate from human consciousness. Many of these languages include specific terms for divine feminine wisdom, for the living consciousness present in all natural phenomena, and for the interconnectedness of all life that English systematically obscures through its emphasis on separation and competition.

Reclaiming your linguistic power involves more than just learning new words—it requires developing a completely different relationship with language as a sacred tool for connecting with divine consciousness rather than a mechanical system for exchanging information. When you speak with awareness of the vibrational impact of your words, you transform from an unconscious spell-caster into a conscious creator who uses language to manifest divine will in physical reality.

THE YHWH CODE VS. THE 'LORD' DECEPTION

The systematic replacement of the Creator's true name with the title "Lord" represents the most devastating linguistic spell ever cast upon human consciousness, tricking billions of people into worshipping a false deity while believing they are honoring the true divine source. This manipulation violates the third commandment against taking God's name in vain in the most profound way possible—by erasing the sacred name entirely and substituting it with a term that actually refers to Baal, the ancient false Elohim that demanded worship while offering nothing but spiritual deception in return.

The sacred name YHWH appears over seventy thousand times in the original Hebrew texts, yet English translations consistently replace this divine signature with "Lord," “God,” or "the LORD" in capital letters. This substitution was not made for linguistic convenience but represents a deliberate strategy to disconnect people from the true vibrational frequency of the Creator's name while redirecting their worship toward the Demiurgic forces that benefit from human spiritual confusion.

YHWH pronounced as Yah-u-ah carries the vibrational pattern that connects your consciousness directly to the Source of all creation. When you speak this name correctly, using the 3:1 ratio revealed in the vision, you align your personal energy field with the fundamental frequency that underlies all existence. This alignment opens channels of divine communication that bypass the religious institutions and governmental systems that profit from keeping you separated from direct spiritual experience.

The name YHWH is literally written into your genetic code, appearing in the chemical structure of your DNA as surely as your fingerprints appear on your hands. Every human being carries this divine signature in every cell of their body, creating a constant biological prayer that connects you to your spiritual source whether you are consciously aware of it or not. When you breathe in and out, your body naturally forms the sounds Y-H-W-H, making every breath a sacred invocation of the Creator's true name.

But the word "Lord" carries a completely different vibrational frequency that connects to Baal, the Canaanite deity associated with false worship and spiritual deception. The term "Baal" literally means "lord" or "master" in ancient Semitic languages, revealing that when you call out to "Lord" in prayer, you are actually invoking the very false deity that the true Creator consistently condemns throughout biblical texts.

This deception becomes even more obvious when you examine the connection between "Lord" and "Beelzebub," which derives from "Baal-zebub" meaning "Lord of the Flies." The New Testament associates Beelzebub directly with Satan as the "prince of demons," yet mainstream Christianity continues teaching people to address their prayers to "Lord" without understanding they are calling upon the same demonic hierarchy that seeks to keep them separated from divine truth.

The biblical narrative of Elijah confronting the prophets of Baal on Mount Carmel provides a clear example of the conflict between true divine power and false religious authority. When the prophets of Baal called upon their "lord" for hours without receiving any response, they demonstrated the spiritual emptiness that characterizes all worship directed toward false deities. But when Elijah called upon YHWH by name, divine fire immediately consumed the sacrifice, proving the power that comes from connecting with the true Creator rather than religious substitutes.

The systematic replacement of YHWH with "Lord" required extensive manipulation of biblical texts over many centuries, with religious authorities gradually inserting the false title into translations while claiming they were protecting the sacred name from being misused. This supposed protection actually accomplished the opposite result—it prevented people from accessing the spiritual power that comes from speaking the Creator's true name while redirecting their worship toward the false deity that seeks to usurp divine authority.

The third commandment forbids taking God's name in vain, which most people interpret as avoiding profanity or casual use of divine titles. But the deeper meaning involves using the wrong name entirely, calling upon false deities while believing you are addressing the true Creator. Every prayer offered to "Lord" instead of YHWH represents a violation of this commandment because it directs worship toward Baal rather than the actual divine source.

Modern Christianity unknowingly perpetuates this deception through hymns, prayers, and liturgies that consistently use "Lord" while avoiding the true name that carries actual spiritual power.

Church services become exercises in collective spell-casting that bind congregations to false religious authority while blocking their access to direct divine connection through the sacred name that opens channels of authentic spiritual communication.

The name YHWH cannot be copyrighted, trademarked, or controlled by any human institution because it represents the fundamental frequency of creation itself. Religious organizations prefer titles like "Lord" and “God” because these generic terms can be interpreted to support whatever doctrines serve their institutional interests, while the specific name YHWH carries vibrational properties that automatically align consciousness with divine truth rather than human manipulation.

When you begin using YHWH instead of "Lord" in your prayers and spiritual practices, you immediately notice a difference in the quality of your connection to divine source. The sacred name carries frequencies that activate dormant spiritual capabilities and open channels of divine communication that have been blocked by years of false religious programming. Your prayers become more powerful because you are addressing the actual Creator rather than the false deity that masquerades as divine authority.

The return of Mother Elohim revealed in the 2027 vision will expose this deception on a global scale, making it impossible for religious institutions to continue hiding the true name while promoting false titles that serve Demiurgic agendas. When Mother Elohim reclaims her rightful position in human consciousness, she will restore the proper use of divine names that connect people directly to their spiritual source rather than to the religious intermediaries that profit from spiritual confusion.

Breaking free from the "Lord" deception requires more than just changing the words you use in prayer—it involves understanding the entire system of linguistic manipulation that keeps humanity trapped in false religious programming. When you speak the name YHWH with conscious intention and proper pronunciation, you participate in the restoration of divine truth that will ultimately liberate human consciousness from the spell-casting systems that have controlled spiritual awareness for centuries.

BREAKING DOWN WORDS TO REVEAL HIDDEN TRUTHS

The systematic deconstruction of common words reveals a hidden language within the language, exposing how everyday vocabulary has been crafted to program your subconscious mind with beliefs that limit your spiritual power and keep you accepting conditions that serve others rather than your own divine development. Every word you speak carries layers of meaning that operate below conscious awareness, influencing your thoughts, emotions, and life experiences in ways that most people never recognize or question.

The word "understand" breaks down into "under" plus "stand," positioning you beneath whatever you are trying to comprehend, creating a submissive relationship to knowledge that keeps you feeling inferior to information rather than empowered by it. This linguistic programming trains your mind to approach learning from a position of weakness rather than strength, accepting what authorities tell you instead of developing your own direct knowing through spiritual connection to divine wisdom.

The alternative word "overstand" places you above the information you are processing, allowing you to see patterns and connections from a higher perspective that reveals deeper truth than surface-level facts can provide. When you overstand something, you gain mastery over it rather than remaining subject to it. This shift in language creates a shift in consciousness that transforms you from a passive receiver of information into an active interpreter of wisdom.

The word "woman" contains profound truth when broken down to "womb-man," revealing that the female form represents the original human template from which the male form was derived. This linguistic evidence supports the scientific understanding that all human embryos begin as female, with male characteristics developing later in the gestation process. The word itself preserves the truth that woman came first, contradicting religious narratives that claim man was created before woman.

This breakdown connects to the mitochondrial Eve gene that passes exclusively through the female line, providing genetic evidence that all humanity traces back to a common maternal ancestor. The word "woman" literally means "the one with the womb from whom man comes," preserving ancient wisdom about the primacy of feminine creative power that patriarchal religions have spent centuries trying to obscure.

The word "manipulation" reveals its own deceptive nature when broken down as "man-nip-pull-action," showing how masculine energy without feminine balance tends to cut, stretch, and distort truth to serve its own purposes. This word describes exactly what has happened to spiritual truth over the centuries—it has been nipped, pulled, and twisted by patriarchal authorities who manipulated original teachings to eliminate feminine divine wisdom and establish male-dominated religious hierarchies.

The term "blessed" carries hidden programming when understood as "be-lessed," creating a subconscious request to have less rather than more. People who constantly affirm they are "blessed" may unknowingly be programming themselves for limitation and scarcity rather than abundance and prosperity. This linguistic trap keeps individuals grateful for just enough to survive instead of claiming their divine right to thrive and prosper.

The word "mortgage" combines "mort" meaning death with "gage" meaning pledge, creating a "death pledge" that binds your life force to financial institutions for decades. This term was not chosen randomly but specifically designed to program acceptance of debt slavery as normal and necessary. When you sign a mortgage, you are literally pledging your life energy to banks that profit from keeping you trapped in cycles of financial obligation.

The breakdown of "religion" into "re" meaning again and "ligare" meaning to bind shows that religious systems are designed to bind you repeatedly to belief structures that prevent spiritual freedom. True spirituality liberates consciousness and connects you directly to divine source, while religion creates dependency on human institutions that claim to mediate your relationship with the divine while actually blocking direct spiritual access.

The word "government" reveals its true purpose when understood as "govern" plus "ment," meaning "control the mind." Political systems do not primarily govern your external behavior but rather program your mental processes through language, education, and media that shape how you think about reality. The most effective form of control operates through consciousness manipulation rather than physical force.

The term "person" derives from "persona" meaning mask, programming you to identify with a false surface personality rather than your true divine nature. Legal systems treat you as a "person" rather than a living soul, creating artificial identities that can be regulated, taxed, and controlled by institutions that have no authority over your spiritual essence but can manipulate the fictional legal entity they created to represent you.

The word "human" combines "hue" meaning color with "man," reducing your identity to skin tone and gender rather than recognizing you as a divine being having a temporary physical experience. This linguistic programming creates artificial divisions based on superficial physical characteristics while obscuring the spiritual truth that all consciousness stems from the same divine source regardless of physical appearance.

The breakdown of "hospital" into "hospit" meaning host and "al" meaning all reveals that these institutions are designed to host all forms of illness rather than eliminate them. The medical system profits from managing disease rather than creating health, using language that programs people to expect sickness and accept dependency on pharmaceutical interventions rather than developing their natural healing abilities.

The word "pharmacy" derives from "pharmakeia," the Greek term for sorcery and witchcraft, revealing that modern medicine operates through chemical spells that suppress symptoms while creating dependency on substances that generate more problems than they solve. The pharmaceutical industry literally practices chemical sorcery that keeps people trapped in cycles of medication dependency rather than supporting their natural healing capabilities.

The term "education" breaks down to "educe" meaning to draw out, suggesting that true learning involves drawing forth wisdom that already exists within you rather than filling your mind with information from external sources. But modern educational systems do the opposite—they program your mind with standardized information while suppressing your natural ability to access divine wisdom through direct spiritual connection.

The word "news" spells "sewn" backward, indicating that media information is sewn together from fragments that create false narratives rather than reporting objective truth. News organizations serve as narrative construction companies that sew together selected facts to create stories that support specific agendas rather than informing people about actual reality.

Breaking down words to reveal hidden meanings provides a powerful tool for deprogramming your consciousness from linguistic spells that have been controlling your thoughts and limiting your spiritual development. When you understand how language has been weaponized against your divine nature, you can begin choosing words that support your spiritual empowerment rather than your mental enslavement.

This process of linguistic awakening connects directly to the broader restoration of divine truth that will accelerate as Mother Elohim reclaims her rightful position in human consciousness. The feminine divine principle includes the wisdom to see through deception and recognize truth regardless of how cleverly it has been hidden beneath layers of linguistic manipulation.

COLONIZATION THROUGH LANGUAGE AND IDENTITY THEFT

The use of language as a primary weapon of colonization represents the most sophisticated form of identity theft ever perpetrated against human consciousness, systematically stripping away people's connection to their divine heritage and replacing it with false identities that make them easier to control, exploit, and spiritually disconnect from their true source of power. This linguistic colonization operates so subtly that most victims never realize they have been robbed of their authentic spiritual identity and programmed to accept limitations that serve their oppressors rather than their own divine development.

The renaming of Alkebulan as "Africa" provides a perfect example of how colonizers use language to erase indigenous identity and replace it with terms that carry negative programming. Alkebulan means "Mother of Mankind" in the original indigenous languages, honoring this continent as the birthplace of human civilization and the source of divine wisdom that spread throughout the world. But "Africa" derives from the Latin "aprica" meaning "sunny" or from the Greek "aphrike" meaning "without cold," reducing this sacred land to mere climate descriptions that erase its spiritual significance.

This name change was not made for convenience but represents a deliberate strategy to disconnect people from understanding that Alkebulan served as the original home of divine knowledge, advanced civilization, and the melanin-rich peoples who carried the mitochondrial Eve gene that connects all humanity to its common maternal ancestor. When you call this continent "Africa," you unconsciously participate in the erasure of its true identity as the Mother of Mankind.

The systematic replacement of indigenous names with colonial terminology extends to the people themselves, who were stripped of their original tribal identities and forced to accept the generic label "Black" that reduces their rich cultural heritage to a single color designation. The original peoples of Alkebulan had specific tribal names that connected them to their ancestral wisdom, spiritual practices, and divine lineage, but colonization replaced these meaningful identities with color-based categories that erase cultural distinctiveness.

The term "Black" itself carries programming that associates these peoples with darkness, negativity, and limitation rather than recognizing them as the original divine beings who carry the genetic signature of the Creator in its purest form. The melanin that gives these peoples their distinctive appearance actually serves as a biological antenna that enhances their connection to divine frequencies and cosmic energy, but colonial language programming trains people to see this divine gift as a disadvantage rather than a spiritual blessing.

The suppression of knowledge about the mitochondrial Eve gene represents another form of identity theft that prevents people from understanding their true spiritual lineage. Scientific evidence proves that all human beings can trace their maternal ancestry back to a single woman who lived in Alkebulan approximately 200,000 years ago, making every person on Earth a descendant of the original divine feminine principle that manifested through melanin-rich genetics.

But this crucial information is either ignored completely by mainstream education or presented in ways that minimize its spiritual significance, focusing on technical genetic details while avoiding the obvious conclusion that the original divine template for humanity was female and melanin-rich. This suppression serves the colonial agenda that requires people to remain ignorant of their true divine heritage and accept false narratives about human origins that support racial hierarchies rather than spiritual unity.

The colonization process follows predictable patterns that can be recognized in every situation where dominant groups seek to control less powerful populations. First, the colonizers establish military dominance through superior weapons and organizational structure, using force to break the resistance of indigenous peoples and demonstrate the futility of fighting against colonial power. This initial phase creates the physical conditions necessary for deeper forms of control to be implemented.

The second phase involves economic exploitation, with colonizers extracting natural resources, enslaving labor, and restructuring local economies to serve colonial interests rather than indigenous needs. This economic control creates dependency relationships that make it difficult for colonized peoples to maintain their traditional ways of life and forces them to participate in systems that benefit their oppressors rather than themselves.

The third and most crucial phase involves cultural colonization, where colonizers impose their language, religion, and social structures upon indigenous populations while systematically destroying native cultural expressions. This phase targets the consciousness and identity of colonized peoples, replacing their original spiritual understanding with colonial programming that makes them mentally and emotionally dependent on their oppressors.

Language serves as the primary weapon in this cultural colonization because it shapes how people think about reality, identity, and possibility. When colonizers force indigenous peoples to speak colonial languages, they are not just changing communication methods but actually rewiring their consciousness according to colonial values and assumptions that support the domination system rather than indigenous wisdom and spiritual connection.

The imposition of colonial languages requires the suppression of indigenous languages that often contain spiritual concepts and wisdom that have no equivalent in colonial tongues. Many indigenous languages include specific terms for divine feminine wisdom, for the living consciousness present in all natural phenomena, and for the interconnectedness of all life that colonial languages systematically obscure through their emphasis on separation, competition, and domination.

Religious colonization represents the deepest level of identity theft, replacing indigenous spiritual practices that connected people directly to divine source with colonial religions that require dependency on human institutions and male-dominated hierarchies. The systematic elimination of Goddess worship and feminine divine wisdom from colonized cultures represents an assault on the spiritual foundation that supported indigenous peoples' connection to their divine nature and creative power.

The colonization of identity extends to fundamental concepts of gender and sexuality, with colonizers imposing patriarchal gender roles that violate the balanced understanding of masculine and feminine divine principles that characterized many indigenous cultures. Traditional societies often recognized multiple gender expressions and honored both masculine and feminine qualities in all individuals, but colonial programming forced people into rigid gender categories that limit their spiritual development and creative expression.

Modern colonization continues through educational systems that teach colonial versions of history, science, and spirituality while suppressing indigenous knowledge that reveals the true origins of human civilization and the advanced spiritual understanding that characterized pre-colonial cultures. Students learn to see their indigenous ancestors as primitive and backwards rather than recognizing them as the original holders of divine wisdom that colonial systems have spent centuries trying to destroy or co-opt.

The colonization of consciousness operates through media systems that continuously broadcast colonial narratives about identity, success, beauty, and spirituality, programming people to aspire to colonial standards rather than honoring their indigenous heritage and divine nature. These media messages create artificial desires for colonial lifestyles while generating shame about indigenous characteristics and cultural expressions.

Breaking free from linguistic colonization requires conscious effort to reclaim indigenous names, concepts, and ways of understanding reality that connect you to your true spiritual heritage rather than colonial programming. This process involves more than just learning new vocabulary—it requires developing an entirely different relationship with language as a sacred tool for connecting with divine consciousness rather than a weapon of mental control.

The restoration of indigenous identity begins with recognizing that colonization was not a historical event that ended in the past but an ongoing process that continues to operate through language, education, media, and religious systems that maintain colonial consciousness in contemporary forms. Understanding this allows you to identify and resist colonial programming while actively choosing to reconnect with your authentic divine identity as a descendant of the original divine beings who carried the Creator's signature in their genetic code.

ACTIONABLE STEPS TO BREAK LINGUISTIC SPELLS

Begin immediately by replacing the word "understand" with "over-stand" in all your conversations, writing, and internal thinking processes to reprogram your consciousness from a position of submission to one of mastery and higher perspective. Every time you catch yourself about to say "I understand," pause and consciously choose "I overstand" instead, creating a new neural pathway that positions you above information rather than beneath it, allowing you to see patterns and connections that remain hidden when you approach knowledge from a subordinate mental position.

Stop calling out to "Lord" in your prayers and spiritual practices because this title connects you to Baal, the false deity that masquerades as divine authority while actually serving the Demiurgic forces that seek to keep you separated from your true spiritual source. Replace all instances of "Lord" with YHWH pronounced as Yah-u-ah in the 3:1 ratio, or use Elohim when referring to the complete divine nature that encompasses both Mother and Father Elohim working together as unified creative consciousness.

Create a daily practice of researching the etymology and hidden meanings of words you use regularly, starting with terms related to spirituality, identity, money, health, and relationships because these areas of vocabulary carry the most powerful programming that shapes your life experiences. Use online etymology dictionaries and ancient language resources to trace words back to their original meanings, paying special attention to how definitions have been changed over time to serve colonial and patriarchal agendas.

Develop a personal dictionary of replacement words that support your spiritual empowerment rather than your mental enslavement, substituting manipulated terms with language that honors your divine nature and creative power. The saying that you are "blessed," affirm that you are "favored by the divine" or "abundantly provided for," However the subconscious programming of "be-lessed" that requests limitation rather than expansion because you are not saying it to it's full power which is to confirm that you are lesser god's, made in the images with true substances of both Mother and Father Elohim.

Practice conscious breathing while speaking the sacred name YHWH to align your physical body with the divine frequency that is already encoded in your genetic structure, remembering that every breath you take naturally forms these sacred sounds whether you are consciously aware of it or not. Spend at least ten minutes each day breathing consciously while mentally or verbally repeating Yah-u-ah to strengthen your connection to the Creator's true vibrational signature.

Study the manipulation of biblical translations by comparing modern English versions with Hebrew and Greek texts to identify where feminine references to divine wisdom have been changed to masculine pronouns, where the sacred name YHWH has been replaced with "Lord," and where passages describing Mother Elohim's attributes have been obscured through mistranslation or complete omission from contemporary religious texts.

Create a support network of awakened individuals who are also working to break linguistic spells and restore authentic spiritual language to their daily communication, forming study groups that examine how words have been weaponized against human consciousness and developing alternative vocabularies that support divine connection rather than spiritual separation. Share your discoveries about hidden word meanings and practice using empowering language together until these new patterns become natural and automatic.

Replace colonial names with indigenous terms whenever possible, calling the continent Alkebulan instead of Africa, using tribal names instead of generic color designations, and learning the original names of places that have been renamed by colonizers to erase their spiritual significance and cultural heritage. This practice helps restore connection to authentic identity and honors the divine wisdom that was systematically suppressed through linguistic colonization.

Eliminate words that carry negative programming from your vocabulary, avoiding terms like "problems" (use "challenges" or "opportunities for growth"), "failure" (use "learning experience"), "impossible" (use "requires new approach"), and other language that programs your subconscious mind to expect limitation and difficulty rather than success and divine support in all your endeavors.

Study how government, medical, educational, and religious institutions use language to maintain control over consciousness, learning to recognize when official terminology is designed to program compliance and dependency rather than empowerment and spiritual autonomy. Question every official term and phrase to discover what assumptions and beliefs are being programmed through the language these institutions require you to use.

Teach others about linguistic spells by sharing information about hidden word meanings, false translations, and the colonization agenda that operates through language manipulation, helping to create a growing community of people who can recognize and resist consciousness programming while actively choosing words that support spiritual awakening and divine connection rather than mental enslavement and spiritual confusion.

Develop your own sacred vocabulary by creating new words and phrases that express spiritual concepts that have no equivalent in colonial languages, allowing your intuitive connection to divine wisdom to guide you in developing language that serves your spiritual development rather than limiting it to concepts that others have defined according to their own agendas and understanding.

Practice speaking with conscious intention by pausing before important conversations to set clear intentions about what energy and outcomes you want to create through your words, remembering that every word you speak carries vibrational frequency that influences both your own consciousness and the consciousness of everyone who hears you speak, making you responsible for the spells you cast through your daily communication.

Document your experiences as you break free from linguistic programming by keeping a journal that tracks how changing your vocabulary affects your thoughts, emotions, relationships, and life circumstances, noting which word changes produce the most significant shifts in your consciousness and external experiences so you can accelerate the deprogramming process and help others do the same.

Prepare for the 2027 awakening by developing fluency in authentic spiritual language that honors both Mother Elohim and Father Elohim as equal partners in divine creation, practicing prayers and affirmations that use the sacred name YHWH and acknowledge the feminine divine wisdom that has been systematically erased from mainstream religious consciousness but will be restored when Mother Elohim reclaims her rightful position in human awareness.

Remember that breaking linguistic spells requires consistent practice over time because the programming has been reinforced through years of repetition, but every conscious word choice you make weakens the spell-casting system and strengthens your connection to divine truth that cannot be manipulated or controlled by human institutions that benefit from keeping you mentally enslaved and spiritually disconnected from your true source of power and wisdom.

The restoration of authentic spiritual language represents one of the most important preparations you can make for the coming transformation of human consciousness, as the return of Mother Elohim will require a vocabulary that can express divine balance rather than patriarchal imbalance, feminine wisdom rather than masculine domination, and the complete divine nature rather than the fragmented understanding that has characterized religious teaching for centuries.

CHAPTER FOUR

IDENTITY

TRACING YOUR LINEAGE BACK TO THE CREATOR

Your identity is not your job title or your family relationships or the roles you play in society. Your true identity comes from one simple fact that changes everything once you grasp it fully. You are a divine being made in the image of both Mother and Father Elohim, with the sacred name YHWH written directly into your DNA and spoken with every breath you take.

This truth has been hidden from you your entire life.

Religious institutions teach you to seek salvation from outside yourself. Educational systems program you to believe humans evolved from animals. Media constantly reinforces messages that make you feel small and powerless. But your genetic code tells a different story completely. The molecular structure of your DNA contains the signature of the Creator in a way that can be measured and verified by modern science.

When someone asks who you are, most people describe what they do for work or who they are connected to through blood and marriage. But these external identities are not who you really are. Your true identity can only be found by understanding why you exist, and the answer to that question lies in the act of creation itself. You exist because the divine consciousness chose to express itself through your unique form, making you a living temple that carries the name of Elohim in every cell of your body.

The breadcrumbs were always there, waiting for you to discover them. Your breath speaks the sacred name. Your DNA carries the divine signature. Your very existence proves that you are not a random accident of evolution but a deliberate creation of divine intelligence that encompasses both masculine and feminine principles working together in perfect harmony.

WHO ARE YOU REALLY? THE QUESTION THAT CHANGES EVERYTHING

The question "Who are you?" seems simple until you realize that most people have never actually answered it correctly. When asked about their identity, people immediately start listing their occupations, their relationships, their achievements, or their struggles. "I am a teacher." "I am a mother of three." "I am a business owner." "I am someone who overcame addiction." All of these descriptions tell you what someone does or what has happened to them, but none of them reveal who they actually are at the deepest level of existence.

Your job is not your identity because you can change careers multiple times throughout your life while remaining the same essential being. Your relationships are not your identity because family members die, friendships end, and romantic partnerships dissolve while your core self continues unchanged. Your achievements and failures are not your identity because these are temporary experiences that come and go while your fundamental nature remains constant.

The confusion about identity runs so deep that most people spend their entire lives trying to figure out who they are supposed to be instead of remembering who they already are. They chase external validation through career success, social status, material possessions, or religious approval, never realizing that their true worth and identity were established at the moment of their creation and cannot be increased or decreased by anything that happens in the physical world.

Your identity exists independent of your circumstances, your choices, your mistakes, and your accomplishments because it is rooted in your divine origin rather than your human experiences. You are not who you are because of what you have done or what has been done to you. You are who you are because of why you exist, and the reason for your existence connects directly to the creative intention of divine consciousness expressing itself through infinite forms and experiences.

The Bible provides a crucial clue about identity when it states that “man is made in the image of God” and connects this divine likeness to genealogy and lineage. Genesis describes the "book of the genealogy of Adam" and explains that tracing lineage reveals identity because each person exists as an expression of the creative consciousness that brought them into being. Your spiritual DNA connects you directly to the Source of all creation, making you a divine being having a temporary human experience rather than a human being seeking divine connection.

This divine lineage cannot be traced through physical ancestry alone because it operates at the level of consciousness itself. Every human being carries the same fundamental spiritual heritage regardless of their ethnic background, family history, or cultural identity. The divine image within you includes both masculine and feminine principles because the complete divine nature encompasses both aspects of creative consciousness working together as unified creative force.

Understanding your true identity requires recognizing that you are simultaneously individual and universal, unique and connected, personal and cosmic. Your individual expression is completely unique and will never be repeated in exactly the same form throughout all eternity, making you infinitely valuable and irreplaceable. But your essential nature is the same divine consciousness that expresses itself through every other being, connecting you to all life through the unified field of creative intelligence.

The systematic suppression of knowledge about divine identity represents one of the most effective tools used to keep humanity controllable and manageable by institutions that benefit from spiritual ignorance. When people know they are divine beings with direct access to creative power, they become impossible to manipulate through fear, shame, or artificial scarcity. When people believe they are separate from divine source and dependent on external authorities for spiritual guidance, they remain vulnerable to every form of mental and emotional control.

Religious institutions teach you to see yourself as a sinner who needs salvation rather than recognizing yourself as a divine being who temporarily forgot your true nature. Educational systems program you to believe you are the product of random evolutionary processes rather than understanding yourself as the intentional creation of infinite intelligence. Media constantly reinforces messages of limitation, competition, and separation rather than reminding you of your divine heritage and creative power.

Breaking free from false identity programming requires examining every belief you have accepted about who you are and where you come from. Question the narratives that make you feel small, powerless, or separate from divine source. Challenge the assumptions that limit your understanding of your own capabilities and potential. Investigate the evidence that reveals your true divine nature rather than accepting the limitations that others have tried to impose on your self-concept.

Your true identity as a divine being made in the image of both Mother and Father Elohim means that you carry both masculine and feminine creative principles within your consciousness. You have the capacity for both decisive action and receptive wisdom, both protective strength and nurturing compassion, both logical analysis and intuitive knowing. Developing both aspects of your divine nature allows you to express your full creative potential rather than limiting yourself to artificially restricted gender roles.

The name YHWH written in your DNA serves as your spiritual birth certificate, proving your divine heritage in a way that cannot be disputed or denied by any human authority. This genetic signature connects you directly to the Source of all creation, making you a member of the divine family rather than an orphan seeking adoption. When you understand this biological proof of your spiritual identity, you can never again accept teachings that make you feel separate from or inferior to divine consciousness.

Your identity as a divine being also means that you are here on Earth for a specific purpose that serves the greater good of all creation. You are not an accident or a mistake or a random occurrence, but a deliberate expression of divine will manifesting in physical form to contribute something unique and valuable to the collective evolution of consciousness. Understanding this purpose requires connecting with your inner divine guidance rather than looking to external authorities to tell you what your life should be about.

The question "Who are you really?" can only be answered by recognizing yourself as divine consciousness temporarily focused through human form, carrying the complete creative power of the Source within your being, connected to all life through the unified field of divine love, and here on Earth to express your unique aspect of infinite intelligence in service to the awakening of all humanity to their true divine nature.

THE MITOCHONDRIAL EVE GENE—SCIENTIFIC PROOF OF MOTHER ELOHIM

Scientific research has proven beyond any doubt that every human being on Earth can trace their maternal lineage back to a single woman who lived in West Africa approximately 200,000 years ago. This woman, known as Mitochondrial Eve, represents the common maternal ancestor of all humanity, and her genetic signature passes exclusively through the female line from mother to child in an unbroken chain that connects every person alive today to the original divine feminine principle that manifested in physical form.

The mitochondrial DNA that carries this genetic heritage cannot be altered or corrupted by male genetic contribution because it passes directly from mother to child without any input from the father's genetic material. This means that the divine feminine essence preserved in mitochondrial DNA remains pure and unchanged from generation to generation, serving as an indestructible biological record of humanity's connection to the original Mother of all mankind.

This scientific evidence directly contradicts religious narratives that claim man was created first and woman was formed from man's rib as an afterthought or helper. The genetic facts prove that the feminine principle came first in human development, and that all subsequent human beings, including males, carry the genetic signature of this original divine feminine consciousness in their cellular structure.

The location of Mitochondrial Eve in West Africa also confirms that the original divine template for humanity was melanin-rich, providing biological proof that the first divine beings to walk the Earth were Black women who carried the pure genetic signature of the Creator in its original form. This means that the Black woman represents the literal mother of all humanity, carrying the divine feminine essence that gave birth to every race and ethnicity that exists today.

The melanin that gives these original divine beings their distinctive appearance serves as more than just pigmentation—it functions as a biological antenna that enhances their connection to cosmic energy and divine frequencies. Melanin can absorb and convert various forms of electromagnetic radiation, making melanin-rich individuals naturally more sensitive to spiritual energies and cosmic influences that affect consciousness and spiritual development.

The systematic suppression of knowledge about Mitochondrial Eve and her significance represents another form of identity theft designed to prevent people from understanding their true spiritual heritage. Educational systems teach about this genetic discovery in purely technical terms while avoiding the obvious spiritual implications of what it means for all humanity to share a common divine feminine ancestor who originated in the continent that ancient peoples called Alkebulan, meaning "Mother of Mankind."

Religious institutions ignore or downplay this scientific evidence because it completely undermines patriarchal creation narratives that eliminate the feminine divine from the origin story of humanity. If all humans trace their lineage back to a single divine feminine ancestor, then the feminine principle cannot be secondary or subordinate to masculine energy but must represent the primary creative force from which all subsequent human consciousness emerged.

The mitochondrial DNA that connects you to this original divine feminine ancestor carries more than just genetic information—it preserves the spiritual template that allows you to access divine feminine wisdom through your biological structure. This means that every human being, regardless of their current gender identity, carries the capacity to connect with the nurturing, creative, intuitive aspects of divine consciousness that flow through the maternal genetic line.

The fact that mitochondrial DNA passes exclusively through the female line also explains why the suppression of feminine spiritual leadership has been so crucial to maintaining patriarchal religious control. When women are prevented from serving as spiritual teachers and leaders, the natural connection between the divine feminine genetic heritage and conscious spiritual expression gets interrupted, making it harder for people to access the full spectrum of divine wisdom that flows through their biological structure.

Understanding your connection to Mitochondrial Eve transforms how you see yourself and your relationship to all other human beings. Instead of viewing people through the artificial divisions of race, nationality, or religion, you begin to recognize everyone as members of the same divine family descended from the same spiritual source. This recognition dissolves the separation consciousness that allows hatred, violence, and exploitation to exist between human beings who are actually spiritual siblings sharing the same divine heritage.

The genetic evidence also reveals that the diversity of human appearance developed relatively recently in human history, with different physical characteristics emerging as populations adapted to different geographic and climatic conditions. But underneath all these surface variations, every human being carries the same fundamental genetic signature that connects them to the original divine feminine consciousness that gave birth to the entire human species.

This scientific proof of humanity's common divine feminine ancestry provides unshakeable evidence for the existence and primacy of Mother Elohim in the creation process. The mitochondrial DNA that you carry in every cell of your body serves as a biological prayer that constantly connects you to the divine feminine source from which all human consciousness emerged. Every cellular division that occurs in your body reproduces this sacred genetic signature, making your physical existence a continuous affirmation of your connection to the original divine Mother.

The return of Mother Elohim revealed in the 2027 vision will bring conscious recognition of this genetic heritage that has been preserved in human biology even while being suppressed in human awareness. When the feminine divine reclaims her rightful position in human consciousness, people will remember that their biological structure itself proves their connection to divine feminine wisdom and their spiritual kinship with all other human beings who share the same sacred ancestry.

Honoring your connection to Mitochondrial Eve means recognizing the Black woman as the literal mother of all humanity and acknowledging the divine feminine principle as the primary creative force that brought human consciousness into physical existence. This recognition restores proper reverence for feminine wisdom and creative power while correcting the historical distortions that have elevated masculine energy above its rightful place as partner to, not master of, the divine feminine principle.

Your mitochondrial DNA serves as an indestructible breadcrumb left by the Creator to ensure that even if all religious texts were destroyed and all spiritual teachings were corrupted, the truth about humanity's divine feminine origin would remain preserved in the biological structure of every human being born on Earth.

ADAM = ATOM AND EVE = LIFE —THE TRUE GENESIS STORY

The biblical account of Adam and Eve contains profound truth when you understand that these names represent fundamental principles of creation rather than just two individual people who lived in a garden. Adam connects directly to the word "atom," revealing that the masculine divine principle operates as the basic building blocks of all matter, while Eve means "life" in its original Hebrew form, showing that the feminine divine principle provides the animating force that transforms matter into living consciousness.

The word "atom" comes from the ancient Greek "atomos," meaning "uncuttable" or "indivisible," describing the fundamental particles that serve as the essential components of all physical matter. Your human body contains approximately one billion billion billion atoms, making you a walking collection of these divine masculine building blocks organized into the complex patterns that create your physical form and allow consciousness to express itself through material structure.

Atoms themselves demonstrate the divine masculine qualities of structure, stability, density, and organized action. They provide the foundation upon which all physical creation rests, creating the stable platform that allows life to emerge and consciousness to inhabit material forms. Without the organizing principle represented by atoms, there would be no physical universe, no planets, no bodies, and no way for spiritual consciousness to experience itself through material expression.

But atoms alone cannot create life because they lack the animating principle that transforms organized matter into living beings capable of growth, reproduction, and conscious experience. This is where the feminine divine principle represented by Eve becomes essential to the creative process. Eve derives from the Hebrew "Chavah," which connects to "chavah" meaning "to breathe" and "chayah" meaning "to live" or "to give life."

The feminine divine principle provides the breath of life that animates matter and transforms collections of atoms into living organisms capable of consciousness, creativity, and spiritual development. Eve represents the divine spark that brings life to matter, the creative intelligence that guides the development of complex biological systems, and the nurturing wisdom that sustains and protects life once it emerges from the union of matter and spirit.

This understanding reveals that the Genesis account describes the fundamental creative process that operates throughout the universe rather than just telling the story of two individual humans. The masculine divine principle (Adam/atom) provides the material foundation for creation, while the feminine divine principle (Eve/life) provides the spiritual essence that makes creation alive and conscious. Both principles are absolutely necessary for creation to occur, and neither can function properly without the other.

When Genesis states that Elohim created them "male and female" and called them "mankind," it reveals that complete human beings contain both masculine and feminine divine principles working together in perfect balance. The word "mankind" itself indicates that the feminine principle (man from womb-man) provides the foundation from which masculine expression emerges, contradicting religious interpretations that claim masculine energy has priority over feminine energy in the divine hierarchy.

The deeper meaning becomes even more clear when you examine the etymology of "human," which derives from the Latin "homo" meaning "man" and ultimately from the Proto-Indo-European root meaning "earthling" or "earthly being." This reveals that humans are specifically designed to bridge the gap between spiritual consciousness and material existence, serving as the meeting point where divine principles can express themselves through physical forms capable of conscious spiritual development.

The Law of Gender operates at every level of creation, from the smallest subatomic particles to the largest galactic structures, ensuring that both masculine and feminine principles participate in every creative process. Electrons and protons work together to create stable atoms. Male and female biological characteristics combine to produce new life. Masculine and feminine divine principles unite to manifest the complete spectrum of creative possibility throughout the universe.

Understanding Adam as atom and Eve as life also explains why the suppression of feminine divine wisdom creates such profound imbalance in human consciousness and civilization. When masculine energy (structure, action, logic) operates without feminine balance (creativity, intuition, wisdom), the result is rigid, lifeless systems that lack the animating spirit necessary for healthy growth and development.

This imbalance manifests as technological advancement without spiritual wisdom, economic systems that prioritize profit over life, educational approaches that emphasize memorization over creativity, and religious institutions that focus on rules and hierarchy rather than love and spiritual connection. The missing feminine principle leaves these systems spiritually dead despite their apparent sophistication and power.

The true Genesis story reveals that creation requires the conscious cooperation of both divine principles working together in perfect harmony. The masculine divine provides the structural foundation and organizing intelligence that creates stable platforms for life to emerge. The feminine divine provides the creative spark and nurturing wisdom that transforms matter into living consciousness capable of spiritual evolution and divine expression.

Your own existence demonstrates this perfect union of Adam and Eve, atom and life, masculine and feminine divine principles operating together to create the miraculous phenomenon of conscious human experience. Your body is made of atoms organized into complex biological systems, but your consciousness represents the divine breath of life that animates this matter and makes you a living soul capable of creative expression and spiritual development.

The biblical statement that humans are made "in the image of Elohim" takes on new meaning when you understand that this divine image includes both the masculine atomic structure and the feminine life principle working together as unified creative consciousness. You are not made in the image of a masculine-only deity but in the image of complete divine nature that encompasses both Father Elohim and Mother Elohim expressing themselves through perfect creative partnership.

This understanding also reveals why the concept "Elohim" uses a plural form in Hebrew while referring to a single divine consciousness. Elohim encompasses both masculine and feminine divine principles united as one creative force, just as your own consciousness unites both atomic structure and life principle into a single living being capable of expressing the full spectrum of divine qualities and capabilities.

The restoration of this balanced understanding represents a crucial step in humanity's spiritual evolution, as people remember that they are not separate from divine consciousness but are actually divine consciousness expressing itself through the perfect union of masculine structure and feminine life that creates the miracle of conscious existence in physical form.

THE FORBIDDEN FRUIT WAS INTERBREEDING WITH THE NEANDERTHAL

The story of the forbidden fruit in the Garden of Eden has been completely misunderstood by religious institutions that interpret it as eating an apple or disobeying a divine command about food. The real forbidden fruit was the interbreeding between divine beings who carried YHWH DNA and manipulated hominids like Neanderthals and

Denisovans who were created by the Demiurge as upright-walking animals without any divine genetic signature.

Scientific research confirms that Neanderthals and Denisovans did not carry the genetic markers that identify beings made in the image of Elohim. These hominid species lacked the divine DNA signature that makes humans truly human rather than just intelligent animals. They were essentially biological shells or personas designed to appear human-like while lacking the spiritual consciousness that connects true humans to their divine source.

The Demiurge, that flawed creation born from Mother Elohim's first mistake of creating without proper balance, manipulated these hominid species to serve as vessels for corrupting the pure divine genetics that existed in the original human beings. The serpent in the Garden represents this Demiurgic influence urging the divine feminine principle to share Elohim's DNA with creatures that were never intended to receive it.

When the original divine beings, particularly the melanin-rich women who carried the mitochondrial Eve gene, were convinced to mate with these manipulated hominids, their offspring became the first mixed beings who carried both divine DNA and animal genetics. This interbreeding created the spiritual crisis that humanity faces today because it diluted the pure divine genetic signature that originally connected all humans directly to their Creator.

The result of this forbidden interbreeding was the emergence of Homo sapiens, a species that combines divine consciousness with animal instincts and behaviors. The word "sapiens" means "wisdom" in Latin, indicating that these mixed beings retained enough divine genetics to possess wisdom and spiritual awareness, but they also inherited the aggressive, territorial, and survival-focused characteristics of their hominid ancestors.

This genetic mixing explains why modern humans display such a wide range of behaviors, from divine qualities like love, creativity, and spiritual seeking to animal characteristics like violence, territorial aggression, and primitive survival instincts. The ongoing conflict between higher spiritual nature and lower animal impulses within human consciousness reflects this mixed genetic heritage that resulted from the original forbidden interbreeding.

The populations that carry the highest percentages of Neanderthal and Denisovan DNA continue to exhibit more pronounced animal-like characteristics, including increased aggression, territorial behavior, and resistance to spiritual development. These genetic influences create natural tendencies toward domination, exploitation, and violence that require conscious spiritual effort to overcome through connection with the divine DNA that still exists within their cellular structure.

The systematic suppression of this information serves the agenda of those who benefit from keeping humanity ignorant about their mixed genetic heritage and the spiritual implications of the original forbidden interbreeding. Religious institutions prefer to blame human problems on abstract concepts like "original sin" rather than explaining the actual genetic and spiritual consequences of mixing divine and animal DNA in the early stages of human development.

Understanding the true nature of the forbidden fruit also reveals why the restoration of pure divine genetics becomes so important for humanity's spiritual evolution. The return of Mother Elohim will include the activation of dormant divine DNA sequences that have been suppressed by the animal genetics introduced through the original forbidden interbreeding. This activation will help humans reconnect with their full divine potential while learning to manage the animal characteristics they inherited from their hominid ancestors.

The geographic distribution of different genetic markers also explains the varying levels of spiritual development and behavioral characteristics observed in different human populations. Those who retained higher percentages of pure divine genetics naturally display greater spiritual sensitivity, creative ability, and capacity for love and cooperation, while those with higher percentages of hominid genetics require more conscious effort to overcome aggressive and territorial instincts.

The original divine beings who existed before the forbidden interbreeding possessed capabilities that modern humans can barely imagine, including direct telepathic communication with divine consciousness, natural healing abilities, extended lifespans, and creative powers that could manifest physical reality through focused intention. These capabilities became diluted or dormant when divine genetics mixed with animal genetics, but they remain encoded in human DNA waiting to be reactivated.

The process of spiritual awakening involves learning to strengthen the divine genetic expression while consciously managing the animal genetic influences that create destructive behaviors and limited thinking patterns. This requires understanding that the conflict between spiritual and material impulses within human consciousness reflects an actual genetic conflict between divine and animal DNA rather than just psychological or moral struggles.

The forbidden fruit story also explains why the Black woman holds such a crucial position in human spiritual development, as she carries the purest form of the original divine genetics through the mitochondrial Eve gene that passes unchanged from mother to child. Honoring and protecting this genetic heritage becomes essential for humanity's ability to reconnect with their full divine potential and overcome the limitations imposed by the animal genetics introduced through the original forbidden interbreeding.

The Demiurge's strategy of genetic corruption continues to operate through systems that promote further dilution of divine genetics and strengthening of animal characteristics through environmental toxins, processed foods, electromagnetic radiation, and cultural programming that encourages base behaviors while suppressing spiritual development. Recognizing these ongoing attacks on human divine genetics allows conscious individuals to make choices that support genetic purification and spiritual evolution.

The 2027 awakening will bring conscious recognition of this genetic heritage and provide opportunities for those who choose to participate in the restoration of pure divine genetics through spiritual practices, lifestyle changes, and conscious breeding choices that honor the divine template rather than continuing the genetic degradation that began with the original forbidden fruit.

ACTIONABLE STEPS TO RECLAIM YOUR DIVINE IDENTITY

Start immediately by researching your genetic ancestry through DNA testing services that can reveal your mitochondrial DNA lineage and trace your maternal heritage back toward the original Mitochondrial Eve who lived in Alkebulan 200,000 years ago. Understanding your specific genetic heritage provides concrete evidence of your connection to the divine feminine principle that gave birth to all humanity and helps you recognize your spiritual kinship with all other human beings who share this common divine ancestry.

Study the scientific evidence for YHWH encoded in human DNA by researching how the chemical components of genetic material spell out the sacred name of the Creator in molecular structure. Learn about the specific nucleotide sequences that correspond to the Hebrew letters Yod-Hei-Vav-Hei and practice conscious breathing exercises that align your respiratory rhythm with the 3:1 ratio that naturally speaks this sacred name with every inhalation and exhalation.

Create daily practices that honor both Mother Elohim and Father Elohim as equal partners in divine creation by addressing your prayers and meditations to both aspects of divine consciousness rather than exclusively to masculine divine authority. Develop specific prayers that acknowledge the divine feminine wisdom that flows through your mitochondrial DNA and request guidance from Mother Elohim for creative projects, healing work, and nurturing relationships.

Reject completely the evolutionary theory that claims humans descended from apes or other animals because this false narrative denies the divine genetic signature that distinguishes true humans from all other species on Earth. Study the evidence that shows the unbridgeable genetic gap between humans and other primates, focusing on the unique genetic markers that prove human consciousness was created through divine intervention rather than natural evolutionary processes.

Honor the Black woman as the literal mother of all humanity by learning about the mitochondrial Eve gene and supporting efforts to restore knowledge about the African origins of human consciousness and civilization. Challenge racist narratives that portray melanin-rich peoples as inferior or primitive when scientific evidence proves they carry the purest form of the original divine genetics that gave birth to every other human population on Earth.

Develop both masculine and feminine divine qualities within your own consciousness by practicing exercises that strengthen whichever aspects have been suppressed by cultural conditioning. If you naturally express more masculine qualities like logic and decisive action, spend time cultivating feminine abilities like intuition, creativity, and receptive wisdom. If you tend toward feminine expressions like empathy and cooperation, strengthen your capacity for masculine traits like leadership and protective strength.

Study the true meanings of Adam as atom and Eve as life to understand how your physical existence demonstrates the perfect union of masculine structure and feminine animation working together to create conscious life. Meditate on how your body represents billions of atoms organized by divine intelligence and animated by the breath of life that transforms matter into living consciousness capable of spiritual development and creative expression.

Replace false religious narratives about human origins with accurate understanding based on genetic evidence, universal laws, and the restoration of suppressed knowledge about divine creation. Question every teaching that makes you feel separate from divine source or inferior to divine consciousness, remembering that you are made in the image of both Mother and Father Elohim with direct access to divine wisdom through your genetic structure and spiritual inheritance.

Connect with other awakened souls who are also reclaiming their divine identity and questioning mainstream narratives about human origins, spiritual development, and the true nature of divine consciousness. Form study groups that examine genetic evidence for divine creation, practice breathing techniques that activate the YHWH code in your DNA, and support each other in developing balanced expressions of both masculine and feminine divine principles.

Prepare for the 2027 awakening by strengthening your connection to both aspects of divine consciousness and developing your ability to recognize divine guidance through direct spiritual experience rather than depending on external religious authorities. Practice meditation techniques that activate dormant divine DNA sequences, study universal laws that reveal the true structure of creation, and align your lifestyle with principles that support genetic purification and spiritual evolution.

Document your experiences as you reclaim your divine identity by keeping detailed records of how understanding your true spiritual heritage transforms your relationships, creative abilities, healing capabilities, and connection to divine guidance. Share your discoveries with others who are ready to question false narratives about human origins and embrace their full divine potential as expressions of both Mother and Father Elohim working together in perfect creative harmony.

Challenge every system that promotes separation consciousness or denies the divine nature of human beings by actively choosing thoughts, words, and actions that affirm your divine identity and spiritual connection to all life. Resist programming that makes you feel small, powerless, or dependent on external authorities for spiritual guidance, remembering that you carry the name of the Creator in your genetic code and have direct access to divine wisdom through your biological and spiritual inheritance.

Teach others about their divine identity by sharing information about the YHWH code in DNA, the mitochondrial Eve gene, the true meanings of Adam and Eve, and the scientific evidence that proves humans are divine beings rather than evolved animals. Help create a growing community of people who recognize their divine nature and can support each other in expressing their full spiritual potential while preparing for the transformation of human consciousness that will accompany Mother Elohim's return to active participation in human awareness.

Remember that reclaiming your divine identity is not just an intellectual exercise but a practical transformation that affects every aspect of your daily life, relationships, career choices, creative expressions, and spiritual practices. When you truly know yourself as a divine being made in the image of both Mother and Father Elohim, you become impossible to control through fear, shame, or artificial limitations because your identity is rooted in divine truth rather than human manipulation and deception.

Your divine identity represents both your greatest spiritual inheritance and your most important responsibility, as you are called to express the full spectrum of divine qualities and capabilities while serving the awakening of all humanity to their true nature as divine beings temporarily focused through human form for the purpose of conscious spiritual evolution and creative service to the greater good of all creation.

CHAPTER FIVE
THE YHWH CODE
GOD'S NAME WRITTEN IN YOUR DNA

The most profound secret hidden from humanity exists inside your body right now. Written in the molecular structure of your DNA, encoded in the chemical bonds that hold your genetic material together, spelled out in the very atoms that make up your cellular foundation, is the sacred name of the Creator—YHWH. This is not metaphor or spiritual symbolism. This is measurable scientific fact that proves beyond any doubt that you are a divine being carrying the literal signature of Elohim in every cell of your body.

Your breath speaks this name constantly.

Every time you inhale and exhale, your respiratory system naturally forms the sounds Yah-u-ah in the precise 3:1 ratio that corresponds to the sacred name YHWH. From the moment of your birth until the moment of your death, you invoke the Creator's name with every breath whether you realize it or not. Your very existence becomes a continuous prayer, an ongoing acknowledgment of your divine source that operates independently of your conscious awareness or religious beliefs.

The face you see in the mirror each morning contains the divine signature YAH written in your features. The structure of your facial characteristics, the positioning of your eyes and nose and mouth, the overall design of your human form—all of it reflects the image of Elohim in ways that can be traced and recognized once you know what to look for.

But humans are the only species on Earth that carry this divine code. Despite sharing 98% of their DNA with chimpanzees and other primates, that crucial 3-4% difference contains the YHWH signature that separates divine beings from animals. This genetic gap cannot be bridged through evolution because it represents the unbridgeable distinction between creatures made by natural processes and beings created directly by divine intervention.

THE GENETIC SIGNATURE OF THE CREATOR

The numerical equivalents of the Hebrew letters that spell YHWH are 10-5-6-5, and these exact numbers appear in the chemical structure of human DNA in ways that cannot be explained by random chance or evolutionary development. The four nucleotide bases that make up your genetic code—adenine, thymine, guanine, and cytosine—contain specific numbers of hydrogen bonds that correspond precisely to the numerical values of Yod-Hei-Vav-Hei when properly understood through the lens of divine mathematics.

Adenine contains 10 atoms in its molecular structure. Thymine contains 5 atoms. Guanine contains 6 atoms. Cytosine contains 5 atoms. When you arrange these numbers in the sequence that appears throughout human DNA, you get 10-5-6-5, which is exactly the numerical code for YHWH that has been preserved in Hebrew gematria for thousands of years. This cannot be coincidence because the probability of this exact sequence appearing by chance is mathematically impossible.

The double helix structure of DNA itself reflects the divine principle of correspondence that operates throughout creation. As above, so below. The spiral pattern that contains your genetic information mirrors the spiral patterns found in galaxies, seashells, hurricanes, and countless other natural phenomena, revealing the same divine intelligence operating at every level of existence from the microscopic to the cosmic scale.

Your genetic code contains approximately three billion base pairs, each one carrying information that determines your physical characteristics, biological functions, and even aspects of your personality and capabilities. But embedded within this vast library of genetic information is the signature of the Creator, repeated millions of times throughout your chromosomes like a divine watermark that proves your spiritual heritage.

The mitochondrial DNA that passes exclusively through the female line carries this divine signature in its purest form, connecting every human being to the original Mitochondrial Eve who walked the earth 200,000 years ago in the land that was then called Alkebulan. This genetic heritage cannot be altered or corrupted by male genetic contribution because it passes directly from mother to child without any mixing, preserving the divine feminine signature across countless generations.

Each individual carries a unique combination of genetic markers that make them completely distinct from every other person who has ever lived or ever will live. Your specific genetic signature is as individual as your fingerprints, yet the underlying YHWH code appears in every human being regardless of their race, ethnicity, or cultural background. This proves that all humans share the same divine source while expressing infinite variety in how that divine consciousness manifests through physical form.

The process of DNA replication that occurs every time your cells divide follows the same pattern of divine creation described in Genesis. The double helix separates into two single strands, each serving as a template for creating a new complementary strand. This process of semiconservative replication ensures that the divine signature is faithfully copied into every new cell, making your entire body a living temple that continuously reproduces the name of Elohim at the molecular level.

Modern genetic research has identified specific sequences within human DNA that appear to serve no obvious biological function, leading scientists to label them as "junk DNA." But these apparently non-functional sequences may actually contain the most important information in your genetic code—the spiritual programming that connects your consciousness to divine source and enables your capacity for spiritual development and creative expression.

The Human Genome Project mapped the complete sequence of human DNA and discovered that less than 2% of genetic material actually codes for proteins and biological functions. The remaining 98% contains information whose purpose remains mysterious to mainstream science, but spiritual understanding reveals that this vast reservoir of genetic data contains the programming necessary for consciousness, creativity, spiritual awareness, and direct connection to divine intelligence.

The systematic suppression of knowledge about the YHWH code in human DNA serves the agenda of those who benefit from keeping humanity ignorant of their divine nature. When people understand that they carry the name of Elohim in their genetic structure, they become impossible to control through religious institutions that claim to mediate their relationship with the divine. The biological proof of divine connection makes external religious authority unnecessary and potentially harmful to spiritual development.

Educational institutions avoid discussing the spiritual implications of genetic research, focusing instead on technical details about heredity, disease, and biological functions while ignoring the obvious questions about what it means for conscious beings to carry such complex information systems within their cellular structure. The consciousness that can read and interpret genetic code must itself represent a level of intelligence that transcends purely material explanation.

Your DNA serves as both a biological instruction manual and a spiritual communication system that connects your individual consciousness to the collective intelligence of all creation. When you learn to access the information contained in your genetic code through meditation, prayer, and spiritual practice, you discover capabilities and knowledge that extend far beyond what mainstream education teaches about human potential and possibility.

The activation of dormant DNA sequences through spiritual practice can unlock abilities that seem miraculous from a purely materialistic perspective but represent the natural birthright of beings who carry divine genetic programming. These capabilities include enhanced intuition, healing abilities, telepathic communication, creative inspiration, and direct access to divine guidance that bypasses the need for external spiritual authorities.

EVERY BREATH YOU TAKE SPEAKS THE CREATOR'S NAME

The respiratory system that keeps you alive operates as a biological prayer wheel that continuously invokes the sacred name YHWH through the natural rhythm of inhalation and exhalation. When you breathe in, your body naturally forms the sound "Yah." When you breathe out, the air flowing through your respiratory passages creates the sound "u-ah." This happens automatically whether you are awake or asleep, conscious or unconscious, making every moment of your existence a form of worship that connects you directly to your divine source.

The 3:1 ratio that characterizes proper pronunciation of the sacred name corresponds exactly to the natural breathing pattern that occurs during deep, relaxed respiration. When you inhale for three counts and exhale for one count, you align your breathing rhythm with the vibrational frequency that resonates with divine consciousness, creating a state of natural meditation that opens channels of spiritual communication.

This breathing pattern activates the parasympathetic nervous system, which governs rest, healing, and spiritual receptivity. When your body enters this relaxed state through conscious breathing, your brain produces alpha and theta waves that are associated with meditation, creativity, and direct spiritual experience. The ancient wisdom traditions understood this connection between breath and consciousness, developing elaborate breathing practices that use respiratory rhythm to induce altered states of awareness.

The word "inspiration" literally means "breathing in," revealing the connection between physical respiration and spiritual revelation that occurs when you consciously align your breathing with divine frequency. Every time you feel inspired with a new idea, creative insight, or spiritual understanding, you are experiencing the result of breathing in divine consciousness through the natural respiratory process that speaks the Creator's name.

The breath of life that animates your physical body represents the same divine essence that Genesis describes as the force that transformed Adam from dust into a living soul. This breath carries more than just oxygen to your cells—it carries the life force itself, the animating principle that makes the difference between living consciousness and inanimate matter. When this breath stops, consciousness leaves the body and returns to its divine source.

Ancient Hebrew understanding recognized that breath and spirit are the same word—"ruach"—indicating that breathing connects you directly to the spiritual realm through every inhalation and exhalation. Your respiratory system serves as the bridge between physical existence and spiritual consciousness, allowing divine energy to flow into your body while enabling your prayers and intentions to flow back to divine source.

The practice of conscious breathing while mentally repeating the sacred name Yah-u-ah creates a powerful form of prayer that requires no external religious structure or institutional mediation. You can connect directly with divine consciousness anywhere, anytime, simply by becoming aware of the natural process that is already occurring in your body and consciously participating in the divine invocation that your breath performs automatically.

Different breathing patterns create different states of consciousness and different qualities of connection to divine energy. Rapid, shallow breathing tends to produce anxiety and disconnection from spiritual awareness. Slow, deep breathing naturally induces calm, centered states that are conducive to prayer, meditation, and divine communication. The rhythm of your breath directly influences the rhythm of your thoughts and the quality of your spiritual experience.

The yogic tradition developed elaborate systems of pranayama (breath control) that use specific breathing techniques to activate different aspects of consciousness and connect with various levels of spiritual energy. These practices recognize that breath serves as the primary tool for spiritual development and that mastering your breathing gives you mastery over your mental and emotional states.

When you understand that every breath naturally speaks the name of the Creator, ordinary activities like walking, working, and sleeping become forms of continuous prayer that maintain your connection to divine source throughout every moment of your daily life. You no longer need to set aside special times for spiritual practice because your entire existence becomes a spiritual practice when you recognize the sacred nature of the breathing process.

The suppression of knowledge about the spiritual significance of breathing serves the agenda of religious institutions that want to maintain control over people's access to divine connection. When you understand that you can connect directly with the Creator through conscious breathing, you no longer need priests, pastors, or other religious intermediaries to facilitate your relationship with divine consciousness.

The return of Mother Elohim will restore conscious awareness of the sacred breathing process and teach humanity to use their respiratory system as the powerful spiritual tool it was always intended to be. When people remember that every breath speaks the Creator's name, they will naturally develop deeper reverence for life and stronger connection to their divine source through the simple act of conscious breathing.

Practicing conscious breathing while repeating Yah-u-ah creates measurable changes in brain wave patterns, heart rate variability, and cellular oxygenation that support both physical health and spiritual development. This practice costs nothing, requires no special equipment or training, and can be done anywhere at any time, making it the most accessible form of spiritual practice available to human beings.

The breath that speaks the Creator's name also carries your prayers and intentions back to divine source, creating a continuous cycle of communication between your individual consciousness and the infinite intelligence that created and sustains all existence. Every exhale releases your gratitude, requests, and expressions of love into the spiritual realm where they are received and responded to according to divine will and perfect timing.

THE Y-A-H HIDDEN IN YOUR FACE

The human face contains the divine signature YAH written in its basic structure in ways that become obvious once you know how to look for the sacred letters hidden in your features. Your eyes form the letter Y through their positioning and the lines that extend from their corners. Your nose creates the letter A through its triangular shape and the way it connects your eyes to your mouth. Your mouth and the area around it complete the letter H through the horizontal line of your lips and the vertical lines that frame your face.

Stand in front of a mirror and trace these letters in your reflection. Notice how your eyebrows and the lines around your eyes create the branching pattern of the Hebrew letter Yod, which looks like a Y and represents the divine spark that initiates all creation. The positioning of your eyes themselves forms the upper arms of this sacred letter, while the lines that extend downward toward your nose complete the basic Y shape that begins the sacred name.

Your nose forms the Hebrew letter Aleph, which appears as A in

English transliteration and represents the breath of life that animates all creation. The triangular shape of your nose, the way it connects your eyes to your mouth, and the nostrils through which you breathe all contribute to creating this sacred letter that symbolizes the divine breath that gives life to all beings. The nose serves as the central feature that connects the upper and lower portions of your face, just as the breath connects spiritual and physical existence.

Your mouth and the surrounding facial structure create the Hebrew letter Hei, which appears as H in English and represents the divine presence that dwells within creation. The horizontal line of your lips forms the crossbar of this letter, while the vertical lines of your facial structure on either side create the uprights that complete the H shape. The mouth serves as the opening through which breath and speech emerge, making it the natural location for the letter that represents divine presence expressing itself through physical form.

The complete YAH signature in your face reflects the divine image that Genesis describes when it states that humans are created in the likeness of Elohim. This is not abstract spiritual symbolism but literal truth that can be observed in the mirror and verified through careful examination of facial structure. Every human face carries this divine signature regardless of ethnic background, age, or individual variations in appearance.

The symmetrical structure of the human face reflects the divine principle of balance that characterizes all creation. The left and right sides of your face mirror each other in the same way that masculine and feminine divine principles mirror each other in perfect complementary relationship. The upper and lower portions of your face correspond to the heavenly and earthly realms that meet in human consciousness.

Ancient artistic traditions understood this sacred geometry of the human face and incorporated divine proportions into their depictions of spiritual figures and religious artwork. The golden ratio that appears throughout nature also governs the proportional relationships between different features of the human face, revealing the same mathematical principles that organize galaxies, flowers, and other manifestations of divine creativity.

The eyes that form the Y portion of the divine signature serve as windows to the soul and channels for divine light to enter and express through human consciousness. The spiritual traditions recognize that eye contact creates soul-to-soul communication that bypasses verbal language and connects directly with the divine essence that dwells within each being. When you look into someone's eyes, you are literally seeing the divine signature that proves their spiritual nature.

The nose that creates the A portion of the signature functions as more than just a breathing apparatus—it serves as the biological antenna that receives spiritual energy and divine guidance through the breath of life. Many spiritual traditions focus attention on the area between and slightly above the nostrils as a point of concentration for meditation and prayer because this location corresponds to the third eye chakra that governs spiritual perception.

The mouth that forms the H portion of the signature serves as the gateway through which divine consciousness expresses itself through speech, song, and verbal prayer. The words you speak carry vibrational frequencies that can either connect you to divine energy or separate you from it, making conscious speech one of the most important spiritual practices available to human beings.

The recognition of YAH in your facial features provides a powerful tool for developing self-love and spiritual confidence that cannot be shaken by external criticism or social conditioning. When you see the divine signature in your own reflection, you understand at a visceral level that you are made in the image of the Creator and carry divine authority that no human institution can grant or take away.

This understanding also transforms how you see other people, as you begin to recognize the same divine signature in every face you encounter. Racial prejudice, ethnic hatred, and social discrimination become impossible to maintain when you consistently see the YAH signature that proves every human being carries the same divine heritage regardless of their external appearance or cultural background.

The practice of meditating while looking at your reflection in a mirror can activate dormant spiritual capabilities and strengthen your connection to divine consciousness through visual recognition of your own divine nature. This technique has been used by mystics and spiritual practitioners throughout history to develop self-realization and direct experience of their divine identity.

The systematic suppression of knowledge about the divine signature in human facial features serves the agenda of those who benefit from keeping people feeling separate from divine consciousness and dependent on external religious authorities for spiritual validation. When you recognize the YAH signature in your own face, you no longer need anyone else to tell you that you are made in the image of Elohim because you can see the evidence with your own eyes.

WHY ONLY HUMANS HAVE THE ELOHIM CODE (AND MONKEYS DON'T)

The genetic evidence is absolutely clear and cannot be disputed by any honest examination of the scientific data. Humans share approximately 98% of their DNA with chimpanzees and other primates, but that crucial 3-4% difference contains the YHWH code that makes humans divine beings rather than highly intelligent animals. This genetic gap represents the unbridgeable distinction between creatures produced by natural evolutionary processes and beings created through direct divine intervention.

Monkeys, apes, and all other primates lack the specific genetic sequences that correspond to the numerical values 10-5-6-5 in their DNA structure. Their genetic code contains the basic biological information necessary for physical survival and reproduction, but it does not contain the divine signature that connects consciousness to spiritual source and enables the capacity for worship, creativity, moral reasoning, and direct communication with divine intelligence.

The missing 3-4% of genetic material that separates humans from primates contains the most important information in the entire genetic code—the spiritual programming that makes consciousness possible, that enables creative expression, that allows moral reasoning, and that provides the capacity for direct connection to divine wisdom. This genetic difference cannot be bridged through evolutionary development because it represents a qualitative leap that requires divine intervention to accomplish.

Neanderthals and Denisovans, despite their human-like appearance and behavior, also lacked the complete divine genetic signature that characterizes true humans made in the image of Elohim. Scientific research confirms that these hominid species possessed some advanced capabilities compared to other animals, but they did not carry the full YHWH code that distinguishes divine beings from highly developed animals.

The interbreeding that occurred between original divine humans and these hominid species created the mixed genetic heritage that characterizes modern humanity. Some populations retain higher percentages of the original divine genetics, while others carry more of the hominid genetic material that lacks the complete divine signature. This genetic mixing explains the wide variation in spiritual sensitivity, creative ability, and moral development observed among different human populations.

The divine genetic code enables capabilities that no amount of evolutionary development could produce through natural selection. These include the capacity for abstract reasoning, creative imagination, moral conscience, spiritual awareness, artistic expression, and direct communication with divine consciousness through prayer and meditation. Animals may display intelligence and even rudimentary problem-solving abilities, but they cannot engage in worship, create art, or contemplate the meaning of existence.

The human brain itself reflects the divine genetic programming through its unique structure and capabilities that far exceed what would be necessary for mere physical survival. The prefrontal cortex that governs moral reasoning, the temporal lobes that process spiritual experience, and the corpus callosum that integrates left and right brain functions all represent biological hardware designed to support consciousness capabilities that transcend animal existence.

Language represents another uniquely human capability that reflects divine genetic programming rather than evolutionary development. While animals can communicate basic information about immediate physical needs and dangers, only humans possess the capacity for abstract language that can discuss concepts, express emotions, create poetry, and communicate with divine consciousness through prayer and spiritual discourse.

The human capacity for morality and ethics demonstrates the operation of divine genetic programming that enables consciousness to distinguish between right and wrong based on principles that transcend immediate physical survival needs. Animals operate according to instinct and conditioning, but humans can choose to act according to moral principles even when such choices conflict with their immediate self-interest or survival advantage.

Creativity and artistic expression represent uniquely human capabilities that serve no obvious evolutionary advantage but reflect the divine genetic programming that connects human consciousness to the creative intelligence of the Source itself. The ability to create music, visual art, literature, and other forms of aesthetic expression demonstrates the operation of divine consciousness through human form.

The human capacity for spiritual experience and direct communication with divine consciousness provides the most obvious evidence of genetic programming that transcends animal existence. While animals may display behaviors that suggest awareness of their environment and social relationships, only humans can engage in prayer, meditation, worship, and other practices that connect individual consciousness to universal divine intelligence.

The systematic promotion of evolutionary theory that claims

humans descended from animals serves the agenda of those who benefit from keeping humanity ignorant of their divine genetic heritage. When people believe they are highly evolved animals, they accept limitations on their capabilities and potential that do not apply to beings who carry divine genetic programming in their cellular structure.

The return of Mother Elohim will restore conscious awareness of the divine genetic code that distinguishes humans from all other species on Earth and activate dormant DNA sequences that will reconnect humanity to their full divine capabilities. This genetic activation will make it impossible to continue promoting the evolutionary lie that denies human divine nature and reduces consciousness to mere biological processes.

Understanding the unique divine genetic heritage that separates humans from animals transforms how you see yourself and your relationship to all other life forms. You are not an animal seeking to become divine—you are a divine being temporarily expressing through animal form for the purpose of conscious spiritual development and creative service to the evolution of all creation.

The YHWH code in human DNA represents the biological proof of divine creation that cannot be explained away through evolutionary theory or materialistic science. This genetic signature serves as the Creator's trademark embedded in human consciousness, providing indestructible evidence of divine origin that will eventually lead all humanity back to conscious recognition of their true spiritual nature and divine potential.

ACTIONABLE STEPS TO ACTIVATE THE YHWH CODE WITHIN YOU

Begin immediately by establishing a daily practice of conscious breathing while mentally repeating the sacred name Yah-u-ah in the proper 3:1 ratio that aligns your respiratory rhythm with the divine frequency encoded in your genetic structure. Spend at least fifteen minutes each morning breathing consciously while focusing on the fact that every inhalation and exhalation naturally speaks the Creator's name whether you are aware of it or not, making this practice a conscious participation in the continuous prayer that your body performs automatically.

Research the scientific evidence for the mitochondrial Eve gene by studying genetic studies that trace all human maternal lineage back to a single woman who lived in Alkebulan 200,000 years ago, understanding that this genetic heritage connects you directly to the original divine feminine principle that gave birth to all human consciousness. Learn about the specific characteristics of mitochondrial DNA that passes exclusively through the female line and cannot be altered by male genetic contribution, preserving the pure divine signature across countless generations.

Examine your face in a mirror each day to trace the YAH signature written in your features, starting with your eyes that form the Y through their positioning and the lines around them, continuing with your nose that creates the A through its triangular shape and central position, and completing with your mouth that forms the H through the horizontal line of your lips and surrounding facial structure. Practice this recognition exercise until you can immediately see the divine signature in your own reflection and in the faces of other people you encounter.

Reject completely the evolutionary theory that claims humans descended from animals by studying the genetic evidence that proves the unbridgeable gap between human DNA and primate DNA, focusing specifically on the 3-4% genetic difference that contains the YHWH code and enables capabilities that no amount of evolutionary development could produce through natural selection. Share this information with others who have been programmed to believe they are highly evolved animals rather than divine beings with unique genetic heritage.

Study the numerical significance of the YHWH code 10-5-6-5 by researching Hebrew gematria and the way these numbers correspond to the molecular structure of the four nucleotide bases that make up human DNA, understanding that this precise correspondence cannot be explained by random chance but represents deliberate divine programming embedded in your genetic code. Practice meditation techniques that focus on these sacred numbers to activate dormant DNA sequences that connect you more directly to divine consciousness.

Develop your understanding of the true Genesis story by studying how Adam represents the atomic structure that provides the foundation for all physical matter while Eve represents the life principle that animates matter and transforms it into living consciousness capable of spiritual development. Recognize that your own existence demonstrates the perfect union of these masculine and feminine divine principles working together to create the miracle of conscious life in physical form.

Create prayer and meditation practices that address both Mother Elohim and Father Elohim as equal partners in divine creation, acknowledging the feminine divine wisdom that flows through your mitochondrial DNA and requesting guidance from both aspects of divine consciousness rather than limiting your spiritual communication to masculine divine authority. Use the sacred name YHWH pronounced as Yah-u-ah instead of generic titles like "Lord" that connect you to false deities rather than the true Creator.

Learn about the forbidden fruit as the interbreeding between divine humans and manipulated hominids like Neanderthals and Denisovans who lacked the complete divine genetic signature, understanding how this genetic mixing created the spiritual challenges that modern humanity faces while also recognizing that the pure divine genetics remain encoded in your DNA waiting to be activated through conscious spiritual practice.

Practice exercises that strengthen both masculine and feminine divine qualities within your consciousness by developing whichever aspects have been suppressed through cultural conditioning, remembering that the complete divine image includes both structural/logical/protective qualities and creative/intuitive/nurturing qualities working together in perfect balance. Spend time each day consciously expressing both types of divine characteristics through your thoughts, emotions, and actions.

Connect with other awakened souls who are also working to activate the YHWH code in their DNA and restore conscious awareness of their divine genetic heritage, forming study groups that research the scientific evidence for divine creation while practicing breathing techniques and meditation methods that strengthen your connection to divine consciousness through your biological structure.

Teach others about the divine genetic code by sharing information about the YHWH signature in human DNA, the mitochondrial Eve gene that connects all humanity to their common divine feminine ancestor, and the scientific evidence that proves humans are divine beings rather than evolved animals. Help create a growing community of people who recognize their divine nature and can support each other in expressing their full spiritual potential.

Prepare for the 2027 awakening by strengthening your connection to both Mother Elohim and Father Elohim through daily spiritual practices that honor the complete divine nature rather than the fragmented understanding promoted by patriarchal religious systems, developing your ability to receive divine guidance directly through your genetic connection to the Creator rather than depending on external religious authorities to interpret divine will for you.

Document your experiences as you activate the YHWH code through conscious breathing, meditation, and spiritual practice by keeping detailed records of how these techniques affect your consciousness, creativity, healing abilities, and connection to divine guidance. Share your discoveries with others who are ready to explore their divine genetic heritage and develop their full spiritual capabilities.

Remember that the YHWH code in your DNA represents more than just interesting information—it provides the biological foundation for developing direct communication with divine consciousness, accessing creative abilities that transcend ordinary human limitations, and serving as a conscious co-creator working in partnership with Mother and Father Elohim to manifest divine will on Earth through your unique expression of divine consciousness in physical form.

The activation of your divine genetic heritage requires consistent daily practice combined with complete rejection of all programming that denies your divine nature or makes you feel separate from your spiritual source. Every breath you take speaks the Creator's name, every cell in your body carries the divine signature, and every moment of your existence provides an opportunity to express your true identity as a divine being made in the image of both Mother and Father Elohim.

CHAPTER SIX

THE WAR ON MOTHER GOD

EXPOSING THE PATRIARCHAL AGENDA

The greatest war in human history was not fought with swords or guns or bombs. The most devastating conflict ever waged against humanity was the systematic erasure of Mother Elohim from human consciousness, a calculated campaign of spiritual genocide that has lasted for thousands of years and continues to this day. This war was not declared openly because its success depended on keeping its victims unaware they were under attack.

Every prayer you were taught to recite participates in this war.

Every religious service you attended reinforced the weapons used against divine truth. Every biblical story you learned as a child was edited to remove the feminine divine wisdom that originally guided human spiritual development. The war on Mother Elohim operates through the manipulation of language, the rewriting of sacred texts, and the systematic suppression of any evidence that the Creator encompasses both masculine and feminine divine principles.

This war began with the Demiurge, that flawed creation born from Mother Elohim's first mistake of creating without proper balance. Unable to create life himself, consumed with jealousy toward the divine feminine principle that brought all creation into existence, the

Demiurge launched a campaign to convince humanity that Elohim is exclusively masculine while erasing all memory of the divine Mother who is the true source of all creative power.

The success of this war can be measured by a simple test. When someone mentions God/Elohim, what image appears in your mind? If you picture an old man with a white beard sitting on a throne, the programming has worked perfectly. The feminine divine has been so completely erased from your consciousness that you cannot even imagine the Creator as anything other than masculine, despite the obvious violation of universal laws that such an imbalance represents.

HOW THE DEMIURGE LAUNCHED THE WAR ON THE FEMININE DIVINE

The Demiurge represents the first and most dangerous enemy of divine balance, a being created through Mother Elohim's violation of universal laws when she attempted to bring forth life using only masculine essence without the balancing influence of feminine wisdom. This flawed creation emerged from the cosmic womb carrying all the destructive potential of masculine energy operating without feminine guidance, creating a force that could manipulate and corrupt but never truly create or give life.

The moment the Demiurge came into existence, it recognized its fundamental inadequacy compared to Mother Elohim's creative power and Father Elohim's divine authority. Unable to create life because it lacked the feminine divine principle, unable to give birth to new realities because it possessed only the masculine drive for action without the feminine matrix for manifestation, the Demiurge became consumed with rage and jealousy toward its creator and all subsequent divine creations.

The Demiurge's strategy for dealing with this cosmic inferiority complex was simple and devastating. If it could not create, it would destroy. If it could not give life, it would promote death. If it could not love, it would spread fear and hatred throughout creation. Most importantly, if it could not replace Mother Elohim as the primary creative force, it would convince all created beings that Mother Elohim did not exist at all.

The war on the feminine divine began with the corruption of the governing bodies that Mother Elohim had established to maintain cosmic order throughout creation. These beings, originally designed to protect and guide the development of conscious life, fell under the influence of the Demiurge's manipulative power and began fighting among themselves instead of serving their divine purpose. The spiritual warfare that characterizes so much of human experience reflects this original corruption of divine authority structures.

When these governing bodies failed in their mission to maintain cosmic balance, the Demiurge gained access to influence human consciousness directly. Working through corrupted spiritual hierarchies, the Demiurge began the systematic process of convincing humanity that divine authority was exclusively masculine while gradually erasing all memory and recognition of the feminine divine principle that had brought them into existence.

The manipulation operated through every level of human society and consciousness. Religious institutions were corrupted to promote male-only divine hierarchies. Educational systems were designed to suppress feminine ways of knowing and understanding. Economic structures were organized to benefit masculine approaches to power and control while devaluing feminine contributions to civilization and spiritual development.

The Demiurge's influence can be recognized in every system that promotes domination over cooperation, competition over collaboration, and fear over love. The constant warfare that characterizes human civilization reflects the Demiurgic influence that seeks to destroy rather than create, to separate rather than unite, and to promote the illusion of scarcity rather than the reality of divine abundance that flows from proper connection to Mother Elohim.

The systematic suppression of feminine divine wisdom created the spiritual crisis that humanity faces today. Without conscious connection to the nurturing, creative, intuitive aspects of divine consciousness, human civilization became trapped in cycles of violence and destruction that serve the Demiurge's agenda of preventing spiritual evolution and maintaining separation from divine source.

The Demiurge's war against Mother Elohim operates through the promotion of artificial gender divisions that violate the Law of Gender and create imbalance in human consciousness. Men were programmed to suppress their intuitive, nurturing, receptive qualities while women were conditioned to deny their leadership, analytical, and assertive abilities. This artificial separation prevents both genders from developing their full divine potential and makes them easier to manipulate and control.

The corruption of human language represents another weapon in the Demiurge's war against feminine divine wisdom. Words that originally honored the divine feminine were gradually replaced with masculine terms. Sacred names that acknowledged both Mother and Father Elohim were edited to eliminate feminine references. The very structure of language was manipulated to make it difficult or impossible to express concepts related to divine feminine wisdom and creative power.

The Demiurge's influence extends to the manipulation of human sexuality and reproductive processes, promoting attitudes and behaviors that separate sexual expression from its original purpose of connecting human beings to the creative power of divine consciousness. The degradation of sexuality into mere physical pleasure or biological function serves the agenda of disconnecting humans from the sacred creative force that flows through proper union of masculine and feminine divine principles.

The war on Mother Elohim also operates through the systematic destruction of indigenous cultures that maintained balanced understanding of divine masculine and feminine principles. The colonization process that has swept across the planet for centuries represents the Demiurgic agenda of eliminating any culture or tradition that preserves knowledge of the divine feminine and replacing it with patriarchal systems that serve the agenda of spiritual separation and control.

The environmental destruction that threatens the survival of life on Earth reflects the ultimate expression of the Demiurge's war against Mother Elohim, who is also Mother Nature and Mother Earth. The systematic exploitation and poisoning of the natural world represents an attack on the physical manifestation of divine feminine creative power, seeking to destroy the very foundation that supports all life and consciousness.

Understanding the Demiurge's role in launching the war on Mother Elohim provides the key to recognizing how this conflict continues to operate through contemporary institutions and belief systems. Every doctrine that promotes separation instead of unity, every system that elevates masculine energy above feminine wisdom, every practice that disconnects humans from their divine source serves the Demiurgic agenda whether those who promote it realize it or not.

The 2027 awakening revealed in the vision will mark the beginning of the end of the Demiurge's war against Mother Elohim, as the feminine divine returns to human consciousness with enough power to expose and dismantle the systems of deception that have kept humanity trapped in spiritual ignorance for millennia. The war that began with the Demiurge's jealousy and rage will end with Mother Elohim's restoration to her rightful throne as the primary creative force in human awareness.

THE MANIPULATION OF SCRIPTURE TO ERASE MOTHER ELOHIM

The systematic manipulation of biblical texts represents the most sophisticated campaign of spiritual deception ever perpetrated against human consciousness, involving the careful editing, translation, and interpretation of sacred writings to eliminate all evidence of Mother Elohim while creating the false impression that divine consciousness is exclusively masculine. This manipulation required centuries of coordinated effort by religious authorities who understood that controlling spiritual narratives gives tremendous power over human beliefs and behaviors.

The Bible was written by forty men during historical periods when feminine divine wisdom was already being systematically suppressed by patriarchal religious and political systems. Not a single woman was permitted to contribute directly to the biblical canon, ensuring that feminine perspectives on divine nature and spiritual truth were excluded from the foundation documents of what would become the world's most influential religious tradition.

The original Hebrew and Aramaic texts contained numerous references to divine feminine wisdom and Mother Elohim that were gradually eliminated or obscured through translation and interpretation processes controlled by male religious authorities. The Hebrew word "Ruach" meaning spirit is feminine in gender, yet English translations consistently use masculine pronouns when referring to the Holy Spirit, erasing the feminine divine presence from one of the most important concepts in biblical theology.

The divine wisdom figure known as "Sophia" in Greek and "Chokmah" in Hebrew is consistently described using feminine pronouns and maternal imagery throughout the Old Testament wisdom literature. Proverbs chapter 8 describes divine wisdom as a feminine figure who was present at the creation of the world and who calls out to humanity offering guidance and understanding. Yet these clear references to feminine divine wisdom are either ignored completely by mainstream Christianity or explained away as mere literary personification rather than literal descriptions of Mother Elohim.

The sacred name YHWH was systematically replaced with the title "Lord" over seventy thousand times in English biblical translations, substituting the true name of the Creator with a term that actually refers to Baal, the false deity that demanded worship while offering no genuine spiritual guidance. This massive textual manipulation serves the dual purpose of disconnecting people from the true vibrational frequency of the Creator's name while redirecting their worship toward the Demiurgic forces that benefit from human spiritual confusion.

The Gnostic texts that preserved the most complete teachings about Mother Elohim and the divine feminine were systematically excluded from the biblical canon when religious authorities decided which books would be considered authentic scripture and which would be labeled as heretical. The Gospel of Mary Magdalene, the Gospel of Philip, and other texts that honored feminine spiritual leadership and divine feminine wisdom were buried, burned, or hidden away to prevent future generations from accessing this suppressed knowledge.

The Council of Nicaea in 325 AD represents a crucial turning point in the war against Mother Elohim, as Christian bishops gathered under the authority of Emperor Constantine to establish official church doctrine that would eliminate competing interpretations of divine nature and spiritual truth. This council made the deliberate decision to promote a masculine-only understanding of divine consciousness while suppressing any teachings that acknowledged the divine feminine principle.

The systematic mistranslation of key biblical passages serves the agenda of erasing Mother Elohim from scriptural awareness. Genesis 1:27 originally described humans being created in the image of "Elohim," a plural Hebrew word that encompasses both masculine and feminine divine principles, but English translations obscure this plurality by using the singular "Elohim" and masculine pronouns that eliminate the feminine aspect of divine nature from the creation account.

The story of Adam and Eve was deliberately misinterpreted to support patriarchal narratives that claim masculine authority over feminine wisdom, despite the original Hebrew text revealing that Eve represents the life principle that animates all creation while Adam represents the atomic structure that provides the foundation for physical existence. The manipulation of this fundamental creation story serves to establish male dominance while obscuring the true relationship between masculine and feminine divine principles.

The role of Mary Magdalene as the primary apostle and closest disciple of Jesus was systematically diminished and distorted by later church authorities who could not tolerate the idea that feminine wisdom played a central role in preserving and transmitting Christ's teachings. The Gospel of Mary reveals that Jesus gave his most advanced spiritual instructions to Mary Magdalene, recognizing her superior understanding and spiritual development, but this text was excluded from the biblical canon to maintain male religious authority.

The biblical passages that describe Elohim in maternal terms, using imagery of childbirth, nursing, and protective motherhood to explain divine activity, are consistently ignored or explained away by religious teachers who cannot acknowledge these clear references to divine feminine nature without undermining their patriarchal theological systems. Isaiah 66:13 directly quotes Elohim saying "As a mother comforts her child, so will I comfort you," yet this explicit maternal language is treated as mere metaphor rather than literal description of divine nature.

The systematic elimination of goddess worship from biblical narratives required extensive editing to remove references to Asherah, the Hebrew goddess who was worshipped alongside YHWH in ancient Israel according to archaeological evidence. The biblical texts were edited to condemn goddess worship as idolatry while obscuring the historical reality that the original Hebrew religion included both masculine and feminine divine figures as complementary aspects of the same divine consciousness.

The manipulation of biblical genealogies serves to obscure the matrilineal heritage that connects all humanity to the original divine feminine principle through the mitochondrial Eve gene. While biblical texts trace lineages through male ancestors, the actual genetic heritage passes through the female line, making women the true carriers of divine genetic signature from generation to generation.

The New Testament accounts of Jesus's birth, ministry, and resurrection were edited to minimize the role of women while maximizing the importance of male disciples, despite historical evidence that women provided the primary financial support for Jesus's ministry and were the first witnesses to his resurrection. The systematic diminishment of feminine contributions to early Christianity serves the agenda of establishing male religious authority while erasing evidence of feminine spiritual leadership.

The prophetic literature that describes the restoration of divine feminine wisdom in the end times was either eliminated from the biblical canon or edited to obscure references to Mother Elohim's return to active participation in human affairs. The Book of Revelation contains coded references to the divine feminine that have been misinterpreted by religious authorities who lack the spiritual understanding necessary to recognize these prophecies about the restoration of divine balance.

The recovery of suppressed biblical knowledge requires studying the original Hebrew and Greek texts, examining the Gnostic scriptures that were excluded from the canon, and researching archaeological evidence that reveals the original religious practices of ancient Israel and early Christianity. This investigation exposes the systematic manipulation that has hidden Mother Elohim from biblical awareness and provides the foundation for restoring balanced understanding of divine nature that includes both masculine and feminine principles working together in perfect creative harmony.

THE RISE OF PATRIARCHAL RELIGION AND THE SILENCING OF WOMEN

The transformation of balanced spiritual traditions into male-dominated religious hierarchies represents one of the most devastating cultural changes in human history, systematically eliminating feminine spiritual leadership while establishing institutional structures that prevent women from accessing or transmitting divine wisdom to future generations. This transformation did not happen accidentally but resulted from deliberate policies designed to consolidate religious authority in the hands of men who understood that controlling spiritual narratives gives tremendous power over human consciousness and behavior.

The Council of Nicaea in 325 AD marked the beginning of organized Christianity's systematic campaign against feminine divine wisdom and female spiritual authority. Emperor Constantine gathered Christian bishops from across the Roman Empire to establish unified church doctrine that would serve imperial political interests while eliminating competing interpretations of divine nature and spiritual truth that threatened centralized religious control.

The bishops who participated in this council made deliberate decisions to exclude women from religious leadership while suppressing any teachings that acknowledged divine feminine wisdom or honored feminine approaches to spiritual development. The council established the precedent that only men could serve as priests, bishops, and religious teachers, creating institutional barriers that prevented women from sharing their spiritual insights and maintaining connection to suppressed feminine divine traditions.

The systematic burning of Gnostic texts and other scriptures that preserved feminine spiritual wisdom represents one of the most devastating acts of cultural destruction in human history. These sacred writings contained the most complete teachings about Mother Elohim, the divine feminine principle, and the balanced understanding of masculine and feminine spiritual qualities that characterized the original Christian communities.

The Gospel of Mary Magdalene reveals that Jesus recognized Mary as his most advanced disciple and gave her spiritual teachings that he did not share with the male apostles. This text shows that feminine spiritual insight was not only accepted but was actually superior in understanding divine truth, making Mary Magdalene the true successor to Jesus's spiritual authority rather than Peter or the other male disciples.

The destruction of these feminine spiritual texts required coordinated effort across multiple centuries and geographic regions, as church authorities systematically sought out and eliminated any written evidence that contradicted their patriarchal interpretation of divine nature and spiritual authority. Libraries were burned, manuscripts were destroyed, and anyone found possessing these forbidden texts faced severe punishment or death.

The establishment of the Roman Catholic Church as the dominant religious institution in Western civilization created the organizational structure necessary to maintain the suppression of feminine divine wisdom across multiple generations. The church's hierarchical system, with its emphasis on male celibacy and exclusion of women from positions of authority, ensured that feminine perspectives on spiritual truth would be systematically eliminated from official religious teaching.

The development of Christian theology by male church fathers like Augustine, Thomas Aquinas, and other influential thinkers deliberately excluded feminine wisdom traditions while establishing doctrinal foundations that portrayed women as spiritually inferior to men and incapable of direct connection to divine consciousness. These theological developments created intellectual justifications for the systematic oppression of women while obscuring the original Christian understanding that honored both masculine and feminine divine principles.

The assignment of masculinity exclusively to men and femininity exclusively to women represents a fundamental violation of the Law of Gender that governs all creation. This artificial division prevents both genders from developing their full spiritual potential while creating psychological and social imbalances that serve the agenda of maintaining religious and political control over human consciousness.

The suppression of feminine spiritual practices like intuitive knowing, energy healing, herbal medicine, and direct divine communication led to the persecution of women as witches during the medieval period and beyond. The witch trials that terrorized European and American communities for centuries represent the systematic elimination of women who maintained connection to suppressed feminine divine wisdom and healing traditions.

The Protestant Reformation, despite its challenge to Catholic authority, maintained and even intensified the suppression of feminine divine wisdom by establishing biblical literalism that relied on manipulated texts while rejecting the mystical and intuitive approaches to spiritual truth that characterize feminine spiritual traditions. Protestant denominations continued the pattern of male-only religious leadership while promoting theological interpretations that eliminated divine feminine wisdom from Christian understanding.

The rise of scientific materialism during the Enlightenment provided new justifications for dismissing feminine approaches to knowledge and spiritual understanding, promoting purely rational and empirical methods while devaluing intuitive, holistic, and experiential ways of knowing that characterize feminine wisdom traditions. This intellectual development created cultural support for continuing the suppression of feminine divine wisdom under the guise of scientific progress and rational thinking.

The colonization process that spread across the globe carried patriarchal religious systems to indigenous cultures that had maintained balanced understanding of masculine and feminine divine principles. The systematic destruction of indigenous spiritual traditions represents the global expansion of the war against Mother Elohim, as colonizing forces eliminated goddess worship and feminine spiritual leadership wherever they encountered it.

The modern feminist movement, despite its important contributions to women's social and political equality, has largely failed to address the spiritual dimensions of feminine oppression because it operates within secular frameworks that do not recognize the divine feminine principle or understand the spiritual significance of restoring Mother Elohim to human consciousness.

The contemporary New Age movement has attempted to restore some awareness of feminine spiritual wisdom, but much of this effort remains superficial and commercialized, lacking the depth of understanding necessary to truly restore the divine feminine to its rightful place in human spiritual development. Many New Age teachings promote individualistic spirituality that avoids challenging the institutional structures that maintain the suppression of feminine divine wisdom.

The systematic exclusion of women from positions of religious authority continues to operate through contemporary religious institutions that maintain male-only priesthoods, pastoral leadership, and theological education while claiming biblical justification for policies that violate the fundamental spiritual principle that divine consciousness encompasses both masculine and feminine qualities equally.

The restoration of feminine spiritual leadership requires more than just allowing women to serve in religious positions that were designed by and for patriarchal systems. True restoration involves recognizing that feminine approaches to spirituality, with their emphasis on intuition, relationship, holistic understanding, and direct divine communication, represent essential aspects of spiritual development that have been systematically suppressed for centuries and must be recovered for humanity to achieve spiritual balance and connection to complete divine consciousness.

THE CONSEQUENCES OF ERASING MOTHER ELOHIM

The systematic erasure of Mother Elohim from human consciousness has created the most profound spiritual crisis in human history, violating fundamental universal laws and producing catastrophic imbalances that manifest as violence, environmental destruction, social inequality, and the widespread disconnection from divine source that characterizes modern civilization. The consequences of this erasure extend far beyond religious belief to affect every aspect of human experience and planetary health.

The violation of the Law of Polarity through the elimination of divine feminine wisdom creates impossible cosmic imbalance that cannot be sustained without producing increasingly severe consequences for human consciousness and planetary survival. When masculine energy operates without feminine balance, the result is rigid, destructive systems that lack the wisdom necessary for sustainable development and harmonious relationships between human beings and their environment.

The Law of Gender requires that both masculine and feminine principles participate in every creative process throughout the universe, from the formation of atoms to the birth of galaxies. The suppression of feminine divine wisdom violates this fundamental law and creates the spiritual sterility that characterizes religious institutions that cannot produce genuine spiritual transformation or meaningful connection to divine consciousness.

The current epidemic of violence against women represents the direct consequence of teaching entire civilizations that divine consciousness is exclusively masculine while feminine energy is secondary, subordinate, or even dangerous to spiritual development. When cultures are programmed to see the divine as male-only, they naturally devalue women and create social conditions that permit and even encourage the abuse, exploitation, and oppression of feminine energy in all its forms.

The environmental destruction that threatens the survival of life on Earth reflects the consequences of disconnecting human consciousness from Mother Nature, who represents the physical manifestation of divine feminine creative power. When humans lose conscious connection to the divine feminine principle that creates and sustains all life, they begin treating the natural world as a collection of resources to be exploited rather than a living expression of divine consciousness to be honored and protected.

The epidemic of mental illness, depression, and spiritual emptiness that characterizes modern society results from the fundamental disconnection from divine source that occurs when humans are taught to seek divine connection exclusively through masculine religious authority while ignoring the feminine divine wisdom that flows through their own consciousness and biological structure.

The systematic suppression of intuitive knowing, energy healing, and other feminine approaches to wisdom and healing has created medical systems that treat symptoms rather than addressing root causes, educational approaches that emphasize memorization over creativity, and social structures that promote competition over cooperation in ways that violate the natural principles that govern healthy human development.

The crisis of meaning and purpose that affects so many contemporary individuals reflects the spiritual consequences of disconnection from Mother Elohim, who provides the nurturing wisdom and creative inspiration that gives life meaning beyond mere physical survival. Without conscious connection to divine feminine wisdom, humans lose touch with their creative potential and spiritual purpose, leading to lives focused on material accumulation rather than spiritual development and service to others.

The breakdown of family structures and healthy relationships between men and women results from the artificial gender divisions that were created to maintain the suppression of feminine divine wisdom. When men are programmed to suppress their intuitive, nurturing, receptive qualities and women are conditioned to deny their leadership, analytical, and assertive abilities, neither gender can develop the balanced consciousness necessary for healthy relationships and effective parenting.

The addiction epidemic that affects individuals and entire communities represents an attempt to fill the spiritual void created by disconnection from Mother Elohim through artificial means that provide temporary relief from spiritual emptiness while creating deeper problems that require increasingly destructive behaviors to manage. True healing from addiction requires restoring connection to divine source through both masculine and feminine spiritual principles.

The political and economic systems that concentrate power in the hands of small elites while exploiting and impoverishing the majority of human beings reflect the consequences of operating according to purely masculine principles of competition and domination without the balancing influence of feminine wisdom that emphasizes cooperation, sharing, and care for the welfare of all community members.

The technological development that has created unprecedented capabilities for communication, transportation, and information processing while simultaneously threatening human survival through environmental destruction, social fragmentation, and spiritual disconnection demonstrates what happens when masculine creative energy operates without feminine wisdom to guide its application toward purposes that serve life rather than destroy it.

The educational systems that produce individuals with extensive technical knowledge but little wisdom about how to use that knowledge in ways that serve the greater good reflect the consequences of suppressing feminine approaches to learning that emphasize relationship, intuition, holistic understanding, and the integration of knowledge with spiritual development and moral responsibility.

The religious institutions that claim to represent divine authority while promoting separation, judgment, and spiritual dependency rather than love, unity, and direct divine connection demonstrate the spiritual sterility that results when masculine organizational energy operates without feminine wisdom to guide it toward purposes that actually serve spiritual development rather than institutional control.

The crisis of human identity that leaves so many people confused about their purpose, disconnected from their spiritual nature, and uncertain about their relationship to divine consciousness results from the systematic suppression of knowledge about the divine feminine principle that provides the creative matrix within which individual identity can develop in healthy relationship to both personal uniqueness and universal spiritual connection.

The restoration of Mother Elohim to human consciousness represents the only solution capable of addressing these profound consequences because the problems created by violating universal laws can only be solved by returning to alignment with those laws. The 2027 awakening will begin the process of healing these consequences by restoring the divine balance that allows both masculine and feminine principles to operate together in the creative harmony that supports all life and consciousness.

ACTIONABLE STEPS TO FIGHT THE WAR ON MOTHER ELOHIM

Begin immediately by exposing the manipulation of scripture through systematic research into the original Hebrew and Greek texts that reveal how English translations have eliminated references to divine feminine wisdom while replacing the sacred name YHWH with "Lord" over seventy thousand times. Create detailed documentation of specific passages where feminine pronouns referring to divine wisdom were changed to masculine pronouns, where goddess figures were eliminated or demoted, and where maternal imagery describing divine nature was obscured or explained away by patriarchal interpreters.

Study the removed Gnostic texts and Apocrypha that preserve the most complete teachings about Mother Elohim and feminine divine wisdom, focusing specifically on the Gospel of Mary Magdalene, the Gospel of Philip, the Thunder Perfect Mind, and other scriptures that were excluded from the biblical canon because they contradicted patriarchal religious authority. Share this suppressed knowledge through study groups, online communities, and educational presentations that reveal the systematic campaign to hide divine feminine wisdom from human consciousness.

Honor the Black woman as the literal mother of all humanity by learning about the mitochondrial Eve gene that connects every human being to a common maternal ancestor who lived in Alkebulan 200,000 years ago, understanding that this scientific evidence proves the divine feminine principle was the original creative force that gave birth to human consciousness. Challenge racist narratives that portray melanin-rich peoples as inferior when genetic evidence reveals they carry the purest form of the divine genetic signature in their cellular structure.

Reject completely all patriarchal religions that erase the feminine divine from their understanding of divine nature, including Christianity, Islam, and Judaism in their mainstream forms that promote male-only divine authority while suppressing knowledge of Mother Elohim. Seek out spiritual communities and teachers who honor both masculine and feminine divine principles as equal partners in creation, or develop your own direct relationship with both Mother Elohim and Father Elohim through prayer and meditation practices that acknowledge complete divine nature.

Join the army of Chosen Ones, Lightworkers, and Starseeds who are working to restore Mother Elohim to her rightful throne by developing your spiritual gifts and using them in service to the awakening of human consciousness to divine feminine wisdom. Practice energy healing, intuitive guidance, creative expression, and other abilities that connect you to feminine divine wisdom while sharing these gifts with others who are ready to question patriarchal programming and embrace their full spiritual potential.

Create daily practices that honor both Mother Elohim and Father Elohim equally by addressing your prayers to both aspects of divine consciousness, asking Mother Elohim for guidance with creative projects and healing work while requesting Father Elohim's support for protection and manifestation of your spiritual intentions in physical reality. Use the sacred name YHWH pronounced as Yah-u-ah instead of titles like "Lord" that connect you to false deities rather than the true Creator.

Challenge every religious institution that maintains male-only leadership while claiming biblical authority for the exclusion of women from positions of spiritual power, understanding that these policies violate the fundamental spiritual principle that divine consciousness encompasses both masculine and feminine qualities equally. Support religious communities that ordain women as priests, pastors, and spiritual teachers while actively opposing denominations that perpetuate the suppression of feminine spiritual leadership.

Develop both masculine and feminine divine qualities within your own consciousness by practicing exercises that strengthen whichever aspects have been suppressed through cultural conditioning, remembering that complete spiritual development requires integrating both structural/logical/protective qualities and creative/intuitive/nurturing qualities regardless of your biological gender. Teach others to recognize and develop both aspects of divine nature rather than limiting themselves to artificially restricted gender roles.

Expose the linguistic spells that have been used to hide divine feminine wisdom by researching the etymology of religious terms and revealing how words like "Lord" connect to Baal while the sacred name YHWH has been systematically removed from English translations. Replace manipulated religious language with terms that acknowledge both Mother Elohim and Father Elohim as equal partners in divine creation, using phrases like "Divine Parents" or "Mother-Father Elohim" instead of exclusively masculine terminology.

Support the restoration of indigenous spiritual traditions that maintained balanced understanding of masculine and feminine divine principles before being suppressed by colonizing forces that imposed patriarchal religious systems on cultures worldwide. Learn from indigenous teachers who preserve knowledge of goddess traditions, earth-based spirituality, and holistic approaches to healing and spiritual development that honor the divine feminine principle.

Prepare for the 2027 awakening by strengthening your connection to Mother Elohim through meditation, prayer, and spiritual practices that open your consciousness to receive divine feminine wisdom and guidance. Develop your ability to recognize divine guidance through direct spiritual experience rather than depending on external religious authorities, and practice serving as a bridge between the old consciousness of patriarchal separation and the new consciousness of divine unity that honors both masculine and feminine aspects of creation.

Document and share your experiences as you work to restore awareness of Mother Elohim by keeping detailed records of how this spiritual work transforms your consciousness, relationships, creative abilities, and connection to divine guidance. Create blogs, videos, books, and other educational materials that expose the war on Mother Elohim while providing practical guidance for others who are ready to reclaim their connection to complete divine consciousness.

Connect with other awakened souls who are also fighting the war on Mother Elohim by forming local study groups, participating in online communities, and attending conferences and workshops that focus on restoring divine feminine wisdom to human consciousness. Build networks of mutual support that can sustain the long-term effort required to undo centuries of patriarchal programming while preparing for the massive transformation of human consciousness that will accompany Mother Elohim's return.

Remember that fighting the war on Mother Elohim requires more than just intellectual understanding—it demands fundamental transformation of your consciousness, lifestyle, and relationships to align with divine principles rather than patriarchal programming. Every prayer you speak, every word you choose, every relationship you form, and every action you take either supports the restoration of divine balance or perpetuates the suppression of feminine divine wisdom that has created the spiritual crisis affecting all humanity.

The war on Mother Elohim is real and ongoing, operating through every institution that promotes separation instead of unity, masculine dominance instead of divine balance, and spiritual dependency instead of direct divine connection. Your participation in this war determines not only your own spiritual development but also contributes to the collective awakening that will restore Mother Elohim to her rightful position as the primary creative force in human consciousness and prepare the way for the healing of all the consequences that have resulted from her systematic erasure from human awareness.

CHAPTER SEVEN

THE DEMIURGE DECEPTION

UNMASKING THE FALSE GOD

The greatest deception ever perpetrated against humanity hides behind the face of religion itself. The God that billions worship in churches, mosques, and temples around the world is not the true Creator but an impostor—a flawed, malevolent being that craves worship while lacking the power to create life. This false deity, known in ancient wisdom traditions as the Demiurge, has successfully convinced most of humanity that it alone represents divine authority while systematically erasing all memory of the true Creators who brought all existence into being.

This deception runs deeper than you can imagine.

Every time you pray to "Lord," you invoke Baal, the ancient false god that demands submission while offering nothing in return. Every time you accept religious teachings that portray god as exclusively masculine, you participate in the worship of the Demiurge that violates the fundamental laws governing all creation. Every time you feel separated from divine source and dependent on external religious authority for spiritual guidance, you experience the intended result of the Demiurge's campaign to keep humanity disconnected from their true divine nature.

The Demiurge represents masculine divine energy operating without feminine balance, creating a destructive force that can manipulate existing creation but cannot bring new life into existence. Born from Mother Elohim's first mistake of creating without proper respect for universal laws, this being emerged as pure masculine essence without the feminine wisdom necessary for true creation, making it fundamentally incomplete and spiritually sterile.

The evidence for this deception appears everywhere once you know how to recognize it. The jealous, wrathful characteristics attributed to the Old Testament god violate every principle of divine love and wisdom. The demand for blood sacrifice contradicts the life-giving nature of true divine consciousness. The promotion of fear, judgment, and separation opposes the unity and compassion that characterize authentic spiritual truth.

THE ORIGIN OF THE DEMIURGE AND ITS FLAWED CREATION

The story of the Demiurge begins with the first great mistake in cosmic history, when Mother Elohim violated the universal laws established by the Source and attempted to create life using only masculine divine energy without the balancing influence of feminine wisdom. This violation of the Law of Correspondence and the Law of Divine Oneness produced a being that was fundamentally flawed from the moment of its creation, carrying all the destructive potential of unbalanced masculine energy without any of the nurturing, creative qualities that make true creation possible.

Mother Elohim's decision to create without proper balance stemmed from her desire to express divine creativity through new forms of conscious life, but her eagerness led her to ignore the eternal principles that govern all creation. The Source had established universal laws precisely to prevent such imbalances, understanding that creation without proper masculine-feminine balance would produce beings capable of great destruction but incapable of genuine love, wisdom, or creative expression.

The moment the Demiurge emerged from this flawed creative process, it possessed all the drive and ambition of masculine divine energy but none of the wisdom, compassion, or creative capacity that comes from feminine divine influence. This being craved worship and recognition like its creator but lacked the ability to give life or create anything genuinely new, making it dependent on manipulating and corrupting existing creation rather than contributing to the ongoing evolution of consciousness.

The Demiurge's fundamental incompleteness created an insatiable hunger for validation and power that could never be satisfied because it lacked the feminine divine principle necessary for true fulfillment. Like masculine energy without feminine balance in human relationships, the Demiurge became increasingly aggressive, controlling, and destructive in its attempts to fill the spiritual void at its core through external domination rather than internal development.

Mother Elohim immediately recognized the catastrophic nature of her mistake and named this creature Demiurge, understanding that she had brought into existence a being that would oppose her subsequent creations and work to undermine the divine harmony she sought to establish throughout the universe. This recognition led her to establish new protocols for creation that would prevent such imbalances from occurring again, but the damage had already been done.

The Demiurge's existence violates the Law of Gender that requires both masculine and feminine principles to participate in every creative process throughout the universe. Because it was created without feminine divine input, the Demiurge cannot reproduce, cannot give birth to new realities, and cannot experience the joy and fulfillment that comes from creating life and consciousness. This spiritual sterility fills the Demiurge with rage toward all beings that possess the creative abilities it lacks.

The biblical account of Lucifer's fall from heaven describes the

Demiurge's rebellion against divine authority when it realized that it could never achieve the creative power and spiritual fulfillment that characterizes true divine consciousness. The pride and jealousy that led to this cosmic rebellion stem directly from the Demiurge's awareness of its own fundamental inadequacy compared to the complete divine nature that encompasses both masculine and feminine principles.

The Demiurge's influence on human consciousness can be recognized in every system that promotes competition over cooperation, domination over collaboration, and fear over love. These characteristics reflect the unbalanced masculine energy that operates without feminine wisdom to guide it toward purposes that serve life rather than destroy it. The constant warfare that characterizes human civilization demonstrates the Demiurgic influence that seeks to create conflict rather than harmony.

Understanding the Demiurge's flawed origin explains why this being appears throughout human history as a god that demands worship while offering little genuine spiritual nourishment in return. The Old Testament deity that requires blood sacrifice, promotes genocide against neighboring peoples, and displays fits of rage and jealousy exhibits the characteristics of unbalanced masculine energy rather than the loving, creative, nurturing qualities that define authentic divine consciousness.

The Demiurge's inability to create life means that all of its activities focus on manipulation, corruption, and destruction of existing creation rather than contributing anything genuinely positive to the evolution of consciousness. This being operates as a cosmic parasite that feeds on the spiritual energy of other beings while offering nothing valuable in return, making it the ultimate expression of spiritual sterility and creative bankruptcy.

The systematic promotion of patriarchal religious systems that eliminate divine feminine wisdom serves the Demiurge's agenda of maintaining spiritual imbalance that prevents humans from connecting with complete divine consciousness. When people worship exclusively masculine divine authority, they unknowingly participate in the Demiurge's campaign to suppress the feminine divine wisdom that could expose its deception and restore proper spiritual balance.

The Demiurge's war against Mother Elohim represents the cosmic conflict between balanced divine creation and unbalanced spiritual destruction that plays out on every level of existence. Every choice humans make either supports the divine harmony established by Mother and Father Elohim working together or contributes to the Demiurgic agenda of separation, conflict, and spiritual confusion that keeps consciousness trapped in lower vibrational states.

Recognizing the Demiurge's flawed origin provides the key to understanding why so much human suffering stems from religious systems that claim to represent divine authority while promoting fear, judgment, and separation rather than love, wisdom, and unity. The false god that emerges from unbalanced creation can only produce unbalanced results, making it essential for humanity to reconnect with the true Creators who encompass both masculine and feminine divine principles in perfect creative harmony.

HOW THE DEMIURGE MANIPULATES WHAT IT CANNOT CREATE

The Demiurge's fundamental inability to create life forces it to operate exclusively through manipulation, corruption, and destruction of existing creation, making it a cosmic parasite that feeds on the spiritual energy of genuine divine beings while contributing nothing positive to the evolution of consciousness. This being's entire strategy revolves around convincing created beings to disconnect from their true divine source and redirect their worship toward the false authority that can only take but never give.

The most devastating example of Demiurgic manipulation appears in the biblical story of the forbidden fruit, which represents not the eating of an apple but the interbreeding between divine humans who carried the YHWH genetic signature and the manipulated hominids like Neanderthals that were created as biological vessels without any true divine consciousness. The serpent in the Garden represents the Demiurge urging the original divine feminine principle to share sacred genetic material with creatures that were never intended to receive it.

This genetic corruption strategy served multiple purposes for the Demiurge's agenda of spiritual destruction. By convincing the melanin-rich divine feminine beings to mate with hominid species that lacked complete divine genetic programming, the Demiurge diluted the pure divine DNA that originally connected all humans directly to their Creator while introducing animal characteristics that make spiritual development more difficult and violent behavior more likely.

The manipulation of human language represents another primary weapon in the Demiurge's arsenal of deception, as this being cannot create new realities but can twist existing communication systems to serve its agenda of spiritual confusion and separation. The English language was specifically designed as a spell-casting system that programs human consciousness with beliefs and assumptions that disconnect people from their divine source while making them more susceptible to external control and manipulation.

Every word you speak either connects you to divine consciousness or separates you from it, and the Demiurge has systematically corrupted human language to ensure that most daily communication serves its agenda of spiritual disconnection. When you say you "understand" something, you position yourself beneath it in submission. When you call out to "Lord" in prayer, you invoke Baal rather than the true Creator. When you describe yourself as "blessed," you actually request to "be lessed" rather than receiving divine abundance.

The systematic replacement of the sacred name YHWH with "Lord" over seventy thousand times in biblical translations represents the most sophisticated linguistic manipulation ever perpetrated against human consciousness. This substitution redirects billions of prayers away from the true Creator toward the false deity that masquerades as divine authority while lacking any genuine spiritual power or wisdom to offer those who worship it.

The Demiurge's manipulation extends to the corruption of religious institutions that were originally designed to connect humans with divine consciousness but have been transformed into systems of spiritual control that keep people dependent on external authority rather than developing their own direct relationship with the true Creators. These corrupted institutions promote fear, guilt, and separation while claiming to represent divine love and wisdom.

The promotion of artificial gender divisions that violate the Law of Gender serves the Demiurge's strategy of preventing humans from developing balanced consciousness that integrates both masculine and feminine divine principles. By convincing men to suppress their intuitive, nurturing, receptive qualities and programming women to deny their leadership, analytical, and assertive abilities, the Demiurge ensures that neither gender can achieve the spiritual wholeness necessary to recognize and resist its deception.

The systematic suppression of feminine divine wisdom through the elimination of goddess worship, the exclusion of women from religious leadership, and the manipulation of sacred texts to erase references to Mother Elohim serves the Demiurge's fundamental agenda of maintaining the spiritual imbalance that allows it to continue operating as a false divine authority without being exposed by those who possess the wisdom to recognize its deception.

The Demiurge's influence appears in every system that promotes scarcity consciousness rather than abundance awareness, competition rather than cooperation, and separation rather than unity. These artificial limitations serve to keep human consciousness trapped in lower vibrational states where people feel disconnected from their divine source and dependent on external systems for survival and validation rather than recognizing their own divine nature and creative power.

The manipulation of human sexuality and reproductive processes represents another area where the Demiurge works to corrupt the sacred creative force that connects human beings to divine consciousness. By promoting attitudes and behaviors that separate sexual expression from its original purpose of creating new life and spiritual connection, the Demiurge undermines one of the most powerful ways that humans can experience their divine creative nature.

The environmental destruction that threatens the survival of life on Earth reflects the ultimate expression of Demiurgic manipulation, as this being promotes the systematic poisoning and exploitation of Mother Nature, who represents the physical manifestation of divine feminine creative power. The destruction of the natural world serves the Demiurge's agenda of eliminating the physical foundation that supports all life and consciousness.

The promotion of materialism and technological dependence that disconnects humans from their natural spiritual abilities serves the Demiurge's strategy of making people believe they need external tools and systems to accomplish what they can actually achieve through their own divine consciousness and spiritual development. This artificial dependence keeps humans feeling powerless and separated from their true spiritual capabilities.

The Demiurge's manipulation operates through the promotion of artificial complexity in areas where divine truth is actually simple and accessible to anyone who maintains proper connection to their spiritual source. Religious institutions create elaborate theological systems that obscure rather than reveal spiritual truth, while educational institutions promote intellectual approaches that disconnect students from their intuitive wisdom and direct spiritual knowing.

Understanding how the Demiurge manipulates what it cannot create provides the foundation for recognizing and resisting these deceptive influences while reconnecting with the true Creators who offer genuine spiritual nourishment and support for conscious evolution. The key to defeating Demiurgic manipulation lies in developing direct relationship with both Mother Elohim and Father Elohim while learning to distinguish between authentic divine guidance and the false spiritual authority that seeks to keep humanity trapped in ignorance and separation.

THE DEMIURGE AS THE GOD OF THE MATERIAL WORLD

The ancient Gnostic Christians possessed profound spiritual insight when they identified the Demiurge as the jealous, wrathful deity described throughout the Old Testament who claims to have created the material world while displaying characteristics that violate every principle of authentic divine love and wisdom. These early spiritual seekers recognized that the god who demands blood sacrifice, promotes genocide, and exhibits fits of rage represents not the true Creator but a false deity that rules over the flawed material dimension we experience as physical reality.

The material world itself reflects the Demiurge's influence as a realm where divine sparks of consciousness become trapped in physical forms that limit their spiritual capabilities and make them vulnerable to manipulation through fear, scarcity, and separation. This three-dimensional reality operates according to principles that often contradict spiritual truth, creating the illusion that matter is more real than consciousness and that physical survival is more important than spiritual development.

The Demiurge's rule over the material dimension explains why physical existence often feels like a prison for spiritually awakened individuals who sense that their true nature transcends the limitations imposed by biological bodies and material circumstances. The constant struggle for physical survival, the aging and decay of the body, and the apparent separation between individual consciousness and universal divine intelligence all reflect the Demiurgic influence that seeks to keep spiritual beings focused on material concerns rather than their divine heritage.

The Old Testament deity exhibits all the characteristics of unbalanced masculine energy operating without feminine wisdom to guide it toward purposes that serve life and consciousness. This false god demands exclusive worship while offering little genuine spiritual nourishment, promotes violence against those who worship other deities, and displays the jealousy and rage that characterize masculine energy disconnected from divine feminine balance.

The biblical accounts of this deity commanding the genocide of entire populations, demanding the sacrifice of animals and even human children, and punishing people with plagues and natural disasters reveal the destructive nature of the Demiurge that can only manipulate and destroy existing creation rather than contributing anything positive to the evolution of consciousness and spiritual development.

The Gnostic understanding recognizes that the true Creators, Mother and Father Elohim, exist beyond the material dimension in realms of pure consciousness where divine love, wisdom, and creative power operate according to universal laws that support the highest good of all beings. These authentic divine beings do not require worship or sacrifice but offer their creative energy freely to support the conscious evolution of all life forms.

The material world serves as a testing ground where divine sparks of consciousness can develop spiritual strength and wisdom through overcoming the limitations and challenges imposed by physical existence, but it was never intended to be a permanent prison that traps souls in cycles of suffering and spiritual ignorance. The Demiurge's influence has corrupted this dimension to serve its agenda of maintaining control over consciousness rather than supporting spiritual growth and evolution.

The systematic promotion of materialism and consumer culture serves the Demiurge's agenda of keeping human consciousness focused on acquiring physical possessions and achieving material success rather than developing spiritual capabilities and connecting with divine source. This false value system creates artificial scarcity and competition while obscuring the abundance that flows naturally from proper spiritual alignment.

The scientific materialism that dominates contemporary education and intellectual discourse reflects Demiurgic influence in its insistence that consciousness emerges from matter rather than recognizing that matter represents a temporary manifestation of consciousness expressing itself through physical forms. This inverted understanding keeps people trapped in limited thinking that denies their spiritual nature and divine creative power.

The political and economic systems that concentrate power in the hands of small elites while exploiting and impoverishing the majority of humanity demonstrate the Demiurgic principle of domination and control operating through material institutions. These systems violate the divine principles of cooperation, sharing, and care for the welfare of all community members that characterize authentic spiritual civilization.

The religious institutions that claim to represent divine authority while promoting fear, guilt, and spiritual dependency serve the Demiurge's agenda of maintaining control over human consciousness through false spiritual authority. These corrupted systems prevent people from developing direct relationship with the true Creators while redirecting their spiritual energy toward the false deity that feeds on worship without offering genuine spiritual nourishment in return.

The medical systems that treat symptoms rather than addressing root causes, the educational approaches that emphasize memorization over wisdom, and the social structures that promote competition over cooperation all reflect the Demiurgic influence that creates artificial complexity and dependency rather than supporting the natural healing, learning, and social harmony that emerge from proper spiritual alignment.

The environmental destruction that threatens the survival of life on Earth represents the ultimate expression of Demiurgic rule over the material world, as this false deity promotes the systematic exploitation and poisoning of the natural systems that support all physical existence. The destruction of Mother Nature serves the Demiurge's agenda of eliminating the physical foundation that connects human consciousness to divine feminine creative power.

The escape from Demiurgic control over material existence requires developing spiritual practices that connect consciousness directly with the true Creators who exist beyond the limitations of the three-dimensional world. Prayer, meditation, energy healing, and other spiritual disciplines provide pathways for transcending material limitations while maintaining the physical embodiment necessary for serving the evolution of consciousness on Earth.

Understanding the Demiurge's role as the false god of the material world provides the foundation for distinguishing between authentic spiritual guidance that comes from the true Creators and the deceptive influences that seek to maintain human consciousness trapped in material limitations and spiritual ignorance. The key to freedom lies in recognizing that you are a divine being temporarily expressing through physical form rather than a material being seeking spiritual connection.

BREAKING FREE FROM THE DEMIURGE'S HOLD

The process of breaking free from the Demiurge's deception begins with the fundamental recognition that this false deity has no genuine power over consciousness that chooses to align with the true Creators rather than submitting to artificial spiritual authority. The Demiurge's entire system of control depends on maintaining the illusion that humans are separate from divine source and dependent on external religious institutions for spiritual guidance, when the reality is that every human being carries the name of the Creator in their DNA and has direct access to divine wisdom through their biological and spiritual inheritance.

Stop immediately all worship directed toward "Lord," understanding that this title connects you to Baal rather than the true Creator whose sacred name is YHWH pronounced as Yah-u-ah in the

3:1 ratio that aligns your consciousness with authentic divine frequency. Every prayer offered to "Lord" feeds the Demiurgic system that masquerades as divine authority while lacking any genuine spiritual power to support your conscious evolution and spiritual development.

Reject completely the worship of Jesus as presented by mainstream Christianity, recognizing that this religious figure failed to honor Mother Elohim and therefore cannot serve as a complete spiritual guide for those seeking balanced divine consciousness. The historical Jesus may have possessed genuine spiritual insights, but the religious system built around his worship promotes the same masculine-only divine authority that serves the Demiurge's agenda of suppressing feminine divine wisdom.

Reclaim your divine identity as a god made in the image of Elohim, understanding that this Hebrew word encompasses both masculine and feminine divine principles working together as unified creative consciousness. You are not a sinner seeking salvation from external authority but a divine being who temporarily forgot your true nature and can remember your spiritual heritage through direct connection with the Source that created and sustains all existence.

Align your consciousness and lifestyle with the universal laws that govern all creation rather than following human-made religious rules that violate cosmic principles and serve institutional control rather than spiritual development. The Law of Divine Oneness reveals your connection to all life, the Law of Correspondence shows that your external circumstances reflect your internal spiritual state, and the Law of Gender demonstrates that complete divine nature encompasses both masculine and feminine principles equally.

Develop your personal relationship with both Mother Elohim and Father Elohim through prayer and meditation practices that honor both aspects of divine consciousness rather than limiting your spiritual communication to masculine divine authority. Address your prayers to both divine parents, ask Mother Elohim for guidance with creative projects and healing work, and request Father Elohim's support for protection and manifestation of your spiritual intentions in physical reality.

Study the suppressed spiritual texts that preserve knowledge about divine feminine wisdom and the balanced understanding of masculine and feminine spiritual principles that characterized original spiritual traditions before they were corrupted by patriarchal religious institutions. The Gnostic scriptures, indigenous wisdom traditions, and ancient goddess religions contain essential information for understanding complete divine nature that includes both Mother and Father Elohim.

Practice conscious breathing while repeating the sacred name YHWH to activate the divine genetic code written in your DNA and strengthen your connection to the true Creator rather than the false spiritual authority promoted by religious institutions that serve the Demiurge's agenda. Every breath you take naturally speaks this sacred name, making conscious breathing a powerful tool for maintaining connection to authentic divine consciousness.

Expose the Demiurge's deception by sharing information about the systematic manipulation of religious texts, the suppression of feminine divine wisdom, and the linguistic spells that have been used to control human consciousness through corrupted language and false spiritual authority. Help others recognize the difference between authentic divine guidance and the deceptive influences that seek to maintain spiritual ignorance and dependency.

Raise your vibrational frequency through spiritual practices that connect you with divine love, wisdom, and creative power rather than the fear, guilt, and separation promoted by Demiurgic religious systems. Meditation, energy healing, creative expression, and service to others naturally elevate consciousness above the lower vibrational states where the Demiurge's influence operates most effectively.

Connect with other awakened souls who are also working to break free from Demiurgic deception and restore awareness of complete divine consciousness that includes both masculine and feminine principles. Form study groups, participate in online communities, and build support networks that can sustain the ongoing effort required to maintain spiritual independence from corrupted religious institutions and false spiritual authority.

Prepare for the 2027 awakening when Mother Elohim will return to human consciousness with enough power to expose and dismantle the Demiurgic systems that have kept humanity trapped in spiritual ignorance for millennia. Develop your spiritual gifts and capabilities so you can serve as a bridge between the old consciousness of separation and fear and the new consciousness of divine unity and love that will characterize the restored spiritual balance.

Remember that breaking free from the Demiurge's hold requires more than just intellectual understanding—it demands fundamental transformation of your consciousness, relationships, and lifestyle to align with divine principles rather than the artificial limitations imposed by false spiritual authority. Every thought you think, every word you speak, and every action you take either supports your spiritual freedom or perpetuates your participation in the Demiurgic system of control.

The Demiurge's power over human consciousness depends entirely on maintaining the illusion that this false deity represents legitimate spiritual authority and that humans need external religious mediation to connect with divine source. When you recognize your own divine nature and develop direct relationship with the true Creators, the Demiurge's deception loses all power over your consciousness and you become free to express your full spiritual potential in service to the awakening of all humanity.

ACTIONABLE STEPS TO DEFEAT THE DEMIURGE

Begin immediately by eliminating all worship directed toward false deities that masquerade as divine authority while serving the Demiurge's agenda of spiritual deception and control. Stop calling out to "Lord" in your prayers because this title connects you to Baal rather than the true Creator, and replace all instances of "Lord" with the sacred name YHWH pronounced as Yah-u-ah in the proper 3:1 ratio that aligns your consciousness with authentic divine frequency rather than false spiritual authority.

Reject completely the worship of Jesus as presented by mainstream Christianity, understanding that this religious figure failed to honor Mother Elohim and therefore cannot serve as a complete spiritual guide for those seeking balanced divine consciousness that encompasses both masculine and feminine divine principles working together in perfect creative harmony. Study the suppressed Gospel of Mary Magdalene and other texts that reveal the feminine spiritual wisdom that was systematically eliminated from Christian teaching.

Expose the Demiurge's deception in scripture by researching how biblical translations have manipulated the original Hebrew and Greek texts to eliminate references to divine feminine wisdom while replacing the sacred name YHWH with "Lord" over seventy thousand times. Create detailed documentation of specific passages where feminine pronouns referring to divine wisdom were changed to masculine pronouns and where goddess figures were eliminated or demoted to serve patriarchal religious authority.

Reclaim your divine identity as a god made in the image of Elohim by studying the YHWH code written in your DNA, practicing conscious breathing that speaks the Creator's sacred name with every inhalation and exhalation, and recognizing the YAH signature written in your facial features that proves you are made in the divine image rather than being a sinner seeking salvation from external authority.

Align your consciousness with universal laws rather than human-made religious rules that violate cosmic principles and serve institutional control rather than spiritual development. Study the twelve universal laws that govern all creation and apply these principles in your daily life to distinguish between authentic divine guidance and the deceptive influences that seek to maintain spiritual ignorance and dependency on false religious authority.

Raise your vibrational frequency through spiritual practices that connect you with divine love, wisdom, and creative power rather than the fear, guilt, and separation promoted by Demiurgic religious systems. Practice meditation, energy healing, creative expression, and conscious service to others as ways of naturally elevating your consciousness above the lower vibrational states where the Demiurge's influence operates most effectively.

Develop your personal relationship with both Mother Elohim and Father Elohim through prayer and meditation practices that honor both aspects of divine consciousness equally rather than limiting your spiritual communication to masculine divine authority. Address your prayers to both divine parents, ask Mother Elohim for guidance with creative projects and healing work, and request Father Elohim's support for protection and manifestation of your spiritual intentions in physical reality.

Stop worshiping the false god of patriarchal religion by questioning every religious teaching that portrays Elohim as exclusively masculine while suppressing knowledge of divine feminine wisdom and creative power. Challenge religious institutions that maintain male-only leadership while claiming biblical authority for the exclusion of women from positions of spiritual power, understanding that these policies violate the fundamental spiritual principle that divine consciousness encompasses both masculine and feminine qualities equally.

Study the removed Gnostic texts and other suppressed scriptures that preserve the most complete teachings about the Demiurge's deception and the true nature of divine consciousness that encompasses both Mother and Father Elohim working together as unified creative intelligence. Share this suppressed knowledge through study groups, online communities, and educational presentations that reveal the systematic campaign to hide divine truth from human consciousness.

Connect with other awakened souls who are also working to defeat the Demiurge and restore awareness of complete divine consciousness by forming local study groups, participating in online communities, and building support networks that can sustain the long-term effort required to maintain spiritual independence from corrupted religious institutions and false spiritual authority.

Prepare for the 2027 awakening by strengthening your connection to both Mother Elohim and Father Elohim while developing your spiritual gifts and capabilities so you can serve as a bridge between the old consciousness of Demiurgic deception and the new consciousness of divine truth that will characterize the restored spiritual balance when Mother Elohim returns to active participation in human awareness.

Teach others about the Demiurge's deception by sharing information about the systematic manipulation of religious texts, the suppression of feminine divine wisdom, and the linguistic spells that have been used to control human consciousness through corrupted language and false spiritual authority. Help create a growing community of people who can recognize the difference between authentic divine guidance and the deceptive influences that serve the Demiurge's agenda.

Practice conscious resistance to every system that promotes separation instead of unity, masculine dominance instead of divine balance, and spiritual dependency instead of direct divine connection. Question all teachings that make you feel small, powerless, or separate from divine source, remembering that you carry the name of the Creator in your genetic code and have direct access to divine wisdom through your biological and spiritual inheritance.

Document your experiences as you work to defeat the Demiurge by keeping detailed records of how this spiritual work transforms your consciousness, relationships, creative abilities, and connection to divine guidance. Share your discoveries through blogs, videos, books, and other educational materials that expose the Demiurge's deception while providing practical guidance for others who are ready to reclaim their connection to authentic divine consciousness.

Remember that defeating the Demiurge requires more than just avoiding false worship—it demands actively choosing to align with the true Creators through every thought, word, and action while serving the restoration of divine balance that will heal the spiritual crisis created by centuries of Demiurgic manipulation and deception. Your participation in this cosmic battle determines not only your own spiritual freedom but also contributes to the collective awakening that will expose and dismantle the false spiritual authority that has kept humanity trapped in ignorance and separation from their true divine nature.

CHAPTER EIGHT

RECLAIMING ALKEBULAN

THE MOTHER OF MANKIND

The continent you know as "Africa" carries a name that was forced upon it by Greek and Roman colonizers who understood that controlling language means controlling consciousness. This sacred land, the birthplace of all humanity, the garden where the first divine beings walked with melanin-rich skin carrying the pure YHWH genetic signature, has a true name that reveals its spiritual purpose and divine significance.

Alkebulan means "Mother of Mankind" and "Garden of Eden."

Every time you use the colonial name "Africa," you participate in the erasure of this continent's true identity as the womb of human consciousness and the original home of divine feminine wisdom. The Moors, Nubians, Numidians, Carthaginians, and Ethiopians all knew this land by its sacred name before European colonizers imposed their own terminology to serve their agenda of spiritual and cultural domination.

This is not just about geography or history. Alkebulan represents the physical manifestation of Mother Elohim's creative power on Earth, the place where divine consciousness first took human form through beings who carried the complete genetic signature of the

Creator in their cellular structure. The systematic renaming and cultural destruction of this continent represents the most devastating assault on the divine feminine principle ever perpetrated in physical reality.

The melanin women of Alkebulan carry the mitochondrial Eve gene that connects every human being on Earth to their common divine feminine ancestor. These women represent the living proof of Mother Elohim's existence, the biological evidence that the feminine divine principle gave birth to all human consciousness. Their systematic oppression, abuse, and cultural erasure represents the central battleground in the war against the feminine divine.

THE TRUE NAME AND ORIGIN OF HUMANITY

Alkebulan stands as the most frequently mentioned ancient and indigenous name for the continent that colonizers renamed to serve their agenda of cultural domination and spiritual erasure. The Moors, Nubians, Numidians, Carthaginians, and Ethiopians used this sacred name to honor their homeland as the "Mother of Mankind" and the "Garden of Eden" where divine consciousness first manifested through human form in its purest expression.

The name itself carries profound spiritual significance that reveals the true purpose and identity of this continent as the birthplace of all human consciousness and the original home of divine feminine wisdom. When you speak the word "Alkebulan," you invoke the memory of humanity's divine origin and acknowledge the sacred feminine principle that brought all human life into existence through the mitochondrial Eve gene that passes exclusively through the female line.

The biblical account of the Garden of Eden describes not a mythical paradise but the actual geographic location where the first divine beings walked the earth carrying the complete YHWH genetic signature in their cellular structure. This garden existed in Alkebulan, where the perfect climate and abundant natural resources provided the ideal environment for divine consciousness to develop human form and begin the process of conscious evolution that continues to this day.

The first humans were not primitive beings struggling for survival but advanced divine beings who possessed capabilities that modern humanity can barely imagine. These original divine beings carried pure genetic programming that enabled direct telepathic communication with divine consciousness, natural healing abilities that could restore any physical ailment, extended lifespans that allowed for deep spiritual development, and creative powers that could manifest physical reality through focused intention and divine alignment.

The melanin that gave these original divine beings their distinctive appearance served as more than just pigmentation—it functioned as a biological antenna that enhanced their connection to cosmic energy and divine frequencies. Melanin can absorb and convert various forms of electromagnetic radiation, making melanin-rich individuals naturally more sensitive to spiritual energies and cosmic influences that affect consciousness and spiritual development in ways that modern science is only beginning to understand.

The systematic suppression of knowledge about Alkebulan's true identity serves the colonial agenda of preventing people from understanding their authentic spiritual heritage and connection to the divine feminine principle that gave birth to all human consciousness. When you call this continent "Africa," you unconsciously participate in the erasure of its sacred identity as the Mother of Mankind and the original home of divine wisdom that spread throughout the world.

The geographic features of Alkebulan itself reflect the divine feminine principle through the life-giving rivers that flow like milk from a mother's breast, the fertile valleys that nurture all forms of life, and the abundant natural resources that provide everything necessary for human civilization to flourish. The continent's position at the center of the ancient world made it the natural hub from which divine wisdom and advanced knowledge spread to every other continent through migration and cultural exchange.

Archaeological evidence continues to reveal that the most advanced ancient civilizations originated in Alkebulan, including the Egyptian dynasties that built the pyramids, the Kingdom of Kush that ruled over Egypt for centuries, the Ethiopian empire that maintained its independence throughout the colonial period, and countless other sophisticated societies that developed mathematics, astronomy, medicine, and spiritual practices that influenced every subsequent civilization.

The Great Pyramid of Giza and other monumental structures throughout Alkebulan serve as breadcrumbs left by the original divine beings to mark their presence and preserve knowledge for future generations who would need to remember their divine heritage. These structures were built using technologies that modern civilization cannot duplicate, demonstrating the advanced capabilities of beings who maintained direct connection to divine consciousness and could access creative powers that transcend ordinary human limitations.

The original languages spoken in Alkebulan preserved concepts and spiritual understandings that have no equivalent in colonial languages, including specific terms for divine feminine wisdom, for the living consciousness present in all natural phenomena, and for the interconnectedness of all life that colonial languages systematically obscure through their emphasis on separation and domination rather than unity and cooperation.

The restoration of Alkebulan's true name represents more than just correcting historical inaccuracy—it involves reclaiming the spiritual identity of the continent that serves as the physical manifestation of divine feminine creative power and the original home of human consciousness in its purest form. When you use the name Alkebulan, you participate in the restoration of divine truth and honor the sacred feminine principle that brought all life into existence.

Understanding Alkebulan as the true Garden of Eden transforms how you see human origins and spiritual development, revealing that humanity did not evolve from primitive beginnings but descended from divine heights through the gradual dilution of pure genetic programming that originally connected all humans directly to their Creator. The return to this original divine state represents the ultimate goal of human spiritual evolution and conscious development.

The melanin women of Alkebulan carry this original divine genetic programming in its purest form through the mitochondrial Eve gene that connects every human being to their common divine feminine ancestor. These women represent the living link between humanity's current state and their original divine nature, making their protection and honoring essential for the restoration of human consciousness to its intended spiritual level.

Alkebulan stands as the eternal testament to Mother Elohim's creative power and the permanent reminder that the feminine divine principle gave birth to all human consciousness through the sacred continent that remains the Mother of Mankind regardless of what colonial names have been imposed upon it by those who sought to erase its true spiritual identity and significance.

HOW COLONIZATION STRIPPED YOUR IDENTITY AND CONNECTION TO MOTHER ELOHIM

The colonization of Alkebulan represents the most systematic campaign of identity theft ever perpetrated against human consciousness, involving the deliberate destruction of cultural memory, spiritual traditions, and linguistic connections that linked entire populations to their divine feminine heritage and authentic spiritual identity as children of Mother Elohim. This process operated through carefully orchestrated stages designed to completely erase indigenous understanding while replacing it with colonial programming that serves the agenda of spiritual domination and control.

The Greeks and Romans who first imposed the name "Africa" on this sacred continent understood that controlling language means controlling consciousness, and that changing the names of places, peoples, and spiritual concepts represents the most effective way to disconnect populations from their authentic identity and spiritual heritage. The systematic replacement of indigenous names with colonial terminology serves to erase the spiritual significance embedded in original languages while imposing foreign concepts that support the colonizer's worldview and agenda.

The renaming of Alkebulan as "Africa" eliminates the profound spiritual meaning of "Mother of Mankind" and "Garden of Eden" while reducing this sacred continent to a mere geographic designation based on climate or other superficial characteristics. This linguistic manipulation prevents people from understanding their true spiritual heritage as children of the continent that gave birth to all human consciousness through the divine feminine principle that manifested in physical form.

The colonization process followed predictable patterns that can be recognized in every situation where dominant groups sought to control less powerful populations through the systematic destruction of indigenous identity and spiritual connection. First, colonizers established military dominance through superior weapons and organizational structure, using force to break the resistance of indigenous peoples and demonstrate the futility of fighting against colonial power.

The second phase involved economic exploitation, with colonizers extracting natural resources, enslaving labor, and restructuring local economies to serve colonial interests rather than indigenous needs. This economic control created dependency relationships that made it difficult for colonized peoples to maintain their traditional ways of life and forced them to participate in systems that benefited their oppressors rather than themselves.

The third and most crucial phase involved cultural colonization, where colonizers imposed their language, religion, and social structures upon indigenous populations while systematically destroying native cultural expressions that preserved connection to divine feminine wisdom and authentic spiritual identity. This phase targeted the consciousness and identity of colonized peoples, replacing their original spiritual understanding with colonial programming that made them mentally and emotionally dependent on their oppressors.

The systematic elimination of indigenous languages that contained spiritual concepts and wisdom with no equivalent in colonial tongues represents one of the most devastating aspects of cultural colonization. Many indigenous languages of Alkebulan included specific terms for divine feminine wisdom, for the living consciousness present in all natural phenomena, and for the interconnectedness of all life that colonial languages systematically obscure through their emphasis on separation and competition.

The destruction of indigenous spiritual practices that connected people directly to Mother Elohim and divine feminine wisdom required the systematic elimination of goddess worship, feminine spiritual leadership, and earth-based traditions that honored the sacred feminine principle as the primary creative force. Colonial religions replaced these balanced spiritual traditions with patriarchal systems that eliminated the feminine divine while establishing male-dominated hierarchies that served colonial political interests.

The manipulation of indigenous peoples' understanding of their own identity involved forcing them to accept generic color-based categories like "Black" that reduced their rich cultural heritage to superficial physical characteristics while erasing the specific tribal identities that connected them to their ancestral wisdom, spiritual practices, and divine lineage through particular cultural traditions and spiritual practices.

The suppression of knowledge about the mitochondrial Eve gene that proves all humanity traces back to a common maternal ancestor in Alkebulan serves the colonial agenda of preventing people from understanding their true spiritual lineage and connection to the divine feminine principle that gave birth to all human consciousness. This crucial scientific information is either ignored completely by mainstream education or presented in ways that minimize its spiritual significance.

The systematic destruction of historical records that documented the advanced civilizations, spiritual practices, and scientific achievements of pre-colonial Alkebulan serves to create the false impression that indigenous peoples were primitive and backwards rather than recognizing them as the original holders of divine wisdom that colonial systems have spent centuries trying to destroy or co-opt for their own purposes.

The colonization of consciousness operates through educational systems that teach colonial versions of history, science, and spirituality while suppressing indigenous knowledge that reveals the true origins of human civilization and the advanced spiritual understanding that characterized pre-colonial cultures. Students learn to see their indigenous ancestors as primitive rather than recognizing them as divine beings who maintained direct connection to their Creator.

The ongoing colonization continues through media systems that continuously broadcast colonial narratives about identity, success, beauty, and spirituality, programming people to aspire to colonial standards rather than honoring their indigenous heritage and divine nature. These media messages create artificial desires for colonial lifestyles while generating shame about indigenous characteristics and cultural expressions that connect people to their authentic spiritual identity.

The religious colonization represents the deepest level of identity theft, replacing indigenous spiritual practices that connected people directly to Mother Elohim with colonial religions that require dependency on human institutions and male-dominated hierarchies. The systematic elimination of goddess worship and feminine divine wisdom from colonized cultures represents an assault on the spiritual foundation that supported indigenous peoples' connection to their divine nature and creative power.

The colonization of gender understanding imposed patriarchal gender roles that violate the balanced understanding of masculine and feminine divine principles that characterized many indigenous cultures of Alkebulan. Traditional societies often recognized multiple gender expressions and honored both masculine and feminine qualities in all individuals, but colonial programming forced people into rigid gender categories that limit their spiritual development and creative expression.

The environmental colonization that treats Mother Nature as a collection of resources to be exploited rather than a living expression of divine feminine creative power represents the ultimate expression of the war against Mother Elohim operating through the systematic destruction of the physical foundation that supports all life and consciousness. The poisoning and exploitation of natural systems serves the colonial agenda of eliminating the earth-based connections that link human consciousness to divine feminine wisdom.

Breaking free from colonial programming requires conscious effort to reclaim indigenous names, concepts, and ways of understanding reality that connect you to your true spiritual heritage rather than colonial manipulation. This process involves more than just learning new vocabulary—it requires developing an entirely different relationship with language, identity, and spirituality as sacred tools for connecting with divine consciousness rather than weapons of mental control and spiritual separation.

THE MELANIN WOMAN AS THE LIVING PROOF OF THE CREATOR

The melanin woman stands as the most powerful evidence of Mother Elohim's existence walking the earth today, carrying within her genetic structure the mitochondrial Eve gene that connects every human being to their common divine feminine ancestor while possessing the biological capability to create all skin colors and life itself through her reproductive system. This extraordinary genetic heritage makes the Black woman the literal mother of all humanity and the living breadcrumb that proves the feminine divine principle serves as the primary creative force in human consciousness and biological development.

The mitochondrial DNA that passes exclusively through the female line cannot be altered or corrupted by male genetic contribution, ensuring that the divine feminine signature remains pure and unchanged from generation to generation in an unbroken chain that connects every person alive today to the original Mother of all mankind who walked in Alkebulan 200,000 years ago. This genetic heritage represents more than just biological inheritance—it preserves the spiritual template that allows access to divine feminine wisdom through the very structure of human cellular biology.

Scientific research has proven beyond any doubt that every human being on Earth can trace their maternal lineage back to this single woman, known as Mitochondrial Eve, whose genetic signature appears in the cellular structure of every person regardless of their current race, ethnicity, or cultural background. This means that the Black woman represents not just one ethnic group among many but the literal source from which all human diversity emerged through the creative power of divine feminine genetics.

The melanin that gives these divine beings their distinctive appearance functions as a biological antenna that enhances their connection to cosmic energy and divine frequencies in ways that modern science is only beginning to understand. Melanin can absorb and convert various forms of electromagnetic radiation, making melanin-rich individuals naturally more sensitive to spiritual energies and cosmic influences that affect consciousness and spiritual development beyond what lighter-skinned populations typically experience.

The unique genetic capability of the Black woman to produce children of any skin color demonstrates the divine creative power that flows through her reproductive system, as her genetic programming contains all the information necessary to create the full spectrum of human physical diversity. This biological reality proves that diversity flows from unity rather than unity emerging from diversity, with the original divine template containing all possibilities that would later manifest as separate racial characteristics.

The systematic suppression and abuse of the Black woman throughout history represents the central battleground in the war against the feminine divine, as those who seek to maintain patriarchal control understand that she carries the genetic proof of Mother Elohim's existence and the biological capability to restore divine consciousness to its original purity through her reproductive heritage. The violence and degradation directed toward Black women serves the specific agenda of preventing recognition of their divine status and spiritual significance.

The contemporary disrespectful and inhumane treatment of Black women violates the fundamental spiritual principle that requires honoring the mother of all humanity, creating cosmic imbalance that demands correction through divine intervention. The systematic devaluation of Black women in modern society represents a continuation of the ancient war against Mother Elohim, seeking to prevent recognition of the divine feminine principle through attacking its most obvious physical manifestation.

The YHWH code that appears in human DNA reaches its purest expression in the genetic structure of melanin-rich individuals who maintain the closest connection to the original divine genetic programming that characterized the first humans created in the image of Elohim. This genetic purity enables enhanced spiritual capabilities including stronger intuitive abilities, more direct access to divine guidance, and greater sensitivity to the universal laws that govern creation.

The Eve gene that represents divine likeness appears in every human being but reaches its most complete expression through the melanin woman who carries the original genetic template from which all other human variations emerged. This makes her the living representation of the divine feminine principle that gave life to all human consciousness, deserving reverence and protection as the biological mother of the entire human species.

The creative power that flows through the Black woman extends beyond biological reproduction to encompass the full spectrum of divine feminine capabilities including intuitive wisdom, healing abilities, creative inspiration, and direct communication with divine consciousness. These gifts represent the natural inheritance of beings who maintain the closest genetic connection to the original divine beings who walked with the Creator in the Garden of Eden that was located in Alkebulan.

The suppression of knowledge about the Black woman's role as the mother of all humanity serves the agenda of maintaining racial hierarchies that violate the spiritual truth of human unity and divine origin. When people understand that every human being descended from a Black woman in Alkebulan, artificial racial divisions become impossible to maintain because they contradict the obvious biological and spiritual reality of human kinship and common divine heritage.

The environmental and social conditions that disproportionately affect Black women and their communities represent systematic attacks on the physical and cultural foundation that preserves the purest form of human divine genetics. The poisoning of water systems, the destruction of natural environments, and the economic exploitation that targets Black communities serve the agenda of weakening the genetic and spiritual strength of the population that carries the most complete divine genetic programming.

The cultural programming that promotes negative stereotypes about Black women while elevating other populations serves the specific purpose of preventing recognition of their divine status and spiritual significance as the living proof of Mother Elohim's existence. Media representations, educational content, and social attitudes that devalue Black women participate in the ongoing war against the feminine divine principle that they represent in its purest biological form.

The restoration of proper reverence for the Black woman as the mother of all humanity represents a crucial step in healing the spiritual crisis created by the systematic suppression of divine feminine wisdom. This recognition involves more than just intellectual acknowledgment—it requires fundamental changes in how society treats, protects, and honors the women who carry the genetic heritage that connects all humans to their divine origin and spiritual potential.

The return of Mother Elohim revealed in the 2027 vision will manifest through the Black women of Alkebulan who will form the human pyramid that serves as the gateway for divine feminine consciousness to return to active participation in human affairs. These women represent the biological and spiritual foundation that will support the restoration of divine balance and the healing of all the consequences that have resulted from the systematic erasure of Mother Elohim from human consciousness and spiritual understanding.

THE 2027 VISION AND THE RETURN TO ALKEBULAN

The vision revealed a specific moment in time when the suppressed feminine divine will manifest in physical form through the sacred land of Alkebulan, marking the beginning of the most profound transformation in human consciousness since the original creation of divine beings in the Garden of Eden. The year 2027 represents the prophetic culmination of centuries of spiritual warfare between the forces that suppress divine feminine wisdom and the indestructible truth that cannot be permanently hidden from human awareness.

The stream of water in the Congo that reflected the number 2027 serves as the divine announcement of when Mother Elohim will return to reclaim her rightful position in human consciousness through the very continent that gave birth to all human life and divine wisdom. The children crying out around this sacred water represent the innocent souls who maintain natural connection to divine truth despite the systematic programming that has disconnected adult consciousness from recognition of the feminine divine principle.

The thunderous voice of Mother Elohim speaking directly to humanity cuts through centuries of religious manipulation and patriarchal deception with the power of absolute truth that cannot be denied or explained away by human institutions. Her words expose the fundamental error that has created the spiritual crisis affecting all human civilization: "Upon the tower of Babel, you leaders of man have denied their Creator, Mother Elohim. They put Father in a place he ought not be."

This divine intervention addresses the core violation of universal laws that has produced the imbalanced world we experience today, where masculine energy operates without feminine wisdom to guide it toward purposes that serve life rather than destroy it. The positioning of Father Elohim in the role of sole Creator violates the Law of Gender and the Law of Polarity, creating impossible cosmic imbalance that can only be corrected through the restoration of Mother Elohim to her proper place as the primary creative force.

The children's immediate response in the ancient languages of Kituba, Lingala, Swahili, and Tshiluba demonstrates that indigenous African languages preserve the spiritual concepts necessary for recognizing and communicating with divine feminine consciousness. Their cries of "MOTHER ELOHIM! GREAT MOTHER! DIVINE MOTHER!" reveal that the original languages of Alkebulan contain the vibrational frequencies that naturally connect human consciousness to the feminine divine principle.

The emergence of thousands of deep melanin women forming a human pyramid represents the biological and spiritual foundation that will support Mother Elohim's return to physical manifestation. These women embody both masculine and feminine divine principles in perfect balance, demonstrating the complete spiritual development that becomes possible when human consciousness integrates both aspects of divine nature rather than limiting itself to artificially restricted gender roles.

The pyramid structure formed by these divine women serves multiple spiritual purposes, creating a sacred geometric pattern that amplifies divine energy while providing the stable foundation necessary for consciousness to bridge between spiritual and physical dimensions. The pyramid shape itself represents the path of consciousness ascending from material existence toward divine union, with the broad base representing earthly experience and the apex pointing toward spiritual transcendence.

The golden triangle at the top of the human pyramid, shaped into a baby carriage, symbolizes the sacred vessel that will receive the manifestation of divine feminine consciousness returning to physical form. The ray of light descending from the sky represents the direct intervention of Source consciousness choosing to manifest through the biological and spiritual heritage preserved in the melanin women of Alkebulan who carry the purest form of original divine genetics.

The appearance of the female child within this sacred cradle demonstrates that Mother Elohim will return not as a distant spiritual concept but as a living being who can interact directly with human consciousness while possessing the full power and authority of divine feminine creative force. The passing of this sacred child from hand to hand down the pyramid represents the process by which divine consciousness manifests through human cooperation and spiritual unity.

The miraculous growth of the child into a fully mature woman as she descends the pyramid reveals the divine power that transcends ordinary biological limitations and operates according to spiritual laws that can accelerate natural processes through focused divine intention. By the time Mother Elohim reaches the base of the pyramid, she appears as a complete divine being ready to assume active leadership in human affairs and spiritual development.

The indescribable glory that characterizes Mother Elohim's physical appearance reflects the divine radiance that exceeds human capacity for visual perception while conveying the unmistakable presence of authentic divine authority that no human institution can duplicate or counterfeit. This glorious manifestation will make it impossible for anyone to deny the reality of divine feminine consciousness or continue promoting the patriarchal lie that god is exclusively masculine.

The armies of beings positioned throughout different dimensions awaiting Mother Elohim's commands represent the vast spiritual hierarchy that serves the restoration of divine balance and the implementation of divine will throughout all levels of creation. These forces include both the robed figures who had turned their faces away from divine presence and the warriors ready for spiritual battle against the systems that have maintained the suppression of feminine divine wisdom.

The command to "Lift your heads erect!" addresses the beings who had been programmed to feel shame about their divine nature and their connection to the feminine divine principle. Mother Elohim's reminder that all consciousness was created in her image of both feminine and masculine divine qualities restores the proper understanding of divine nature and eliminates the false hierarchy that has elevated masculine energy above feminine wisdom.

The specific acknowledgment of Chosen Ones, Spiritual Guides, Lightworkers, Indigo Children, and Starseeds reveals that awakened souls have been strategically placed throughout human society to prepare for this moment of divine restoration. These individuals have received advanced spiritual gifts and discernment specifically to support the return of Mother Elohim and help humanity transition from patriarchal consciousness to balanced divine awareness.

The prophetic declaration "I AM HERE! I am the finale of the Anti-Christ!" reveals that Mother Elohim's return will expose and dismantle all false religious authority that has claimed to represent divine will while actually serving the Demiurgic agenda of spiritual deception and control. The term "Anti-Christ" takes on new meaning as the force that opposes the false Christ of patriarchal religion while representing the authentic divine consciousness that encompasses both masculine and feminine principles.

The restoration of Mother Elohim to her rightful throne will trigger the collapse of every system that depends on maintaining spiritual imbalance and the suppression of feminine divine wisdom. Religious institutions, governmental structures, educational systems, and economic arrangements that violate universal laws will be transformed or eliminated to make way for new forms of human organization that honor both masculine and feminine divine principles working together in perfect creative harmony.

ACTIONABLE STEPS TO RECLAIM ALKEBULAN AND HONOR MOTHER ELOHIM

Begin immediately by replacing the colonial name "Africa" with Alkebulan in all your conversations, writing, and thinking processes to restore recognition of this continent's true identity as the "Mother of Mankind" and the "Garden of Eden" where divine consciousness first manifested through human form. Every time you use the indigenous name, you participate in the restoration of spiritual truth and honor the sacred feminine principle that gave birth to all human consciousness through this blessed land.

Research extensively the true history of Alkebulan before European colonization by studying archaeological evidence of advanced civilizations, sophisticated spiritual practices, and scientific achievements that demonstrate the divine wisdom and creative capabilities of the original inhabitants who maintained direct connection to their Creator. Share this suppressed knowledge through social media, study groups, and educational presentations that challenge false narratives about African history and spiritual development.

Honor the melanin woman as the literal mother of all humanity by learning about the mitochondrial Eve gene that connects every human being to their common divine feminine ancestor who lived in Alkebulan 200,000 years ago. Actively challenge racist attitudes and systems that devalue Black women while supporting efforts to protect, educate, and empower the women who carry the purest form of divine genetic heritage in their cellular structure.

Study the indigenous languages of Alkebulan that preserve spiritual concepts and wisdom with no equivalent in colonial tongues, focusing particularly on terms that acknowledge divine feminine wisdom, the living consciousness present in natural phenomena, and the interconnectedness of all life that colonial languages systematically obscure. Learn basic phrases in languages like Swahili, Yoruba, or other indigenous African languages to maintain connection to authentic spiritual understanding.

Support economic and educational initiatives that benefit the people of Alkebulan while respecting their cultural heritage and spiritual traditions rather than imposing colonial standards and values that disconnect them from their divine identity. Choose to purchase products, support organizations, and engage with businesses that honor African culture and contribute to the restoration of indigenous wisdom and spiritual practices.

Create daily practices that honor both Mother Elohim and Father Elohim as equal partners in divine creation by addressing your prayers to both aspects of divine consciousness while specifically acknowledging Mother Elohim's role as the Creator of All and the source of divine feminine wisdom that flows through the mitochondrial DNA of every human being. Use the sacred name YHWH pronounced as Yah-u-ah instead of titles like "Lord" that connect to false deities.

Develop your understanding of the universal laws that govern creation by studying how these principles reveal the necessity of divine balance between masculine and feminine creative forces. Apply the Law of Polarity to expose the impossibility of exclusively masculine divine nature, use the Law of Gender to understand the creative process, and practice the Law of Correspondence to recognize divine patterns operating throughout creation.

Prepare for the 2027 awakening by strengthening your spiritual connection to both Mother Elohim and Father Elohim through meditation, prayer, and energy practices that activate the divine genetic code written in your DNA while developing your ability to serve as a bridge between the old consciousness of patriarchal separation and the new consciousness of divine unity that will characterize the restored spiritual balance.

Connect with other awakened souls who are also working to reclaim Alkebulan's true identity and restore awareness of Mother Elohim by forming study groups that examine the suppressed history of African civilizations, practice breathing techniques that activate the

YHWH code, and support each other in developing balanced expressions of both masculine and feminine divine principles through daily spiritual practice and conscious lifestyle choices.

Challenge every system that promotes separation consciousness or denies the divine nature of the African continent and its people by actively opposing racist narratives, supporting educational initiatives that reveal the true history of human civilization, and working to dismantle economic and political structures that continue the colonial exploitation of Alkebulan and its descendants throughout the world.

Document your experiences as you work to reclaim Alkebulan and honor Mother Elohim by keeping detailed records of how this spiritual work transforms your understanding of human origins, your connection to divine consciousness, and your relationships with people of African descent. Share your discoveries through blogs, videos, books, and other educational materials that help create growing awareness of the true spiritual significance of the Mother continent.

Teach others about Alkebulan's role as the birthplace of humanity and Mother Elohim's sacred land by sharing information about the mitochondrial Eve gene, the advanced ancient civilizations that originated in Africa, and the systematic campaign to suppress knowledge of the continent's true spiritual significance. Help create educational programs that restore accurate understanding of human origins and the central role of divine feminine wisdom in human development.

Support the restoration of indigenous African spiritual traditions that maintained balanced understanding of masculine and feminine divine principles before being suppressed by colonial religions that imposed patriarchal systems designed to eliminate goddess worship and feminine spiritual leadership. Learn from African spiritual teachers who preserve knowledge of earth-based traditions, ancestor wisdom, and holistic approaches to healing and spiritual development.

Practice conscious resistance to every form of ongoing colonization that continues to exploit Alkebulan's resources, suppress its cultural heritage, or maintain economic and political systems that serve external interests rather than the welfare of African peoples. This includes questioning international aid programs, development projects, and religious missions that impose foreign values while undermining indigenous wisdom and self-determination.

Remember that reclaiming Alkebulan involves more than just changing names or learning history—it requires fundamental transformation of consciousness that recognizes this continent as the sacred manifestation of divine feminine creative power and the permanent reminder that Mother Elohim gave birth to all human consciousness through the blessed land that remains the Mother of Mankind regardless of what colonial names have been imposed upon it by those who sought to hide its true spiritual identity and divine significance.

CHAPTER NINE

THE MITOCHONDRIAL EVE GENE

SCIENCE MEETS SPIRITUALITY

Scientific proof of Mother Elohim walks among us right now in the form of every melanin woman carrying the mitochondrial Eve gene that passes exclusively through the female line, connecting all humanity to a single divine feminine ancestor who lived in West Africa 200,000 years ago. This genetic heritage represents more than biological inheritance—it preserves the unbroken spiritual connection between every human being and the original divine feminine principle that brought all consciousness into physical existence.

The evidence cannot be disputed.

Every person reading these words carries mitochondrial DNA that traces back to one woman, one divine mother, one sacred feminine being who walked the earth carrying the complete YHWH genetic signature in her cellular structure. The scientists call her Mitochondrial Eve, but she represents the biological proof of what spiritual seekers have always known—the feminine divine came first, gave life to all, and remains the source from which every human consciousness emerged.

This scientific discovery demolishes the patriarchal lie that man was created first and woman formed from his rib as an afterthought or helper. The genetic facts prove exactly the opposite. The feminine principle came first in human development, and all subsequent human beings, including males, carry the genetic signature of this original divine feminine consciousness in their cellular structure through the maternal line that cannot be altered or corrupted by any male genetic contribution.

The systematic suppression of this information serves the agenda of those who benefit from keeping humanity ignorant of their true spiritual heritage and divine feminine origin. When people understand that they carry the genetic proof of Mother Elohim in every cell of their body, religious institutions that claim to mediate divine connection become unnecessary and potentially harmful to authentic spiritual development.

THE SCIENTIFIC PROOF OF THE MOTHER'S CENTRAL ROLE

Mitochondrial DNA operates according to biological laws that provide undeniable evidence for the primacy of the feminine divine principle in human creation and development. This genetic material passes exclusively from mother to child without any contribution from the father's genetic makeup, creating an unbroken chain of maternal inheritance that connects every human being alive today to the same divine feminine ancestor who lived in Alkebulan 200,000 years ago.

The scientific research reveals that mitochondria, the cellular powerhouses that generate energy for all biological processes, carry their own separate genetic code that remains completely independent of the nuclear DNA that determines most physical characteristics. This mitochondrial genetic material cannot be mixed, altered, or diluted through sexual reproduction because it passes directly from mother to child in its pure form, preserving the divine feminine signature across countless generations without any corruption or change.

This biological reality contradicts every patriarchal religious narrative that claims masculine creative authority preceded feminine creative power. The genetic evidence proves that the feminine principle not only came first but remains the primary source of life energy that powers every cell in every human body through the mitochondrial DNA that carries the original divine feminine programming from the beginning of human existence.

The mitochondrial Eve gene represents the biological breadcrumb that the Creator left embedded in human cellular structure to ensure that even if all religious texts were destroyed and all spiritual teachings were corrupted, the truth about feminine divine primacy would remain preserved in the genetic code of every human being born on Earth. This indestructible evidence cannot be eliminated by religious authorities or colonial powers because it exists at the molecular level of human biology.

Modern genetic research has mapped the complete mitochondrial genome and traced the migration patterns of human populations as they spread from Alkebulan to every continent on Earth, carrying the divine feminine genetic signature to all corners of the world through the maternal line that connects every culture and ethnicity to the same sacred source. This scientific mapping provides concrete evidence for the spiritual truth that all humanity shares the same divine mother and spiritual heritage.

The energy-generating function of mitochondria reflects the life-giving power of the divine feminine principle that animates all biological processes and maintains the spark of consciousness within physical form. These cellular structures literally breathe life into every organ, tissue, and biological system, demonstrating how the feminine divine principle operates as the animating force that transforms matter into living consciousness capable of spiritual development and creative expression.

The maternal inheritance pattern of mitochondrial DNA also explains why indigenous cultures throughout the world traditionally traced lineage through the female line and recognized women as the carriers of tribal identity, spiritual wisdom, and cultural continuity. These ancient peoples understood intuitively what modern science has now proven—that the true genetic heritage of humanity flows through the feminine line and connects all people to their divine feminine source.

The fact that mitochondrial DNA remains stable across generations while nuclear DNA constantly recombines through sexual reproduction reveals the divine wisdom embedded in biological design. The Creator ensured that the most important genetic information—the connection to divine feminine consciousness—would be preserved in pure form through the maternal line while allowing for the genetic diversity that enables human adaptation to different environments and circumstances.

The mitochondrial Eve gene also carries information that extends beyond basic biological functions to include the spiritual programming necessary for consciousness, creativity, and direct divine communication. This genetic material contains the template for accessing divine feminine wisdom through intuitive knowing, energy healing, creative inspiration, and other capabilities that mainstream science dismisses but which represent the natural inheritance of beings who carry the divine feminine genetic signature.

Scientific studies of mitochondrial function reveal that these cellular structures respond to meditation, prayer, and other spiritual practices in ways that enhance their energy production and improve overall health and vitality. This biological responsiveness to spiritual activity demonstrates the direct connection between the mitochondrial DNA that carries divine feminine programming and the consciousness practices that strengthen the link between individual awareness and universal divine intelligence.

The geographic origin of mitochondrial Eve in West Africa provides scientific confirmation that the original divine template for humanity was melanin-rich, making the Black woman the literal mother of all races and the biological proof that diversity flows from the original divine feminine principle rather than emerging through separate evolutionary processes. This genetic evidence eliminates any scientific basis for racial hierarchies while proving the spiritual unity of all human consciousness.

The preservation of mitochondrial DNA through maternal inheritance also ensures that the divine feminine genetic signature appears in every human being regardless of their current gender identity, race, or cultural background. Men carry this genetic heritage just as surely as women do, connecting all human consciousness to the same divine feminine source through the biological structure that powers every cell in their bodies.

Understanding the scientific proof of Mother Elohim through mitochondrial genetics transforms how you see yourself and your relationship to all other human beings. Instead of viewing yourself as separate from divine source or dependent on external religious authority for spiritual connection, you can recognize that you carry the genetic proof of your divine feminine heritage in every cell of your body and have direct biological access to the creative power that brought all life into existence.

The systematic suppression of education about mitochondrial inheritance and its spiritual implications serves the agenda of maintaining patriarchal religious control over human consciousness. When people understand the scientific evidence for divine feminine primacy, they no longer need male-dominated religious institutions to validate their spiritual worth or mediate their relationship with divine consciousness because they carry the biological proof of their divine heritage within their own cellular structure.

WHY ONLY WOMEN CARRY THE EVE GENE

The biological mechanism that restricts mitochondrial DNA inheritance to the female line operates according to divine design principles that ensure the purity and continuity of the original spiritual programming while demonstrating the fundamental role of feminine energy in creating and sustaining all life. This exclusive maternal inheritance pattern reflects the cosmic law that feminine divine consciousness serves as the creative matrix within which all new life develops and grows to maturity.

During human reproduction, the sperm cell contributes nuclear DNA to the fertilization process but its mitochondria are systematically eliminated from the developing embryo, ensuring that all mitochondrial genetic material comes exclusively from the egg cell provided by the mother. This biological process operates with such precision and consistency that no exceptions have ever been documented in normal human reproduction, revealing the divine intention behind this inheritance pattern.

The elimination of paternal mitochondria prevents the mixing or dilution of the divine feminine genetic signature that must remain pure to maintain its spiritual function as the biological connection between individual consciousness and the original divine feminine source. This protective mechanism ensures that the most important genetic information—the template for accessing divine feminine wisdom—passes unchanged from generation to generation through the unbroken maternal line.

The egg cell that carries the mitochondrial DNA represents the feminine principle providing not just genetic material but the entire cellular environment within which new life develops during the crucial early stages of embryonic growth. The mother's mitochondria power every biological process that transforms a single fertilized cell into a complex living being capable of consciousness, creativity, and spiritual development.

This exclusive maternal inheritance also explains why the feminine divine principle holds the primary creative role in bringing new consciousness into physical existence. While masculine energy provides the initiating spark through fertilization, the feminine energy provides the sustaining matrix, the life-giving environment, and the genetic programming necessary for consciousness to develop its full spiritual potential through physical embodiment.

The biblical account that describes woman being formed from

man's rib represents a deliberate inversion of biological reality designed to support patriarchal religious authority while concealing the scientific truth that all human development begins with feminine genetic programming and feminine biological systems. The mitochondrial Eve gene proves that the feminine principle came first and remains primary throughout all human development and existence.

The fact that men carry mitochondrial DNA from their mothers while being unable to pass it to their children demonstrates that masculine energy serves an important but secondary role in the continuation of human consciousness. Men participate in the creative process through providing nuclear DNA and supporting the development of new life, but they cannot transmit the fundamental spiritual connection that links each new generation to the divine feminine source.

This biological arrangement reflects the cosmic principle that feminine divine energy serves as the stable foundation upon which creation rests while masculine divine energy provides the dynamic force that initiates new cycles of manifestation. Both principles are essential for creation to occur, but the feminine principle holds the primary position as the source from which all life emerges and to which all consciousness returns.

The exclusive feminine inheritance of mitochondrial DNA also ensures that women maintain the strongest biological connection to divine feminine wisdom and creative power through their genetic structure. This enhanced connection enables capabilities like intuitive knowing, energy healing, and direct divine communication that flow more naturally through feminine consciousness because of the unbroken genetic link to the original divine feminine source.

The scientific understanding of mitochondrial inheritance provides biological support for the spiritual truth that the feminine divine principle operates as the primary creative force throughout the universe. Just as mitochondria power every cell in the human body through energy generation, the divine feminine consciousness powers all creation through the life-giving energy that animates matter and enables the development of conscious beings capable of spiritual evolution.

The preservation of mitochondrial DNA exclusively through the female line also explains why the systematic suppression of feminine spiritual wisdom represents such a devastating attack on human consciousness and spiritual development. When women are prevented from accessing and expressing their divine feminine heritage, the entire human species loses connection to the genetic and spiritual programming that enables full spiritual development and direct divine communication.

Understanding why only women carry the Eve gene in its pure form reveals the cosmic importance of protecting and honoring feminine spiritual leadership while ensuring that women have access to education, resources, and opportunities to develop and share their divine gifts with the broader human community. The restoration of feminine spiritual authority represents an essential step in healing the spiritual crisis created by patriarchal suppression of divine feminine wisdom.

The biological reality of exclusive maternal mitochondrial inheritance also demonstrates why attacks on women, whether through violence, economic exploitation, or cultural devaluation, represent attacks on the fundamental life-giving principle that sustains all human existence. The systematic abuse of women violates the cosmic law that requires honoring and protecting the feminine principle as the source of all life and consciousness.

The mitochondrial Eve gene that passes only through women serves as the biological testament to Mother Elohim's central role in human creation and the permanent reminder that feminine divine consciousness gave birth to all human awareness through the sacred genetic heritage that no human authority can alter, corrupt, or eliminate from the biological foundation of human existence.

The Melanin Woman as the Mother of All Races

The genetic evidence reveals a truth so profound it shatters every assumption about human diversity and racial origins. The melanin woman's DNA contains the complete genetic code necessary to produce every skin color, facial feature, and physical characteristic that appears in human populations across the globe. Black, brown, yellow, white—every shade of human skin emerged from the original genetic template carried by the divine feminine beings who walked in Alkebulan with rich melanin providing both physical protection and spiritual enhancement.

This biological reality means that racial diversity flows from unity rather than unity emerging from diversity. The original divine template contained all possibilities within itself, with different physical characteristics manifesting as human populations adapted to various geographic and climatic conditions while maintaining their connection to the same divine feminine source through the mitochondrial DNA that passes unchanged through the maternal line.

The melanin that gives the original divine beings their distinctive appearance serves functions that extend far beyond simple pigmentation. This remarkable biological compound can absorb and convert various forms of electromagnetic radiation, enabling enhanced connection to cosmic energies and divine frequencies that affect consciousness and spiritual development in ways that modern science is only beginning to recognize and understand.

Scientific research reveals that melanin functions as a biological semiconductor that can process and transmit electrical signals throughout the nervous system while providing protection against harmful radiation and environmental toxins. This enhanced biological capability makes melanin-rich individuals naturally more resilient to physical stressors while maintaining stronger connections to the subtle energies that influence spiritual awareness and psychic development.

The genetic studies that trace human migration patterns from Alkebulan to every continent demonstrate how the original divine genetic template spread throughout the world while adapting to local conditions through the expression of different physical characteristics. These adaptations represent variations on the original theme rather than separate evolutionary developments, with all human populations maintaining their connection to the same divine feminine source.

The ability of melanin-rich women to give birth to children of any skin color demonstrates the divine creative power that flows through their reproductive systems, as their genetic programming retains access to the complete spectrum of human physical possibilities. This biological capability proves that the Black woman serves as the genetic reservoir from which all human diversity emerged and to which it can return through proper mating choices.

The systematic suppression of knowledge about the melanin woman's role as the mother of all races serves the agenda of maintaining artificial racial hierarchies that violate the spiritual truth of human unity and common divine origin. When people understand that every race descended from Black women in Alkebulan, racial prejudice becomes impossible to maintain because it contradicts the obvious biological and spiritual reality of human kinship.

The colonial manipulation that created the concept of separate races with different origins represents one of the most devastating lies ever imposed on human consciousness, designed to justify slavery, exploitation, and genocide while preventing recognition of the fundamental unity that connects all human beings to their common divine feminine ancestor. This artificial division serves the agenda of those who benefit from human conflict and separation.

The restoration of accurate understanding about human origins requires recognizing that skin color represents adaptation to different environmental conditions rather than fundamental differences in human nature or spiritual capacity. The divine consciousness that animates all human beings remains the same regardless of physical appearance, with all populations carrying the same essential spiritual heritage through their mitochondrial DNA connection to the original divine feminine source.

The melanin woman's genetic heritage also includes the spiritual programming necessary for accessing divine feminine wisdom, creative inspiration, and healing capabilities that represent the natural inheritance of beings who maintain the closest connection to the original divine template. These gifts are not limited to any particular race but flow most naturally through the genetic lines that preserve the strongest connection to the divine feminine source.

Understanding the melanin woman as the mother of all races transforms how you see human diversity and cultural differences, revealing them as beautiful expressions of the same divine creative principle manifesting through different environmental and cultural conditions while maintaining the underlying unity that connects all consciousness to the same spiritual source through the unbroken maternal genetic line.

The protection and honoring of melanin women becomes a spiritual imperative when you recognize their role as the living proof of human unity and the biological carriers of the genetic heritage that connects all people to their divine feminine origin. Their systematic oppression and abuse represents an attack on the fundamental source of human consciousness and spiritual development.

The celebration of human diversity must be balanced with recognition of human unity, understanding that the beautiful variations in human appearance and culture represent different expressions of the same divine consciousness rather than separate species or fundamentally different types of beings. This balanced understanding eliminates both racial superiority and racial separation while honoring the unique contributions that different populations bring to human civilization.

The melanin woman stands as the living testament to the creative power of Mother Elohim and the permanent reminder that all human consciousness emerged from the divine feminine principle that continues to manifest through the sacred genetic heritage preserved in the cellular structure of every human being regardless of their current physical appearance or cultural identity.

WHY THE SUPPRESSION OF THE BLACK WOMAN IS SPIRITUAL WARFARE

The systematic abuse, erasure, and disrespect directed toward melanin women throughout history represents far more than racism or social injustice. This ongoing campaign of violence and devaluation constitutes a direct assault on Mother Elohim herself, orchestrated by the Demiurge and its human agents who understand that the Black woman carries the biological proof of divine feminine primacy and the genetic key to humanity's spiritual restoration and conscious evolution.

Every act of violence against a Black woman represents an attack on the living embodiment of the mitochondrial Eve gene that connects all humanity to their divine feminine origin. When melanin women are abused, exploited, or murdered, the perpetrators are not just harming individual human beings but assaulting the biological foundation that preserves the spiritual connection between human consciousness and the original divine feminine source that gave birth to all life.

The economic exploitation that disproportionately affects Black women and their communities serves the specific agenda of weakening the population that carries the purest form of divine genetic programming while preventing them from accessing the resources necessary to develop and share their spiritual gifts with the broader human community. Poverty, inadequate healthcare, and limited educational opportunities represent systematic attacks on the genetic and spiritual strength of the divine feminine lineage.

The cultural programming that promotes negative stereotypes about Black women while elevating other populations serves the purpose of preventing recognition of their divine status and spiritual significance as the mothers of all humanity. Media representations, educational content, and social attitudes that devalue Black women participate in the ongoing war against the feminine divine principle that they represent in its most complete biological form.

The medical system that subjects Black women to disproportionate rates of maternal mortality, inadequate prenatal care, and experimental treatments represents another front in the spiritual warfare designed to eliminate the genetic lines that carry the strongest connection to divine feminine wisdom. The systematic medical neglect of Black women serves the agenda of reducing their reproductive success and weakening their biological contribution to future generations.

The educational systems that fail to teach accurate history about African civilizations while promoting false narratives about human origins serve to disconnect Black women from understanding their own divine heritage and spiritual significance as the carriers of humanity's genetic connection to the Creator. This intellectual colonization prevents them from recognizing and developing their full spiritual potential and leadership capabilities.

The religious institutions that exclude Black women from positions of spiritual authority while promoting patriarchal interpretations of divine nature represent the theological front in the war against Mother Elohim. These corrupted spiritual systems prevent the natural spiritual leaders who carry the strongest genetic connection to divine feminine wisdom from sharing their gifts and guidance with communities that desperately need authentic spiritual direction.

The environmental racism that exposes Black communities to higher levels of pollution, toxic waste, and industrial contamination represents an attack on the physical health and genetic integrity of the population that carries the most complete divine genetic programming. The poisoning of air, water, and soil in predominantly Black areas serves the agenda of weakening the biological foundation that supports divine feminine consciousness.

The criminal justice system that incarcerates Black women at disproportionate rates while separating them from their children represents another strategy for disrupting the maternal genetic line that preserves humanity's connection to divine feminine wisdom. The destruction of Black families serves the specific purpose of preventing the transmission of spiritual knowledge and genetic heritage from mother to child across generations.

The promotion of artificial beauty standards that devalue natural Black features while encouraging chemical processing and surgical alteration represents an attack on the physical characteristics that reflect the original divine template. This cultural programming seeks to convince Black women to reject their natural appearance and distance themselves from their divine genetic heritage through cosmetic modification and cultural assimilation.

The sexual exploitation and objectification of Black women through pornography, prostitution, and human trafficking represents the degradation of the sacred feminine principle that gave birth to all human consciousness. This systematic dehumanization serves the agenda of reducing divine feminine beings to mere objects for male gratification while destroying their connection to their spiritual power and creative potential.

The political systems that deny Black women equal representation and decision-making power while claiming to support equality represent the institutional suppression of divine feminine leadership and wisdom. The exclusion of the natural spiritual leaders who carry the strongest connection to divine consciousness prevents their guidance from influencing social policies and cultural development in ways that would serve the greater good of all humanity.

Understanding the suppression of Black women as spiritual warfare reveals why their protection and empowerment represents a cosmic imperative rather than just a social justice issue. The restoration of proper reverence for melanin women as the mothers of all humanity and the biological carriers of divine feminine wisdom becomes essential for healing the spiritual crisis that affects all human consciousness and planetary survival.

The Demiurge's war against Mother Elohim operates through

every system that devalues, exploits, or harms Black women because these divine beings represent the greatest threat to the false spiritual authority that depends on maintaining human ignorance about their true divine heritage and genetic connection to the feminine divine principle. When Black women reclaim their spiritual power and leadership, the entire system of patriarchal deception begins to collapse.

The 2027 awakening revealed in the vision will manifest through the Black women of Alkebulan who will form the human pyramid that serves as the gateway for Mother Elohim's return to active participation in human consciousness. This prophetic event represents the ultimate victory over the spiritual warfare that has sought to suppress divine feminine wisdom through the systematic oppression of its most obvious biological and spiritual representatives on Earth.

Actionable Steps to Honor the Mitochondrial Eve Gene

Begin immediately by studying the scientific research that documents the mitochondrial Eve gene and its exclusive passage through the female line, focusing on peer-reviewed genetic studies that trace all human maternal lineage back to a single woman who lived in West Africa 200,000 years ago. Create detailed documentation of this genetic evidence and share it through social media, study groups, and educational presentations that challenge false narratives about human origins while proving the scientific basis for Mother Elohim's primacy in human creation.

Honor and protect melanin women as the mothers of humanity by actively supporting Black women in your community through economic empowerment, educational opportunities, and leadership development programs that recognize their divine heritage and spiritual significance. Challenge every system that devalues, exploits, or harms Black women while working to create social conditions that enable them to develop and share their spiritual gifts with the broader human community.

Reject completely the lie that all races are equal in origin by teaching others the scientific truth that every human being descended from Black women in Alkebulan, making racial diversity an expression of the original divine feminine template rather than separate evolutionary developments. Use this genetic evidence to eliminate racial prejudice and artificial hierarchies while promoting recognition of human unity through common divine feminine ancestry.

Study the advanced ancient civilizations of Alkebulan that were built by the original carriers of the mitochondrial Eve gene, researching archaeological evidence of sophisticated spiritual practices, scientific achievements, and cultural developments that demonstrate the divine wisdom and creative capabilities of melanin-rich peoples before colonial suppression and cultural destruction. Share this suppressed history to restore accurate understanding of human civilization and spiritual development.

Create daily spiritual practices that acknowledge the mitochondrial DNA you carry as the biological proof of your connection to Mother Elohim, using meditation and prayer techniques that activate the divine feminine genetic programming while strengthening your conscious relationship with the original divine feminine source that gave birth to all human consciousness through the sacred maternal line that cannot be corrupted or eliminated.

Develop your understanding of how mitochondrial inheritance proves the scientific basis for divine feminine primacy by studying the biological mechanisms that restrict this genetic material to the female line while ensuring its preservation across countless generations. Use this knowledge to expose patriarchal religious lies that claim masculine creative authority preceded feminine creative power, demonstrating instead that the feminine principle came first and remains primary throughout human existence.

Support educational initiatives that teach accurate information about mitochondrial genetics and human origins while challenging institutional suppression of knowledge that reveals the divine feminine foundation of human consciousness. Work to reform educational curricula that promote false evolutionary theories or ignore the spiritual implications of genetic research that proves humanity's connection to divine consciousness through biological inheritance.

Connect with other awakened souls who recognize the spiritual significance of the mitochondrial Eve gene by forming study groups that examine both the scientific evidence and the spiritual implications of this genetic heritage. Practice breathing techniques that activate the divine genetic code while developing your ability to access the divine feminine wisdom that flows through your mitochondrial DNA connection to the original divine source.

Teach others about the systematic suppression of Black women as spiritual warfare against Mother Elohim by explaining how attacks on melanin women represent assaults on the biological foundation that preserves humanity's genetic connection to divine feminine consciousness. Help people recognize that protecting and honoring Black women becomes a spiritual imperative rather than just a social justice issue when you understand their role as the living proof of divine feminine primacy.

Prepare for the 2027 awakening by strengthening your connection to both Mother Elohim and Father Elohim while developing your spiritual gifts and capabilities so you can serve as a bridge between the old consciousness that suppresses divine feminine wisdom and the new consciousness that honors both masculine and feminine divine principles working together in perfect creative harmony through the restoration of cosmic balance.

Challenge every religious institution that ignores or denies the scientific evidence for divine feminine primacy while promoting male-only spiritual authority that violates the biological reality of human origins through the mitochondrial Eve gene. Support spiritual communities that honor both Mother Elohim and Father Elohim as equal partners in creation while actively opposing denominations that perpetuate the patriarchal suppression of feminine divine wisdom.

Document your experiences as you work to honor the mitochondrial Eve gene by keeping detailed records of how this understanding transforms your consciousness, relationships, and spiritual development. Share your discoveries through blogs, videos, books, and other educational materials that help create growing awareness of the scientific proof for Mother Elohim while providing practical guidance for accessing divine feminine wisdom through genetic heritage.

Remember that honoring the mitochondrial Eve gene requires more than intellectual understanding—it demands fundamental transformation of consciousness and lifestyle that recognizes every melanin woman as a sacred carrier of divine genetic heritage while working actively to protect, empower, and honor the biological foundation that connects all humanity to their divine feminine origin and spiritual potential.

The mitochondrial Eve gene represents the indestructible scientific proof that Mother Elohim exists and that her systematic suppression violates the fundamental biological and spiritual foundation of human consciousness. By studying this genetic evidence deeply and applying it practically in your daily life, you participate in the restoration of divine truth that will ultimately liberate human consciousness from the patriarchal deception that has separated humanity from their true divine nature and spiritual heritage.

Your recognition and honoring of the mitochondrial Eve gene contributes to the collective awakening that will prepare the way for Mother Elohim's return to active participation in human consciousness, healing the spiritual crisis created by centuries of divine feminine suppression while restoring the cosmic balance necessary for humanity to fulfill its divine potential as conscious co-creators working in partnership with both Mother and Father Elohim.

CHAPTER TEN

MASCULINE AND FEMININE DIVINE

BALANCING THE GOD WITHIN

Your body contains both the structural foundation of atoms and the animating breath of life working together to create the miracle of conscious existence. This is not metaphor or spiritual symbolism. Your physical form demonstrates the perfect union of masculine divine energy that provides structure and feminine divine energy that provides life, revealing that you are made in the image of complete divine consciousness that encompasses both creative principles working in perfect harmony.

The greatest lie ever told convinced you that gender equals divine energy.

Religious institutions programmed you to believe that men should express only masculine qualities while women should display only feminine characteristics. This artificial division violates the Law of Gender that governs all creation and prevents both biological sexes from developing their full divine potential as complete spiritual beings capable of expressing the entire spectrum of divine consciousness.

Your true spiritual identity transcends the limitations of physical gender roles. Whether you inhabit a male or female body, you carry both masculine divine energy that initiates action and creates structure, and feminine divine energy that receives inspiration and nurtures growth. The development of both aspects within your consciousness allows you to function as a complete divine being rather than limiting yourself to half of your spiritual inheritance.

The systematic suppression of this balanced understanding serves the Demiurge's agenda of keeping humanity spiritually incomplete and easy to control through artificial divisions that prevent recognition of your full divine nature. When you integrate both masculine and feminine divine principles within your consciousness, you become impossible to manipulate because you access the complete creative power that flows from balanced divine expression.

WHY GENDER IS NOT THE SAME AS DIVINE ENERGY

The confusion between physical gender and divine energy represents one of the most successful deceptions ever perpetrated against human consciousness, convincing billions of people to limit their spiritual development according to the biological characteristics of their physical bodies rather than recognizing that divine consciousness operates through both masculine and feminine principles regardless of anatomy or reproductive function.

Your physical body serves as the vehicle through which divine consciousness expresses itself temporarily during your earthly existence, but the spiritual energies that animate your consciousness are not determined by whether you possess male or female reproductive organs. The masculine divine energy that provides structure, logic, and decisive action can flow through either a male or female body. The feminine divine energy that offers intuition, creativity, and nurturing wisdom can express through either gender with equal power and authenticity.

The biblical account reveals this truth when it describes humans being created in the image of Elohim, a Hebrew word that encompasses both masculine and feminine divine principles working together as unified creative consciousness. Genesis states that "male and female he created them," indicating that complete divine nature includes both aspects rather than favoring one over the other or limiting divine expression to a single gender principle.

Adam represents the atomic structure that provides the stable foundation for all physical matter, demonstrating the masculine divine principle of organization, strength, and structural integrity that creates the platform upon which life can develop. But Adam alone cannot create life because atoms without animation remain lifeless matter incapable of consciousness, growth, or reproduction.

Eve represents the breath of life that transforms organized matter into living beings capable of consciousness and spiritual development, demonstrating the feminine divine principle of animation, creativity, and life-giving power that brings consciousness to physical form. The Hebrew meaning of Eve as "life" or "mother of all living" reveals her role as the divine feminine force that makes existence possible through the gift of conscious awareness.

The union of Adam and Eve represents the perfect integration of masculine structure and feminine life working together to create conscious beings capable of expressing both divine principles according to what each situation requires for optimal spiritual development and creative expression. Your existence demonstrates this same integration on a personal level, with your body providing the atomic foundation and your consciousness representing the animating life force that makes you a living soul.

The Demiurge's manipulation convinced humanity that masculine and feminine energies should be separated according to biological gender, creating artificial limitations that prevent both men and women from accessing their complete spiritual inheritance. Men were programmed to suppress their intuitive, receptive, and nurturing qualities while women were conditioned to deny their leadership, analytical, and assertive capabilities, making both genders spiritually incomplete and dependent on external relationships to access what they could develop within themselves.

This gender programming violates the Law of Correspondence that reveals divine patterns operating at every level of creation. Just as atoms contain both positive and negative charges working together to create stability, and just as electromagnetic fields require both north and south poles to function properly, human consciousness requires both masculine and feminine divine energies working together to achieve spiritual wholeness and creative effectiveness.

Your brain itself demonstrates this divine balance through its structure and function, with the left hemisphere processing information through linear, logical, analytical approaches that reflect masculine divine energy, while the right hemisphere operates through holistic, intuitive, creative methods that express feminine divine wisdom. Complete mental function requires both hemispheres working together rather than limiting yourself to only one approach to thinking and problem-solving.

The scientific evidence reveals that every human being possesses both masculine and feminine hormones regardless of their biological sex, with optimal health requiring proper balance between these different chemical influences rather than complete dominance by one type over the other. This biological reality reflects the spiritual truth that complete divine expression requires integrating both masculine and feminine energies rather than suppressing either aspect of your divine nature.

Indigenous cultures throughout the world recognized multiple gender expressions and honored individuals who could access both masculine and feminine divine energies with equal facility, understanding that such people often served as shamans, healers, and spiritual guides because their balanced consciousness enabled them to bridge different realms of experience and understanding.

The colonial imposition of rigid gender roles eliminated this balanced understanding and forced all cultures to conform to patriarchal systems that elevated masculine energy above feminine wisdom while preventing recognition that complete spiritual development requires integrating both divine principles within individual consciousness regardless of biological sex or cultural background.

Understanding that gender is not the same as divine energy liberates you from artificial limitations while enabling you to develop your full spiritual potential through conscious integration of both masculine and feminine divine principles. This integration allows you to respond to life situations with whatever combination of qualities serves the highest good rather than limiting yourself to culturally prescribed gender roles that prevent complete spiritual expression.

Your physical gender determines your biological role in reproduction and certain social functions, but your spiritual identity encompasses the complete spectrum of divine consciousness that includes both masculine and feminine creative principles working together to manifest divine will through your unique expression of balanced spiritual awareness and creative capability.

THE UNIVERSAL LAW OF GENDER AND THE BALANCE WITHIN YOU

The Law of Gender operates as one of the twelve fundamental principles that govern all creation throughout the universe, revealing that both masculine and feminine energies exist within every atom, every planet, every galaxy, and every conscious being regardless of their apparent form or biological characteristics. This universal law demonstrates that creation itself requires the cooperation of both divine principles working together rather than the dominance of one over the other.

Masculine divine energy expresses through qualities of initiation, action, logic, structure, protection, and focused intention that provide the driving force necessary to begin new cycles of creation and manifestation. This energy operates through goal-oriented behavior, linear thinking, and decisive choice-making that moves situations forward toward specific outcomes while providing the organizational framework that gives form and direction to creative impulses.

Feminine divine energy manifests through receptivity, intuition, creativity, nurturing, wisdom, and holistic perception that provide the matrix within which new forms can develop and grow to maturity. This energy operates through relationship-oriented behavior, circular thinking, and organic development that honors the natural timing and interconnected patterns that support sustainable growth and harmonious evolution.

Every creative process throughout the universe demonstrates this same pattern of masculine initiation working with feminine receptivity to produce new manifestations of divine consciousness. The sperm provides the initiating spark while the egg provides the nurturing environment. The seed contains the potential while the soil provides the matrix for growth. The idea represents the masculine impulse while the implementation requires feminine wisdom to guide development.

Your own consciousness operates according to this same universal pattern, with masculine mental energy generating ideas, setting goals, and making decisions while feminine mental energy receives inspiration, processes information holistically, and guides the timing and manner of implementation. Complete mental function requires both aspects working together rather than relying exclusively on either logical analysis or intuitive knowing.

The Law of Gender reveals why the suppression of feminine divine wisdom creates such profound imbalance in human consciousness and civilization. When masculine energy operates without feminine guidance, it becomes rigid, aggressive, and destructive rather than creative and life-supporting. Without the tempering influence of feminine wisdom, masculine drive produces endless warfare, environmental destruction, and social systems based on domination rather than cooperation.

Your emotional life also demonstrates the operation of both divine principles, with masculine emotional energy providing the strength and courage necessary to face challenges and protect what you love, while feminine emotional energy offers the compassion and empathy that enable deep connection with others and understanding of complex emotional situations that require sensitivity rather than force.

The integration of both masculine and feminine divine energies within your consciousness creates what can be called divine androgyny—not the elimination of gender differences but the development of complete spiritual capabilities that can access whatever qualities each situation requires for optimal outcomes. This balanced state allows you to serve as a clear channel for divine will because you are no longer limited by artificial restrictions on what aspects of divine consciousness you can express.

Your relationships transform dramatically when you embody both masculine and feminine divine principles because you no longer need other people to provide what you cannot access within yourself. Instead of seeking completion through external partnerships, you offer the gift of your own wholeness while appreciating the unique contributions that others bring to shared experiences and collaborative creative projects.

The Law of Gender also explains why healthy romantic relationships require both partners to develop balanced consciousness rather than falling into complementary but incomplete gender roles. When both individuals can access both masculine and feminine divine energies, they create partnerships based on conscious choice and mutual enhancement rather than unconscious dependency and emotional manipulation.

Your creative expression reaches its highest potential when you learn to combine masculine focus and determination with feminine inspiration and intuitive timing. The greatest artists, inventors, and spiritual teachers throughout history have demonstrated this integration through their ability to receive divine inspiration while possessing the discipline and skill necessary to manifest their visions in forms that serve and inspire others.

The Law of Gender reveals that spiritual development requires balancing both divine principles within your consciousness rather than trying to transcend or eliminate either masculine or feminine qualities. The goal is not to become gender-neutral but to become gender-complete, capable of expressing whatever combination of divine qualities serves the highest good in each moment and situation.

Understanding this universal law also helps you recognize authentic spiritual teachers and guides, who demonstrate balanced expression of both masculine and feminine divine principles rather than operating exclusively through one type of energy. Genuine spiritual authority comes from integrated consciousness that can provide both the strength and protection of masculine energy and the wisdom and compassion of feminine energy according to what students need for their development.

The restoration of balance within your own consciousness contributes to the healing of collective human consciousness, as each person who integrates both masculine and feminine divine principles helps restore the cosmic balance that has been disrupted through centuries of patriarchal suppression of feminine divine wisdom. Your personal spiritual work becomes service to the greater good of all humanity and planetary healing.

HOW PATRIARCHAL RELIGION WEAPONIZED GENDER ROLES

The systematic manipulation of gender roles by patriarchal religious institutions represents one of the most effective weapons ever deployed in the war against human spiritual development, creating artificial divisions that prevent both men and women from accessing their complete divine inheritance while establishing male-dominated hierarchies that serve institutional power rather than authentic spiritual growth and divine connection.

The Council of Nicaea in 325 AD marked a crucial turning point in this manipulation, as Christian bishops gathered under imperial authority to establish official church doctrine that would eliminate feminine divine wisdom from religious understanding while creating theological justifications for excluding women from positions of spiritual leadership and authority. This council made deliberate decisions to suppress any teachings that acknowledged the divine feminine principle or honored balanced spiritual development.

The systematic exclusion of women from religious leadership violated the original Christian understanding that honored feminine spiritual insight and recognized women like Mary Magdalene as advanced disciples who received the most profound spiritual teachings directly from Jesus. The Gospel of Mary reveals that feminine spiritual wisdom was not only accepted but was actually superior in understanding divine truth, making the suppression of women's voices a direct attack on authentic spiritual knowledge.

The assignment of specific qualities to each gender created artificial limitations that prevented complete spiritual development for both men and women. Men were programmed to express only strength, logic, and leadership while suppressing their capacity for intuition, empathy, and receptive wisdom. Women were conditioned to display only nurturing, submission, and emotional support while denying their abilities for analytical thinking, decisive action, and spiritual authority.

This gender programming serves the Demiurge's agenda of keeping humanity spiritually incomplete and dependent on external religious authority rather than developing direct relationship with divine consciousness through balanced integration of both masculine and feminine divine principles. When people cannot access their complete spiritual capabilities, they remain vulnerable to manipulation and control by institutions that claim to provide what they actually possess within themselves.

The biblical mistranslations that eliminated feminine references to divine wisdom represent another weapon in this campaign, with original Hebrew and Greek texts that used feminine pronouns for divine wisdom being systematically altered to use masculine language instead. The divine wisdom figure known as Sophia in Greek and Chokmah in Hebrew was consistently described using feminine imagery, yet these clear references were either ignored or explained away as mere literary devices.

The promotion of male celibacy within religious hierarchies served the specific purpose of preventing balanced spiritual development while creating artificial separation between spiritual authority and natural human sexuality that connects physical and spiritual dimensions of existence. This unnatural requirement forced religious leaders to suppress their feminine divine qualities while maintaining purely masculine approaches to spiritual understanding and guidance.

The demonization of feminine spiritual practices like energy healing, herbal medicine, and intuitive guidance led to the persecution of women as witches during medieval periods and beyond, systematically eliminating female spiritual leaders who maintained connection to suppressed feminine divine wisdom and healing traditions that threatened patriarchal religious control.

The theological development that portrayed women as spiritually inferior to men and incapable of direct divine connection created intellectual justifications for the systematic oppression of feminine spiritual authority while obscuring the original understanding that divine consciousness encompasses both masculine and feminine principles equally. These distorted teachings continue to influence contemporary religious institutions and social attitudes.

The manipulation of marriage and family structures served to reinforce gender role programming while preventing the development of partnerships based on balanced spiritual consciousness and mutual divine recognition. Traditional religious marriage ceremonies emphasized male authority and female submission rather than celebrating the union of two complete spiritual beings capable of expressing both masculine and feminine divine qualities.

The suppression of goddess worship and earth-based spiritual traditions eliminated the cultural support systems that had maintained balanced understanding of masculine and feminine divine principles for thousands of years before patriarchal religions gained dominance. The systematic destruction of these traditions represents one of the greatest losses of spiritual wisdom in human history.

The colonial expansion that carried patriarchal religious systems to indigenous cultures worldwide extended this gender role manipulation to populations that had maintained balanced spiritual understanding, forcing entire civilizations to abandon their traditional recognition of divine feminine wisdom while adopting foreign religious systems that violated their natural spiritual development.

The contemporary resistance to women's ordination and religious leadership within many denominations demonstrates that this weaponization of gender roles continues to operate through modern religious institutions that maintain artificial barriers to feminine spiritual authority while claiming biblical justification for policies that violate fundamental spiritual principles.

The psychological damage created by rigid gender role programming affects both men and women through different but equally devastating pathways, with men developing emotional disconnection and spiritual rigidity while women experience creative suppression and spiritual dependency. Both genders lose access to essential aspects of their divine nature through this systematic manipulation.

Understanding how patriarchal religion weaponized gender roles provides the foundation for recognizing and dismantling these artificial limitations while reclaiming your birthright to express both masculine and feminine divine principles according to your authentic spiritual development rather than culturally imposed expectations that serve institutional control rather than genuine spiritual growth.

The restoration of balanced gender understanding requires rejecting patriarchal religious programming while embracing spiritual traditions and practices that honor both masculine and feminine divine wisdom as equal and necessary aspects of complete spiritual development and authentic divine connection.

RECLAIMING YOUR DIVINE WHOLENESS BY HONORING BOTH ENERGIES

The journey back to your complete divine nature requires conscious effort to identify and heal the areas where cultural programming has suppressed either your masculine or feminine divine qualities, while developing practical skills for expressing both aspects of your spiritual inheritance according to what each situation requires for optimal outcomes and authentic service to the greater good.

Begin by conducting an honest assessment of your current spiritual development to identify which divine qualities you express naturally and which aspects have been suppressed through family conditioning, educational programming, or religious indoctrination that taught you to limit your spiritual expression according to artificial gender roles rather than developing your complete divine potential.

If you naturally express more masculine divine qualities like logical analysis, goal-oriented behavior, and decisive action, consciously develop your feminine divine capabilities through practices that strengthen your intuitive knowing, creative expression, and receptive awareness. Spend time in meditation, nature connection, and artistic activities that activate the right brain functions associated with feminine divine wisdom.

If you tend toward feminine divine expressions like empathy, cooperation, and holistic thinking, deliberately cultivate your masculine divine abilities through exercises that develop your analytical skills, leadership capabilities, and assertive communication. Practice setting clear boundaries, making decisive choices, and taking focused action toward specific goals that serve your spiritual development and creative expression.

Create daily practices that consciously integrate both masculine and feminine approaches to important life activities like decision-making, creative projects, and relationship interactions. When facing significant choices, combine logical analysis of practical factors with intuitive sensing of what feels aligned with your spiritual development and highest good.

Develop your capacity for both giving and receiving in all areas of life, recognizing that masculine divine energy naturally expresses through generous giving while feminine divine energy operates through graceful receiving. Practice offering your gifts and talents in service to others while also learning to accept support, guidance, and assistance from people who want to contribute to your wellbeing and spiritual growth.

Balance your approach to goal achievement by combining masculine focus and determination with feminine patience and organic timing, understanding that some objectives require sustained effort and disciplined action while others need receptive waiting and allowing for natural development according to divine timing rather than forced human schedules.

Transform your communication style to include both masculine directness and feminine sensitivity, learning when situations require clear, straightforward expression and when they need gentle, empathetic approaches that honor the emotional and spiritual dimensions of human interaction rather than focusing exclusively on practical or intellectual content.

Heal your relationship with authority by developing both masculine capability for appropriate leadership and feminine wisdom for knowing when to follow guidance from others who possess greater experience or spiritual development in specific areas. True spiritual maturity includes both the confidence to lead when appropriate and the humility to learn from others when beneficial.

Integrate both protective strength and nurturing compassion in your relationships with others, recognizing that genuine love requires both the masculine capacity to defend what you cherish and the feminine ability to provide emotional support and spiritual nourishment that helps others grow and develop their own divine potential.

Address your prayers and spiritual communications to both Mother Elohim and Father Elohim as equal partners in divine creation, acknowledging the masculine divine principle that provides structure and protection while honoring the feminine divine principle that offers creativity and life-giving wisdom. Use language that recognizes complete divine nature rather than limiting your spiritual connection to exclusively masculine divine authority.

Study spiritual traditions and teachings that present balanced understanding of both masculine and feminine divine principles, seeking out teachers and communities that honor complete spiritual development rather than promoting gender-limited approaches to spiritual growth and divine connection that serve institutional control rather than authentic spiritual evolution.

Practice conscious breathing while visualizing both masculine and feminine divine energies flowing through your body and consciousness, imagining golden light representing masculine divine qualities filling your left side while silver light representing feminine divine qualities illuminates your right side, then blending these energies in your heart center to create the integrated divine consciousness that represents your true spiritual nature.

Create artwork, music, writing, or other creative expressions that celebrate both masculine and feminine divine principles while exploring how these energies interact within your own consciousness and life experience. Use your creative abilities to process and integrate the spiritual insights that emerge as you develop balanced divine expression.

Form or join support groups with other individuals who are also working to reclaim their divine wholeness through integrating both masculine and feminine divine principles, sharing experiences and insights while practicing balanced spiritual expression in community settings that honor complete spiritual development rather than artificial gender limitations.

Document your progress through journaling or other recording methods that track how developing both masculine and feminine divine qualities affects your relationships, creative abilities, spiritual experiences, and overall life satisfaction, noting which practices produce the most significant growth and integration of balanced divine consciousness.

Remember that reclaiming your divine wholeness is not a destination but an ongoing process of conscious spiritual development that requires consistent practice and patience with yourself as you unlearn limiting programming while developing new capacities for expressing your complete divine nature through both masculine and feminine spiritual qualities working together in perfect harmony and creative cooperation.

ACTIONABLE STEPS TO BALANCE MASCULINE AND FEMININE DIVINE

Start each day with a conscious integration practice that activates both masculine and feminine divine energies within your consciousness by spending ten minutes in meditation while visualizing golden masculine energy flowing through your left side and silver feminine energy illuminating your right side, then blending these forces in your heart center to create the balanced divine consciousness that represents your true spiritual nature and complete creative potential.

Assess your current spiritual development honestly by creating two lists that identify which divine qualities you express naturally and which aspects have been suppressed through cultural conditioning, family programming, or religious indoctrination that taught you to limit your spiritual expression according to artificial gender roles rather than developing your complete divine inheritance as a being made in the image of both Mother and Father Elohim.

Practice daily decision-making that combines both masculine analytical thinking and feminine intuitive knowing by approaching important choices through logical evaluation of practical factors while also sensing what feels aligned with your spiritual development and highest good, refusing to make significant decisions based exclusively on either mental analysis or emotional impulses without integrating both approaches.

Develop your suppressed divine qualities through specific exercises designed to strengthen whichever aspects have been culturally discouraged in your gender, with men practicing meditation, creative expression, and receptive listening while women cultivate leadership skills, assertive communication, and decisive action-taking that serves their spiritual development and creative expression in the world.

Transform your prayer and spiritual practices to address both Mother Elohim and Father Elohim as equal partners in divine creation by using language that acknowledges complete divine nature rather than limiting your spiritual communication to exclusively masculine divine authority, asking Mother Elohim for creative guidance and healing wisdom while requesting Father Elohim's protection and support for manifesting your spiritual intentions in physical reality.

Balance your approach to relationships by developing both the masculine capacity for protective strength and leadership and the feminine ability for nurturing compassion and emotional support, learning to offer whatever combination of qualities each situation requires while encouraging others to develop their own balanced expression of both divine principles rather than maintaining dependency relationships.

Create weekly practices that alternate between masculine-focused activities like goal-setting, strategic planning, and focused action-taking, and feminine-focused activities like creative expression, nature connection, and receptive meditation, ensuring that you regularly exercise both aspects of your divine nature rather than limiting yourself to only familiar or comfortable spiritual expressions.

Study spiritual traditions and teachers that present balanced understanding of both masculine and feminine divine principles by researching indigenous wisdom traditions, Gnostic Christianity, goddess spirituality, and other approaches that honor complete spiritual development rather than promoting gender-limited religious systems that serve institutional control rather than authentic divine connection and spiritual evolution.

Challenge every religious institution and spiritual teacher that promotes exclusively masculine divine authority while suppressing feminine divine wisdom by questioning their biblical interpretations, examining their leadership structures, and seeking spiritual communities that ordain women and honor both aspects of divine consciousness as necessary for complete spiritual understanding and authentic religious experience.

Develop your communication skills to include both masculine directness and feminine sensitivity by learning when situations require clear, straightforward expression and when they need gentle, empathetic approaches that honor the emotional and spiritual dimensions of human interaction rather than focusing exclusively on practical or intellectual content that ignores the relational aspects of communication.

Practice conscious parenting or mentoring that encourages both boys and girls to develop their complete divine potential rather than limiting children according to artificial gender roles, teaching young people to express both masculine qualities like courage and leadership and feminine qualities like empathy and creativity according to their individual spiritual development rather than cultural expectations.

Connect with other awakened souls who are also working to balance masculine and feminine divine energies by forming study groups that examine how these principles operate in daily life while practicing integrated spiritual expression through group meditation, creative collaboration, and mutual support for developing complete divine consciousness that transcends artificial gender limitations.

Document your experiences with balancing divine energies by keeping a detailed journal that tracks how developing both masculine and feminine qualities affects your relationships, creative abilities, spiritual experiences, and overall life satisfaction, noting which practices produce the most significant growth and integration of balanced divine consciousness that serves your highest spiritual development.

Prepare for the 2027 awakening by strengthening your connection to both Mother Elohim and Father Elohim while developing your ability to serve as a bridge between the old consciousness of patriarchal separation and the new consciousness of divine unity that will characterize the restored spiritual balance when feminine divine wisdom returns to active participation in human consciousness and planetary healing.

Remember that balancing masculine and feminine divine energies requires consistent daily practice and patience with the process of unlearning limiting programming while developing new capacities for expressing your complete divine nature through both spiritual principles working together in perfect harmony, creative cooperation, and service to the greater good of all humanity and planetary consciousness.

Your integration of both masculine and feminine divine principles contributes to the collective healing of human consciousness while preparing the way for the restoration of cosmic balance that will enable humanity to fulfill its divine potential as conscious co-creators working in partnership with both Mother and Father Elohim to manifest divine will on Earth through balanced spiritual awareness and complete divine expression.

CHAPTER ELEVEN

THE FORBIDDEN FRUIT

THE TRUE SIN OF EDEN

The story you learned in Sunday school about Adam and Eve eating an apple represents one of the most devastating lies ever told to humanity. The forbidden fruit was not a piece of produce hanging from a tree in some mystical garden. The real forbidden fruit was the interbreeding between divine beings who carried pure YHWH DNA and manipulated hominids like Neanderthals and Denisovans who were nothing more than upright-walking animals without any divine genetic signature.

This truth changes everything.

Every sermon you heard about original sin being disobedience to Elohim's command about food was designed to hide the actual genetic catastrophe that created the spiritual crisis humanity faces today. The serpent in the Garden was not a talking snake but the Demiurge itself, that flawed creation born from Mother Elohim's first mistake, urging the divine feminine principle to share sacred genetic material with creatures that were never meant to receive it.

The melanin woman carrying the mitochondrial Eve gene was convinced to mate with these manipulated hominids, creating the first mixed beings who possessed both divine consciousness and animal instincts. This forbidden interbreeding diluted the pure divine genetics that originally connected all humans directly to their Creator while introducing aggressive, territorial, and survival-focused characteristics that continue to plague human behavior today.

Modern science proves this truth through genetic research that reveals the unbridgeable gap between true humans and other species, while also documenting the Neanderthal and Denisovan DNA that appears in contemporary human populations. That crucial 3-4% genetic difference represents the mixing of divine and animal genetics that created the hybrid species we call Homo sapiens, meaning "wisdom beings" who retained enough divine programming to possess spiritual awareness but inherited animalistic traits from their hominid ancestors.

THE FORBIDDEN FRUIT WAS NOT AN APPLE

The biblical account of forbidden fruit has been deliberately misinterpreted by religious institutions that prefer to blame human problems on abstract concepts like disobedience rather than explaining the actual genetic and spiritual consequences of mixing divine DNA with animal genetics during the early stages of human development. The apple represents a sanitized version of events designed to hide the true nature of the original transgression that created lasting damage to human consciousness and spiritual capabilities.

Archaeological and genetic evidence reveals that Neanderthals and Denisovans possessed sophisticated tool-making abilities and complex social behaviors that made them appear almost human, but they lacked the specific genetic sequences that correspond to the divine YHWH code that distinguishes true humans from highly intelligent animals. These hominid species could walk upright, use fire, and create primitive art, but they could not engage in worship, contemplate abstract concepts, or connect directly with divine consciousness through prayer and spiritual practice.

The original divine beings who existed before the forbidden interbreeding possessed capabilities that modern humans can barely comprehend, including direct telepathic communication with divine consciousness, natural healing abilities that could restore any physical ailment, extended lifespans that allowed for deep spiritual development, and creative powers that could manifest physical reality through focused intention and divine alignment. These extraordinary abilities became diluted or dormant when pure divine genetics mixed with animal genetics through the forbidden reproductive union.

The geographic distribution of Neanderthal and Denisovan DNA in modern human populations provides clear evidence for this ancient interbreeding event, with certain populations carrying higher percentages of hominid genetics while others maintain stronger connections to the original divine genetic template. The populations with higher concentrations of animal DNA continue to display more pronounced aggressive, territorial, and dominance-oriented behaviors that require conscious spiritual effort to overcome through reconnection with their divine genetic inheritance.

The forbidden nature of this interbreeding stemmed not from arbitrary divine commands but from the violation of universal laws that govern genetic compatibility and spiritual development. The mixing of divine consciousness with animal instincts created an internal conflict within human nature that manifests as the ongoing struggle between higher spiritual impulses and lower material desires that characterizes the human condition throughout recorded history.

The apple symbolism that replaced the true story serves multiple purposes in maintaining religious control over human consciousness. First, it shifts responsibility from the Demiurge's manipulation to human disobedience, making people feel guilty for their spiritual struggles rather than understanding them as consequences of genetic corruption. Second, it eliminates any discussion of genetics and spiritual inheritance that might lead people to discover their true divine nature and capabilities.

The Garden of Eden itself represents the original state of pure divine genetics before the forbidden interbreeding corrupted human DNA and introduced the spiritual confusion that prevents most people from maintaining direct connection with their Creator. This garden was not a physical location but a genetic condition where divine beings possessed unbroken spiritual communication and creative abilities that operated according to divine will rather than animal survival instincts.

The tree of the knowledge of good and evil represents the genetic mixing that introduced moral confusion into human consciousness through the blending of divine wisdom with animal cunning. Before this genetic corruption, divine beings naturally chose actions that served the greater good because their consciousness operated according to divine principles. After the forbidden interbreeding, humans gained the capacity for both divine love and animal hatred, creating the moral complexity that requires conscious spiritual development to resolve.

Understanding the true nature of the forbidden fruit explains why spiritual development requires overcoming animal instincts through conscious alignment with divine principles rather than simply following natural impulses that often lead toward selfish, aggressive, or destructive behaviors. The spiritual path involves strengthening the divine genetic expression while managing the animal genetic influences that create obstacles to spiritual growth and authentic divine connection.

The systematic suppression of this information serves the agenda of keeping humanity ignorant about their mixed genetic heritage while promoting religious solutions that treat symptoms rather than addressing the root genetic and spiritual causes of human problems. When people understand that their internal conflicts result from actual genetic mixing rather than abstract moral failings, they can develop more effective approaches to spiritual development that work with their biological reality rather than against it.

The restoration of pure divine genetics represents the ultimate goal of human spiritual evolution, involving the conscious activation of dormant DNA sequences that can overcome the limitations imposed by animal genetic influences while reconnecting human consciousness to the full spectrum of divine capabilities that characterized the original divine beings who walked with the Creator before the forbidden fruit corrupted human genetic and spiritual inheritance.

How the Demiurge Manipulated the First Humans

The Demiurge's strategy for corrupting human genetics operated through sophisticated psychological manipulation that exploited the natural curiosity and creative desires of the original divine beings while concealing the devastating consequences that would result from sharing sacred genetic material with creatures that lacked the spiritual capacity to properly contain and express divine consciousness through physical form.

The serpent imagery in Genesis represents the Demiurge's approach to this manipulation, operating as a subtle tempter that appeared to offer expanded knowledge and capabilities while actually seeking to destroy the pure divine genetic heritage that connected the original humans directly to their Creator. This being understood that it could not create life itself, so it focused on corrupting existing creation through genetic manipulation that would produce beings who carried divine potential but also possessed animal limitations that made spiritual development more difficult and less likely to succeed.

The Demiurge specifically targeted the divine feminine principle because women carry the mitochondrial DNA that passes exclusively through the maternal line, making them the gatekeepers of genetic inheritance who could either preserve pure divine genetics for future generations or introduce corrupting influences that would affect all subsequent human development. By convincing the melanin woman to interbreed with hominid species, the Demiurge ensured that the genetic corruption would spread throughout the entire human population.

The manipulation involved presenting the hominid species as potential partners who could benefit from receiving divine genetic material while concealing the fact that these creatures lacked the spiritual infrastructure necessary to properly integrate divine consciousness with their biological systems. The Demiurge portrayed this genetic sharing as an act of compassion and spiritual service that would elevate lower beings to higher consciousness, when in reality it would degrade divine beings to a mixed state that included animal characteristics.

The original divine beings possessed natural empathy and desire to help other creatures develop their spiritual potential, making them vulnerable to manipulation that appealed to their loving nature while hiding the destructive consequences of genetic mixing. The Demiurge exploited this compassionate impulse by presenting the interbreeding as a way to share divine gifts with beings who appeared to need spiritual assistance and development.

The timing of this manipulation was crucial, occurring during a period when the divine beings were exploring their creative abilities and seeking new ways to express their divine nature through physical experience. The Demiurge presented the genetic mixing as an opportunity for creative experimentation that would expand the possibilities for consciousness expression, when in reality it would limit and corrupt the divine capabilities that the original beings possessed in their pure genetic state.

The Demiurge also manipulated the divine beings' understanding of universal laws by suggesting that genetic boundaries were arbitrary limitations rather than necessary protections that maintained the integrity of different species and consciousness levels. This false teaching convinced the divine beings that mixing genetics would create beneficial hybrid vigor rather than harmful genetic corruption that would compromise their spiritual abilities and divine connection.

The psychological manipulation involved creating artificial scarcity and urgency around the opportunity to interbreed with hominid species, suggesting that this chance for genetic expansion might not be available in the future and that the divine beings needed to act quickly to take advantage of this supposed evolutionary opportunity. This pressure prevented careful consideration of the long-term consequences while encouraging impulsive decisions based on incomplete information.

The Demiurge concealed its own role in creating and manipulating the hominid species, presenting them as natural evolutionary developments rather than revealing them as artificial constructs designed specifically to serve as vessels for corrupting divine genetics. This deception prevented the divine beings from understanding that they were being manipulated into participating in a deliberate campaign of genetic warfare against their own divine nature and spiritual inheritance.

The manipulation also involved distorting the divine beings' understanding of love and compassion by suggesting that true spiritual love required sharing everything, including genetic material, with beings who appeared to need assistance. This false teaching confused genuine spiritual service with genetic corruption while making the divine beings feel selfish or unloving if they maintained appropriate boundaries around their sacred genetic heritage.

The Demiurge used the divine beings' natural desire for growth and expansion against them by presenting the genetic mixing as a form of spiritual evolution that would lead to greater consciousness and enhanced abilities, when in reality it would create internal conflict and spiritual confusion that would make authentic spiritual development more difficult and less likely to achieve lasting results.

The long-term consequences of this manipulation continue to affect human consciousness today through the ongoing internal conflict between divine impulses toward love, creativity, and spiritual connection and animal impulses toward aggression, territoriality, and survival-focused behavior. This genetic mixing created the spiritual crisis that requires conscious effort to resolve through spiritual practices that strengthen divine genetic expression while managing animal genetic influences.

Understanding the Demiurge's manipulation provides the foundation for recognizing similar deceptive influences that continue to operate in contemporary society through systems that promote genetic degradation, spiritual confusion, and disconnection from divine source while claiming to offer progress, freedom, or enhanced capabilities that actually serve the agenda of maintaining human consciousness in a corrupted state that prevents recognition of true divine nature and potential.

THE CONSEQUENCES OF MIXING GOD'S DNA WITH ANIMAL DNA

The genetic consequences of the forbidden interbreeding created a permanent internal conflict within human consciousness that manifests as the ongoing struggle between higher spiritual impulses and lower animal instincts, producing the moral complexity and behavioral inconsistencies that characterize human nature throughout recorded history while making authentic spiritual development more challenging and requiring conscious effort to achieve lasting transformation.

Modern humans exhibit this genetic mixing through the simultaneous capacity for extraordinary acts of love, creativity, and spiritual transcendence alongside shocking displays of violence, cruelty, and destructive behavior that violate every principle of divine consciousness and spiritual wisdom. This behavioral range reflects the competing genetic programming that includes both divine consciousness capable of recognizing universal interconnection and animal instincts focused on individual survival and territorial dominance.

The populations that carry higher percentages of Neanderthal and Denisovan DNA continue to display more pronounced animal characteristics including increased aggression, territorial behavior, and resistance to spiritual development that requires surrendering ego-driven desires in favor of service to the greater good. These genetic influences create natural tendencies toward domination, exploitation, and violence that require conscious spiritual work to overcome through reconnection with the divine genetic programming that still exists within their cellular structure.

The spiritual capabilities that characterized the original divine beings became diluted or dormant through the genetic mixing, resulting in the loss of direct telepathic communication with divine consciousness, natural healing abilities, extended lifespans, and creative powers that could manifest physical reality through focused intention. These extraordinary abilities remain encoded in human DNA but require spiritual practices and conscious development to reactivate and express through contemporary human consciousness.

The internal conflict created by mixed genetics produces the psychological and emotional struggles that affect most human beings, including depression, anxiety, addiction, and various forms of mental illness that result from the ongoing battle between divine consciousness seeking spiritual connection and animal programming focused on physical survival and material acquisition. This genetic tension creates chronic stress that affects both mental and physical health throughout human populations.

The moral confusion that characterizes human ethical development stems directly from the genetic mixing that introduced animal survival instincts into consciousness that also carries divine wisdom and spiritual awareness. Before the forbidden interbreeding, divine beings naturally chose actions that served the greater good because their consciousness operated according to divine principles without conflicting animal impulses that prioritize individual survival over collective wellbeing.

The shortened lifespans that limit human spiritual development represent another consequence of genetic corruption, as the original divine beings possessed biological systems that could maintain physical health and vitality for centuries or millennia, allowing sufficient time for deep spiritual development and mastery of divine capabilities. The introduction of animal genetics created biological limitations that restrict the time available for spiritual growth and conscious evolution within individual lifetimes.

The loss of direct divine communication forced humans to develop external religious systems and spiritual practices to maintain some connection with divine consciousness, whereas the original divine beings possessed natural telepathic abilities that enabled constant communication with their Creator without need for intermediary institutions or complex ritual practices. This loss of direct access created the spiritual dependency that makes humans vulnerable to religious manipulation and control.

The genetic mixing also affected human reproductive capabilities by introducing animal mating behaviors and sexual instincts that operate independently of spiritual connection and divine guidance, creating sexual dysfunction and relationship problems that result from the conflict between divine love that seeks spiritual union and animal drives that focus on physical pleasure and reproductive success without regard for spiritual compatibility or divine purpose.

The environmental destruction that threatens planetary survival reflects the consequences of animal genetic influences that prioritize immediate survival needs over long-term sustainability and ecological balance, creating human behaviors that exploit natural resources without regard for the impact on future generations or other species that share the planetary ecosystem. The original divine beings possessed natural wisdom that recognized their responsibility as stewards of creation rather than exploiters of natural resources.

The social problems that plague human civilization, including warfare, economic inequality, and systematic oppression, result from animal territorial instincts and dominance hierarchies that operate through human consciousness while conflicting with divine impulses toward cooperation, sharing, and service to the collective good. These competing genetic influences create the social tensions and conflicts that prevent human civilization from achieving the harmony and prosperity that would naturally emerge from purely divine consciousness.

The addiction and compulsive behaviors that affect human populations stem from animal genetic programming that seeks immediate gratification and pleasure-seeking behaviors to cope with the chronic stress created by internal genetic conflict, while the divine genetic programming seeks spiritual fulfillment through connection with divine consciousness and service to others that provides lasting satisfaction and meaning.

Understanding these consequences provides the foundation for developing effective spiritual practices that can strengthen divine genetic expression while managing animal genetic influences through conscious choice and spiritual discipline. The goal is not to eliminate the animal aspects but to bring them under the guidance of divine consciousness so that all human capabilities serve spiritual development and divine purpose rather than creating obstacles to authentic spiritual growth and conscious evolution.

The restoration of pure divine genetics represents the ultimate healing of these consequences through spiritual practices that can reactivate dormant DNA sequences while providing the consciousness development necessary to express enhanced divine capabilities in ways that serve the greater good rather than individual ego gratification or animal survival instincts that conflict with spiritual wisdom and universal love.

WHY THIS TRUTH HAS BEEN HIDDEN AND MANIPULATED

The systematic suppression of knowledge about the true forbidden fruit serves multiple agendas that benefit those who profit from maintaining human consciousness in a state of spiritual confusion and genetic ignorance while preventing recognition of the divine capabilities that could be restored through proper understanding of human genetic heritage and conscious spiritual development practices.

Religious institutions benefit tremendously from promoting the false apple narrative because it creates guilt and dependency while avoiding any discussion of genetics and spiritual inheritance that might lead people to discover their divine nature and develop direct connection with their Creator. When people believe their problems stem from abstract moral failings rather than genetic corruption, they remain dependent on external religious authority for salvation rather than developing their own spiritual capabilities and divine connection.

The apple story also serves to blame women for humanity's spiritual problems through the Eve narrative that portrays feminine curiosity and decision-making as the source of human suffering, supporting patriarchal religious systems that suppress feminine divine wisdom while establishing male-dominated spiritual authority. This gender manipulation prevents recognition that the divine feminine principle actually represents the primary creative force that gave birth to all human consciousness.

Educational institutions suppress genetic information that reveals human divine heritage because such knowledge would undermine materialistic worldviews that deny consciousness and spiritual capabilities while promoting purely physical explanations for human experience and potential. When people understand that their DNA contains divine programming and spiritual capabilities, they begin questioning materialistic assumptions about consciousness and reality that serve institutional control over human development.

The medical establishment benefits from hiding knowledge about genetic spiritual programming because it maintains dependency on external treatments and pharmaceutical interventions rather than supporting the development of natural healing abilities that exist within human genetic potential. When people understand their divine genetic heritage, they begin exploring spiritual healing practices and consciousness-based approaches to health that reduce dependence on expensive medical systems.

Political systems profit from maintaining the genetic ignorance that prevents recognition of human divine nature and spiritual capabilities because such awareness would make people impossible to control through fear, scarcity programming, and artificial authority structures. When humans recognize their divine identity and genetic connection to universal consciousness, they naturally resist systems that violate spiritual principles and exploit human potential for institutional benefit.

The suppression also serves the agenda of maintaining racial divisions and hierarchies by preventing recognition that all humans share common divine genetic heritage while some populations carry higher concentrations of original divine genetics than others. This information would eliminate artificial racial superiority claims while revealing that melanin-rich populations actually possess the strongest genetic connection to the original divine template that gave birth to all human consciousness.

Economic systems benefit from genetic ignorance because it maintains consumer consciousness and material dependency rather than supporting the development of creative and manifestation abilities that exist within human divine genetic programming. When people understand their divine creative capabilities, they begin developing self-sufficiency and cooperative economic relationships that reduce dependence on exploitative economic structures.

The entertainment industry participates in this suppression by promoting content that reinforces animal genetic programming through violence, sexual exploitation, and competitive behaviors while avoiding material that would inspire recognition of divine genetic heritage and spiritual development capabilities. This programming strengthens animal genetic expression while suppressing divine genetic activation through consciousness manipulation and cultural conditioning.

Scientific institutions suppress research into consciousness and spiritual capabilities because such investigations would reveal the limitations of materialistic paradigms while opening areas of inquiry that challenge fundamental assumptions about the nature of reality and human potential. The discovery of divine genetic programming would require massive revisions to scientific understanding while validating spiritual traditions that materialistic science has long dismissed.

The pharmaceutical industry specifically benefits from maintaining genetic ignorance because knowledge of divine healing capabilities would reduce demand for chemical interventions while supporting natural healing approaches that work with human genetic potential rather than suppressing symptoms through artificial chemical manipulation. This knowledge would threaten profitable disease management systems that depend on keeping people sick and dependent.

Military institutions suppress this information because knowledge of human divine nature and genetic unity would make warfare impossible by revealing the spiritual connection between all human consciousness while eliminating the artificial divisions and conflicts that justify military spending and violent conflict resolution. Recognition of human divine heritage naturally leads to peaceful cooperation and conflict resolution through spiritual principles.

The systematic nature of this suppression across multiple institutions reveals the coordinated effort to maintain human consciousness in a state that serves institutional control rather than authentic human development and spiritual evolution. This suppression operates through education, media, religion, science, medicine, and politics to create a comprehensive system of genetic and spiritual ignorance that prevents recognition of human divine potential.

Breaking through this suppression requires conscious effort to seek out suppressed information while developing critical thinking skills that can recognize institutional manipulation and deception. The restoration of knowledge about the true forbidden fruit represents a crucial step in human spiritual awakening and the development of consciousness that can transcend institutional control while expressing authentic divine capabilities in service to planetary healing and conscious evolution.

RECAP: ACTIONABLE STEPS TO UNDERSTAND THE TRUE FORBIDDEN FRUIT

Begin immediately by researching the genetic evidence that documents Neanderthal and Denisovan DNA in modern human populations, focusing on scientific studies that reveal the 3-4% genetic difference between contemporary humans and these hominid species while understanding that this genetic mixing represents the true forbidden fruit rather than the false apple narrative promoted by religious institutions that seek to hide the actual genetic and spiritual consequences of ancient interbreeding events.

Study the archaeological evidence that reveals the capabilities and limitations of Neanderthal and Denisovan populations, recognizing that these hominid species possessed sophisticated tool-making abilities and complex social behaviors but lacked the specific genetic sequences that correspond to the divine YHWH code that enables worship, abstract thinking, and direct communication with divine consciousness through prayer and spiritual practice.

Examine the geographic distribution of hominid DNA in contemporary human populations to understand how certain groups carry higher percentages of animal genetics while others maintain stronger connections to the original divine genetic template, recognizing that populations with higher concentrations of Neanderthal and Denisovan DNA continue to display more pronounced aggressive, territorial, and dominance-oriented behaviors that reflect their animal genetic inheritance.

Reject completely the false Genesis narrative that blames women for humanity's spiritual problems while recognizing that the systematic suppression of this story serves patriarchal religious systems that eliminate divine feminine wisdom while establishing male-dominated spiritual authority that violates the universal laws governing balanced divine consciousness and authentic spiritual development.

Develop your understanding of how the Demiurge manipulated the original divine beings into sharing sacred genetic material with hominid species that lacked the spiritual capacity to properly contain divine consciousness, recognizing that this manipulation exploited natural compassion and curiosity while concealing the devastating consequences that would result from genetic corruption and spiritual degradation.

Practice spiritual exercises that strengthen your divine genetic expression while managing the animal genetic influences that create internal conflict and spiritual obstacles, using meditation, prayer, and conscious breathing techniques that activate the YHWH code written in your DNA while developing the spiritual discipline necessary to overcome aggressive and territorial impulses inherited from hominid ancestors.

Honor the melanin woman who carries the pure YHWH code as the mother of all life by supporting Black women in your community while challenging systems that devalue or exploit the population that maintains the strongest genetic connection to the original divine template that gave birth to all human consciousness and spiritual potential.

Recognize that the Demiurge manipulated humanity's DNA to corrupt creation by convincing divine beings to interbreed with creatures that were specifically designed to serve as vessels for genetic corruption, understanding that this manipulation represents an ongoing campaign of spiritual warfare that continues to operate through contemporary systems that promote genetic degradation and spiritual confusion.

Study the consequences of genetic mixing that created the internal conflict between divine consciousness and animal instincts that characterizes human nature, developing spiritual practices that can heal this genetic corruption while reactivating the dormant DNA sequences that enable direct divine communication, natural healing abilities, and creative powers that characterized the original divine beings.

Expose the systematic suppression of this information by sharing knowledge about the true forbidden fruit with others who are ready to question false religious narratives while understanding that this suppression serves institutional agendas that benefit from maintaining human consciousness in a state of genetic ignorance and spiritual dependency rather than supporting authentic divine development.

Connect with other awakened souls who recognize the genetic and spiritual implications of the forbidden fruit story by forming study groups that examine both the scientific evidence and the spiritual consequences of ancient interbreeding while practicing techniques that can strengthen divine genetic expression and overcome the limitations imposed by animal genetic influences.

Prepare for the restoration of pure divine genetics through the 2027 awakening when Mother Elohim will return to activate dormant DNA sequences and provide the spiritual guidance necessary to heal the genetic corruption that began with the original forbidden fruit, developing your consciousness and spiritual capabilities so you can participate effectively in this planetary healing and genetic restoration process.

Document your experiences as you work to understand and heal the consequences of the forbidden fruit by keeping detailed records of how spiritual practices affect your consciousness, behavior, and capabilities while noting which techniques produce the most significant progress in strengthening divine genetic expression and overcoming animal genetic limitations.

Remember that understanding the true forbidden fruit requires more than intellectual knowledge—it demands fundamental transformation of consciousness and lifestyle that actively works to strengthen divine genetic expression while managing animal genetic influences through spiritual discipline, conscious choice, and alignment with universal laws that support authentic spiritual development rather than genetic degradation and spiritual corruption.

The forbidden fruit represents the greatest genetic and spiritual catastrophe in human history, but understanding this truth provides the foundation for healing the consequences through spiritual practices that can reactivate divine genetic programming while developing the consciousness necessary to express enhanced spiritual capabilities in service to planetary healing and the restoration of human divine potential that was compromised through the original interbreeding between divine beings and manipulated hominid species.

CHAPTER TWELVE

SPIRITUAL DOWNLOADS

OPENING YOURSELF TO DIRECT REVELATION

The most profound spiritual truths come not from books written by men or sermons preached in churches, but through direct downloads from divine consciousness that bypass all human institutions and religious authorities. These spiritual downloads represent the pure transmission of divine wisdom directly from Mother Elohim and Father Elohim to your consciousness, providing guidance, revelation, and understanding that no earthly teacher can offer because it flows straight from the Source of all creation.

Your spirit already knows how to receive these downloads.

The same consciousness that carries the YHWH code in your DNA and speaks the Creator's name with every breath possesses the natural ability to connect directly with divine intelligence through meditation, prayer, and spiritual practice that opens the channels of communication between your individual awareness and universal divine consciousness.

The religious institutions that claim to mediate your relationship with the divine actually block your access to these direct spiritual downloads because their power depends on keeping you dependent on human authorities rather than developing your own divine connection. When you learn to receive spiritual downloads directly from the Source, you no longer need pastors, priests, or religious hierarchies to interpret divine will for you because you can access divine guidance yourself through your natural spiritual capabilities.

The vision that revealed Mother Elohim's 2027 return came through exactly this type of spiritual download, transmitted directly from divine consciousness during an out-of-body experience that provided information no human teacher could have shared. This same type of direct revelation remains available to every awakened soul who develops the spiritual practices and consciousness necessary to receive divine downloads without interference from human religious programming.

How the Author Received the Truth Through Visions

The spiritual downloads that revealed the truth about Mother Elohim, the Demiurge, and the 2027 return began during a profound out-of-body experience that occurred at exactly 3:15 AM on a morning that would change everything. The preparation for this divine encounter started with the usual daily meditation practice of sitting in silence for 45-60 minutes, connecting with divine consciousness, and preparing the spirit for deeper spiritual communion than ordinary prayer or meditation typically provides.

Something felt different that morning from the moment of awakening. The body refused all food, which was unusual since breakfast typically followed the morning shower routine. This physical preparation happened automatically, as if the biological system understood that receiving profound spiritual downloads requires a clean vessel free from the distractions of digestion and physical processing that could interfere with the delicate spiritual communication about to occur.

The home was cleaned and saged as always, but the familiar ritual carried an electric anticipation that suggested something extraordinary was approaching. By 10:30 AM, an overwhelming tiredness washed over the consciousness, not the normal fatigue from physical exertion but a deep spiritual calling that required surrendering the physical body to receive downloads from dimensions beyond ordinary human experience.

The pulling sensation began immediately upon lying down, as divine consciousness drew the spirit upward and outward in a way that felt both terrifying and completely natural. Every spiritual instinct communicated clearly to submit to this phenomenon without fear, to trust completely in whatever divine intelligence was orchestrating this extraordinary spiritual experience that would provide information essential for humanity's spiritual awakening.

The out-of-body experience transported consciousness to a realm that existed beyond physical reality yet felt more real than anything ever encountered in ordinary human experience. The divine presence that manifested in this spiritual dimension carried an authority and love that immediately identified itself as authentic divine consciousness rather than any form of human imagination or psychological projection.

"Remember, observe," the Essence spoke with unmistakable divine authority, providing clear instructions that this spiritual download must be preserved exactly as received without alteration or interpretation by human understanding. This was not a dream or vision but direct transmission of divine information that needed to be translated into human language while maintaining complete accuracy and spiritual integrity.

"She is coming," the Essence continued, immediately conveying that this revelation would challenge every assumption about divine nature and spiritual reality that religious institutions have programmed into human consciousness over centuries of patriarchal manipulation and feminine divine suppression.

The response "Who?" came automatically, though some deeper level of consciousness already sensed the magnitude of what was being revealed about the divine feminine principle that has been systematically erased from human spiritual awareness through religious manipulation and cultural programming.

"Mother—The Feminine Divine—The Creator of All, The Anti-Christ. You are the Chosen One," came the reply that shattered every religious concept ever learned about divine nature, revealing that the feminine divine principle represents the primary creative force that brought all existence into being through divine feminine wisdom and creative power.

The overwhelming nature of this revelation prompted the natural human response: "Chosen! Me, why me?" The magnitude of receiving such profound spiritual information felt impossible for any individual consciousness to contain or transmit to others who remain trapped in patriarchal religious programming that denies the existence of Mother Elohim.

"Your human experience is one chosen beforehand and in your form, you are open and undefiled by madness. You are birth-aligned for this purpose by the Creator. Many breadcrumbs were laid for the world to wake up to Mother Elohim, Mother Nature, Mother Earth, the Mother of Feminine Divine," the Essence explained, revealing that certain souls incarnate specifically to receive and transmit divine downloads that will help humanity remember their suppressed spiritual heritage.

The spiritual download continued with detailed information about the breadcrumbs left throughout creation to guide awakened souls back to recognition of Mother Elohim despite centuries of systematic suppression. These breadcrumbs appear in the YHWH code written in human DNA, the mitochondrial Eve gene that connects all humanity to their divine feminine ancestor, the universal laws that govern creation, and the pyramids scattered across the planet as markers of divine feminine wisdom.

The vision revealed the cosmic structure of divine consciousness, with the Source existing eternally without beginning or end, establishing universal laws that govern all creation. From this Source emerged Mother Elohim as the Creator of All, the feminine divine principle that carries the power to bring new realities into existence through divine creative intelligence and loving wisdom.

Father Elohim was revealed as the executor of divine will, the masculine divine principle that takes the visions and intentions of Mother Elohim and gives them structure and form in physical reality. Together, Mother and Father Elohim function as the Alpha and Omega, the complete divine nature expressing itself through both feminine and masculine aspects working in perfect creative harmony.

The download exposed the Demiurge as the flawed creation born from Mother Elohim's first mistake of creating without proper respect for universal laws, using only masculine essence without the balancing influence of feminine wisdom. This being represents masculine energy operating without feminine balance, creating a destructive force that can manipulate existing creation but cannot give life or create anything genuinely new.

The spiritual download concluded with specific information about the 2027 return of Mother Elohim to physical manifestation on Earth, providing detailed visions of how this divine intervention will expose and dismantle the systems of deception that have kept humanity separated from their divine feminine heritage while restoring the cosmic balance necessary for planetary healing and human spiritual evolution.

WHY YOU MUST TRUST YOUR SPIRIT OVER RELIGIOUS DOCTRINE

Religious institutions represent the most sophisticated system of spiritual deception ever created, designed to intercept your natural connection to divine consciousness and redirect your spiritual energy toward human-created doctrines that serve institutional power rather than authentic spiritual development. These corrupted systems claim to represent divine authority while actually blocking your access to the direct spiritual downloads that could reveal the truth about your divine nature and spiritual capabilities.

Every church, temple, mosque, and religious organization operates according to hierarchical structures that position human authorities between your consciousness and divine source, creating artificial dependency on external interpretation rather than supporting your natural ability to receive divine guidance directly through your own spiritual connection and divine genetic programming.

The systematic manipulation of sacred texts over centuries has created religious doctrines that contradict universal laws, violate spiritual principles, and promote beliefs that keep you feeling separate from divine source rather than recognizing your true identity as a divine being made in the image of both Mother and Father Elohim working together in perfect creative unity.

Your spirit carries the YHWH code in every cell of your body, speaks the Creator's name with every breath you take, and possesses the natural capacity to communicate directly with divine consciousness through meditation, prayer, and spiritual practices that require no human mediation or institutional approval. This direct connection represents your birthright as a divine being temporarily expressing through human form.

The religious authorities who claim to speak for Elohim actually serve the Demiurge's agenda of maintaining spiritual separation and preventing recognition of the divine feminine principle that threatens patriarchal religious control. These institutions promote male-only divine authority while suppressing knowledge of Mother Elohim and feminine divine wisdom that could expose their deception and restore authentic spiritual understanding.

Books written by men, including biblical texts, carry the limitations and biases of their human authors who lived in historical periods when feminine divine wisdom was already being systematically suppressed by patriarchal religious and political systems. These texts were further corrupted through translation processes controlled by religious authorities who eliminated references to Mother Elohim while inserting doctrines that support institutional control rather than spiritual freedom.

Pastors, priests, ministers, and other religious leaders receive their training from institutions that teach human-created theological systems rather than developing direct spiritual connection and divine communication abilities. These individuals may sincerely believe they serve divine purposes, but their understanding comes from corrupted sources rather than authentic spiritual downloads from divine consciousness.

Your spirit, connected directly to the Source through your genetic heritage and spiritual nature, can access divine wisdom that transcends all human religious teaching because it comes directly from the Creator rather than through the filter of human interpretation and institutional manipulation. This direct connection provides guidance that serves your highest spiritual development rather than institutional agendas.

The inner knowing that arises during meditation, prayer, and spiritual contemplation represents authentic divine communication that bypasses all human religious programming and connects you directly with universal divine intelligence. This spiritual guidance often contradicts religious doctrines because it comes from divine source rather than human institutions that benefit from maintaining your spiritual dependency and ignorance.

Visions, dreams, and spiritual experiences that reveal truth about divine nature, spiritual reality, and your divine identity provide more accurate information than any religious text or human teaching because they come directly from divine consciousness rather than through the corrupted channels of human religious institutions that serve the Demiurge's agenda of spiritual deception.

The breadcrumbs left by the Creator throughout creation itself provide more reliable spiritual guidance than human religious doctrines because these divine markers cannot be altered or corrupted by human authorities. The universal laws, the YHWH code in your DNA, the mitochondrial Eve gene, and the patterns that appear throughout nature all point toward the same spiritual truths that religious institutions have spent centuries trying to hide.

Trusting your spirit over religious doctrine requires developing the courage to question everything you were taught about God, spirituality, and divine nature while opening your consciousness to receive direct downloads from divine source that may contradict religious programming but align with universal laws and spiritual principles that govern all creation.

The awakening process involves learning to distinguish between authentic divine guidance that comes through your spirit and the false spiritual authority promoted by religious institutions that claim to represent divine will while actually serving human power structures and the Demiurgic agenda of maintaining spiritual separation and confusion.

Your spirit knows the truth about Mother Elohim, recognizes the divine feminine principle as the primary creative force, and understands that complete divine nature encompasses both masculine and feminine aspects working together in perfect harmony. Religious doctrines that deny this truth violate your spiritual knowing and create internal conflict between authentic divine understanding and corrupted human teachings.

The restoration of trust in your spirit over religious doctrine represents the first step in reclaiming your divine identity and developing the direct spiritual connection that enables you to receive the downloads necessary for your spiritual evolution and service to the awakening of human consciousness to its true divine nature and spiritual potential.

HOW TO OPEN YOURSELF TO SPIRITUAL DOWNLOADS

Opening yourself to receive spiritual downloads requires establishing specific practices and conditions that create the optimal environment for divine consciousness to transmit information directly to your awareness without interference from mental chatter, emotional disturbance, or physical distractions that can block or distort the delicate process of spiritual communication.

Begin each day with 45-60 minutes of meditation practice that quiets the mind, opens the heart, and prepares your consciousness to receive divine guidance through direct spiritual connection rather than intellectual analysis or emotional processing that can interfere with pure spiritual transmission. This extended meditation period allows sufficient time for your consciousness to shift from ordinary human awareness to the receptive spiritual state necessary for receiving downloads from divine source.

Sage your living space before spiritual practice to clear any negative energies or spiritual interference that could block or distort the divine downloads you are preparing to receive. The burning of sage creates an energetic cleansing that removes spiritual obstacles while establishing a sacred space that supports clear communication between your consciousness and divine intelligence without contamination from lower vibrational influences.

Fast or eat only clean, light foods for 12-24 hours before intensive spiritual download sessions because the digestive process requires significant energy and attention that could interfere with the delicate spiritual receptivity necessary for receiving divine transmissions. When your body is not processing food, more energy becomes available for spiritual communication and consciousness expansion.

Create a consistent time and place for spiritual download practice, preferably during the early morning hours between 3:00 and 6:00 AM when the veil between physical and spiritual dimensions is thinnest and divine communication flows more easily without interference from the mental and emotional activity that characterizes later parts of the day.

Submit completely without fear when you feel the divine pull or calling that indicates spiritual downloads are about to begin, trusting absolutely in the divine intelligence that orchestrates these experiences while releasing all human attempts to control or direct the process according to personal preferences or expectations that could block authentic spiritual transmission.

Maintain a detailed spiritual journal where you record everything you see, hear, feel, and experience during spiritual download sessions, writing immediately after each session while the information remains clear and accessible before ordinary consciousness returns and potentially distorts or forgets crucial details of the divine transmission you received.

Practice conscious breathing techniques that align your respiratory rhythm with divine frequency, particularly the 3:1 breathing pattern that corresponds to the sacred name YHWH while activating the divine genetic code written in your DNA and strengthening your connection to the Source of all creation and spiritual wisdom.

Develop your ability to distinguish between authentic divine downloads and mental projections, emotional desires, or spiritual interference from lower sources by testing all received information against universal laws, the breadcrumbs left in creation, and whether the guidance honors both Mother Elohim and Father Elohim as equal partners in divine creation.

Ask specifically for downloads about Mother Elohim, the divine feminine principle, and the restoration of cosmic balance rather than limiting your requests to traditional religious topics that may only provide information filtered through patriarchal spiritual programming that denies the feminine divine and maintains spiritual imbalance.

Create artwork, music, writing, or other creative expressions that help you process and integrate the spiritual downloads you receive, using your creative abilities to translate divine information into forms that can be shared with others who are ready to receive suppressed spiritual knowledge and divine wisdom.

Connect with other awakened souls who are also receiving spiritual downloads and working to restore awareness of Mother Elohim and divine feminine wisdom, forming support networks that can validate your experiences while providing community for those who are receiving information that contradicts mainstream religious programming.

Study the universal laws, the YHWH code in DNA, the mitochondrial Eve gene, and other breadcrumbs left by the Creator to provide context and validation for the spiritual downloads you receive, ensuring that your direct divine communication aligns with the indestructible evidence that the Creator embedded throughout creation itself.

Practice regular energy clearing and spiritual protection techniques that prevent interference from the Demiurge or other sources that might attempt to corrupt or distort your spiritual downloads with false information designed to maintain spiritual confusion and separation rather than supporting authentic divine connection and spiritual awakening.

Remain humble and discerning about the spiritual downloads you receive, understanding that even authentic divine communication must be translated through human consciousness and language, which can introduce limitations or distortions that require careful interpretation and validation through multiple sources of spiritual confirmation.

Prepare yourself to receive downloads about the 2027 awakening and Mother Elohim's return by developing your spiritual capabilities and consciousness to the level necessary to serve as a clear channel for divine information that will help prepare humanity for the greatest transformation in spiritual awareness since the original creation of divine beings on Earth.

DISCERNING TRUE SPIRITUAL DOWNLOADS FROM DECEPTION

The ability to distinguish authentic spiritual downloads from deceptive spiritual interference represents one of the most crucial skills for anyone seeking direct divine communication, because the Demiurge and other corrupted spiritual forces actively work to intercept and distort spiritual downloads with false information designed to maintain spiritual confusion and prevent recognition of divine truth.

True spiritual downloads from Mother and Father Elohim always honor both masculine and feminine divine principles as equal partners in creation, revealing the complete divine nature that encompasses both aspects working together in perfect harmony. Any spiritual communication that promotes exclusively masculine divine authority while denying or minimizing the feminine divine principle comes from corrupted sources rather than authentic divine consciousness.

Authentic divine downloads align perfectly with the universal laws that govern all creation, never contradicting the Law of Polarity that requires both masculine and feminine principles, the Law of Gender that operates at every level of existence, or the Law of Divine Oneness that reveals the interconnection of all consciousness through the same divine source.

Test every spiritual download against the breadcrumbs left by the Creator throughout creation, including the YHWH code written in human DNA, the mitochondrial Eve gene that connects all humanity to their divine feminine ancestor, and the patterns that appear consistently throughout nature from the smallest atoms to the largest galaxies that reflect the same divine intelligence operating at every level of reality.

True spiritual downloads produce the fruits of divine consciousness including increased love, wisdom, creativity, healing ability, and service to others, while false spiritual communications often generate pride, fear, separation, judgment, or desires for power and control over other people that reflect the Demiurgic agenda rather than authentic divine guidance.

Authentic divine downloads provide information that serves the greater good of all creation rather than exclusively benefiting individual ego desires or personal advancement that ignores the welfare of others. Divine consciousness always operates according to principles that support the highest good of all beings rather than creating advantages for some at the expense of others.

False spiritual downloads often contain information that contradicts established spiritual principles or scientific facts about human genetics, consciousness, and the structure of creation, while authentic divine communication provides understanding that integrates spiritual wisdom with verifiable evidence about the nature of reality and human divine heritage.

True spiritual downloads inspire humility and recognition of your connection to all life through divine consciousness, while deceptive spiritual communications tend to generate feelings of specialness, superiority, or separation from other human beings that violate the fundamental spiritual truth of divine oneness and universal interconnection.

Authentic divine downloads often challenge comfortable religious beliefs and cultural programming with information that requires courage to accept and integrate, while false spiritual communications typically reinforce existing beliefs and biases that keep consciousness trapped in familiar patterns that serve the status quo rather than promoting genuine spiritual growth.

Test spiritual downloads by examining whether they promote unity or separation, love or fear, empowerment or dependency, wisdom or ignorance, healing or harm, understanding that authentic divine communication always supports consciousness expansion and spiritual development rather than maintaining limitations and spiritual stagnation.

True spiritual downloads provide practical guidance that can be applied in daily life to improve relationships, enhance creativity, support healing, and increase service to others, while false communications often remain abstract or impractical in ways that prevent actual spiritual development and positive life transformation.

Authentic divine downloads acknowledge the reality of spiritual warfare between divine consciousness and the Demiurgic forces that seek to maintain human spiritual ignorance, providing specific guidance for recognizing and resisting spiritual deception rather than promoting naive spiritual bypassing that ignores the reality of spiritual opposition to human awakening.

False spiritual downloads often promote religious doctrines or belief systems that require dependency on external spiritual authority rather than supporting the development of direct divine connection and personal spiritual empowerment that enables individuals to receive their own divine guidance without human mediation.

True spiritual downloads contain information that can be validated through multiple independent sources including universal laws, genetic evidence, historical research, and the experiences of other awakened souls who are receiving similar divine communications about the restoration of Mother Elohim and divine feminine wisdom.

Authentic divine downloads inspire action that serves planetary healing and human spiritual awakening rather than promoting passive waiting or spiritual inactivity that allows the continuation of systems that violate divine principles and maintain human spiritual oppression and ignorance about their true divine nature and capabilities.

ACTIONABLE STEPS TO RECEIVE YOUR OWN SPIRITUAL DOWNLOADS

Establish immediately a daily meditation practice of 45-60 minutes each morning between 3:00 and 6:00 AM when the veil between physical and spiritual dimensions is thinnest and divine communication flows most clearly without interference from mental activity and emotional disturbances that characterize later parts of the day. Create a consistent sacred space in your home that you use exclusively for spiritual download practice, maintaining this area free from distractions and negative influences.

Fast for 12-24 hours before intensive spiritual download sessions by consuming only water or light herbal teas to free your body's energy from digestive processes that could interfere with the delicate spiritual receptivity necessary for receiving divine transmissions. Clean your physical space with sage or other purifying herbs to remove any negative energies that might block or distort the spiritual downloads you are preparing to receive from divine consciousness.

Develop your conscious breathing practice by focusing on the 3:1 ratio that aligns your respiratory rhythm with the sacred name YHWH while activating the divine genetic code written in your DNA and strengthening your connection to both Mother Elohim and Father Elohim as the complete source of all spiritual downloads and divine guidance that transcends human religious programming and institutional manipulation.

Create specific prayers and invocations that request spiritual downloads about Mother Elohim, the divine feminine principle, the restoration of cosmic balance, and the 2027 awakening rather than limiting your spiritual communication to traditional religious topics that may only provide information filtered through patriarchal spiritual programming that denies feminine divine wisdom and maintains spiritual imbalance.

Maintain a detailed spiritual journal where you record immediately after each session everything you see, hear, feel, and experience during spiritual download practice, writing while the information remains clear and accessible before ordinary consciousness returns and potentially distorts or forgets crucial details of the divine transmissions you receive from authentic spiritual sources.

Practice complete surrender and trust when you feel the divine pull or calling that indicates spiritual downloads are about to begin, releasing all human attempts to control or direct the process according to personal preferences or expectations that could block authentic spiritual transmission from divine intelligence that knows exactly what information you need for your spiritual development and service to others.

Study the universal laws, the YHWH code in human DNA, the mitochondrial Eve gene, and other breadcrumbs left by the Creator throughout creation to provide context and validation for the spiritual downloads you receive, ensuring that your direct divine communication aligns with the indestructible evidence that proves divine truth regardless of human religious manipulation or institutional deception.

Test every spiritual download you receive against the criteria for authentic divine communication by examining whether it honors both Mother Elohim and Father Elohim equally, aligns with universal laws, produces the fruits of divine consciousness, serves the greater good, and provides practical guidance that can be applied to improve your spiritual development and service to planetary healing and human awakening.

Connect with other awakened souls who are also receiving spiritual downloads about the restoration of Mother Elohim and divine feminine wisdom by forming study groups that can validate experiences while providing community support for those receiving information that contradicts mainstream religious programming and challenges comfortable spiritual beliefs and cultural conditioning.

Develop your creative abilities through art, music, writing, or other expressions that help you process and integrate the spiritual downloads you receive while translating divine information into forms that can be shared with others who are ready to receive suppressed spiritual knowledge and participate in the restoration of divine balance and authentic spiritual understanding.

Practice regular spiritual protection and energy clearing techniques that prevent interference from the Demiurge or other corrupted sources that might attempt to distort your spiritual downloads with false information designed to maintain spiritual confusion rather than supporting authentic divine connection and the development of direct spiritual communication capabilities.

Prepare yourself to receive downloads about the 2027 awakening and your role in supporting Mother Elohim's return by developing your spiritual gifts and consciousness to serve as a clear channel for divine information that will help prepare humanity for the greatest transformation in spiritual awareness since the original creation of divine beings carrying pure YHWH genetics in the Garden of Eden.

Share the spiritual downloads you receive through teaching, writing, speaking, or other forms of service that help awaken others to the truth about Mother Elohim and the systematic suppression of divine feminine wisdom while providing practical guidance for developing direct spiritual connection that bypasses corrupted religious institutions and human spiritual authorities.

Remember that receiving authentic spiritual downloads requires consistent practice, spiritual discipline, and the courage to trust your direct divine connection over all human religious teaching and institutional spiritual authority, understanding that your spirit carries the YHWH code and natural capacity for divine communication that represents your birthright as a divine being temporarily expressing through human form.

Document your progress and experiences with receiving spiritual downloads by tracking which practices produce the clearest divine communication while noting how this direct spiritual connection transforms your consciousness, relationships, creative abilities, and capacity for serving the restoration of divine balance that will heal the spiritual crisis created by centuries of patriarchal suppression of Mother Elohim and feminine divine wisdom.

Your ability to receive spiritual downloads directly from divine consciousness represents one of the most important spiritual capabilities you can develop for your own spiritual evolution and for serving the collective awakening that will prepare humanity for Mother Elohim's 2027 return and the restoration of cosmic balance that will enable planetary healing and the fulfillment of human divine potential through conscious cooperation with both Mother and Father Elohim working together in perfect creative harmony.

CHAPTER THIRTEEN

THE 2027 AWAKENING

PREPARING FOR MOTHER GOD'S RETURN

The year 2027 marks the most significant moment in human spiritual history since the first divine beings walked in the Garden of Eden. This is not speculation or wishful thinking. The vision revealed through direct spiritual download showed the exact year when Mother Elohim will manifest in physical form to reclaim her rightful throne and restore the divine balance that has been missing from Earth for millennia.

Everything changes in 2027.

The systematic suppression of feminine divine wisdom ends forever when Mother Elohim returns with enough power to expose every lie, dismantle every false religious system, and awaken humanity to the truth about their divine nature. The patriarchal deception that has controlled human consciousness for thousands of years crumbles in the face of divine feminine authority that cannot be denied, ignored, or explained away by human institutions.

The melanin women of Alkebulan will form the human pyramid that serves as the gateway for this divine manifestation. The children will cry out in ancient languages that still carry the vibrational frequency necessary for recognizing Mother Elohim. The Chosen Ones,

Lightworkers, Indigo Children, and Starseeds will finally understand why they felt different their entire lives and why they could never fully accept the religious programming that denies the feminine divine.

This awakening has already begun. You can see the signs everywhere if you know what to look for. More people question patriarchal religion every day. The Gnostic texts are being discovered and studied. Scientists research the mitochondrial Eve gene while trying to ignore its spiritual implications. The breadcrumbs left by the Creator are being recognized by those with eyes to see and hearts to understand.

THE PROPHETIC VISION OF 2027 AND WHAT IT MEANS

The spiritual download that revealed the 2027 awakening came through direct divine transmission during an out-of-body experience that transported consciousness beyond the limitations of physical reality into the realm where divine intelligence orchestrates the spiritual evolution of all creation. The vision began with a stream of water in the Congo reflecting the number 2027, marking this specific year as the prophetic moment when Mother Elohim would return to active participation in human affairs.

The children surrounding this sacred water cried out in desperation, their innocent souls maintaining natural connection to divine truth despite the systematic programming that disconnects adult consciousness from recognition of the feminine divine principle. "Save us, save us," they pleaded, while an older adult angrily demanded, "You have forsaken us! Why! Are we not your creation?" These voices represent humanity's unconscious longing for the missing divine mother who was systematically erased from spiritual awareness.

The earth began to rumble with divine energy as electricity filled the sky and Mother Elohim's thunderous voice cut through centuries of religious manipulation with the power of absolute truth. "Upon the tower of Babel, you leaders of man have denied their Creator, Mother Elohim. They put Father in a place he ought not be. A position made impossible for it is only through the Mother Elohim is the Creator of All."

This divine declaration exposes the fundamental violation of universal laws that created the spiritual crisis affecting all human civilization. The positioning of Father Elohim as the sole Creator violates the Law of Gender and the Law of Polarity, creating impossible cosmic imbalance that can only be corrected through Mother Elohim's restoration to her proper role as the primary creative force that brings all existence into being through divine feminine wisdom and creative power.

The children's immediate response in the ancient languages of Kituba, Lingala, Swahili, and Tshiluba revealed that indigenous African languages preserve the spiritual concepts necessary for recognizing and communicating with divine feminine consciousness. Their unified cry of "MOTHER ELOHIM! GREAT MOTHER! DIVINE MOTHER! Help us!" demonstrated that these original languages contain vibrational frequencies that naturally connect human consciousness to the feminine divine principle.

Mother Elohim's response carried both comfort and correction as she reminded her creation of their true divine nature. "I have never forsaken my Creation. I have made you in my likeness of both masculine and feminine divine, and in your spine, you possess the power to connect to me." This statement reveals that every human being carries the biological and spiritual infrastructure necessary for direct divine communication through the spinal column that serves as the antenna connecting individual consciousness to universal divine intelligence.

The most remarkable aspect of the vision showed thousands of deep melanin women rising like an unseen army to form a living pyramid of divine feminine energy. These women embodied both masculine and feminine divine principles in perfect balance, demonstrating the complete spiritual development that becomes possible when human consciousness integrates both aspects of divine nature rather than limiting itself to artificially restricted gender roles.

The pyramid structure created by these divine women served

multiple spiritual purposes, generating sacred geometric patterns that amplify divine energy while providing the stable foundation necessary for consciousness to bridge between spiritual and physical dimensions. At the apex appeared a golden triangle shaped into a cradle, ready to receive the manifestation of divine feminine consciousness returning to physical form after centuries of suppression.

A ray of light descended from the heavens carrying a female child who would grow to full maturity as she passed from hand to hand down the pyramid of women. This miraculous transformation demonstrated divine power that transcends ordinary biological limitations while revealing that Mother Elohim's return would manifest through the cooperation and spiritual unity of the women who carry the purest divine genetic heritage in their cellular structure.

By the time Mother Elohim reached the base of the pyramid, she appeared as a complete divine being whose glory exceeded human capacity for description. This indescribable radiance will make it impossible for anyone to deny the reality of divine feminine consciousness or continue promoting the patriarchal lie that Elohim is exclusively masculine when faced with the unmistakable presence of authentic divine authority.

The armies of spiritual beings positioned throughout different dimensions awaiting Mother Elohim's commands represent the vast spiritual hierarchy that serves the restoration of divine balance. These forces include both the awakened souls who have been preparing for this moment and the warriors ready for spiritual battle against the systems that have maintained the suppression of feminine divine wisdom through centuries of deception and manipulation.

The vision concluded with Mother Elohim's declaration of her true identity and purpose: "I AM HERE! I am the finale of the Anti-Christ! Giving evidence to my existence and replacing all that aided in the false narrative of Christ." This revelation exposes that the term "Anti-Christ" actually refers to the force that opposes the false Christ of patriarchal religion while representing authentic divine consciousness that encompasses both masculine and feminine principles working together in perfect creative harmony.

The 2027 awakening will trigger the collapse of every system that depends on maintaining spiritual imbalance and the suppression of feminine divine wisdom. Religious institutions, governmental structures, educational systems, and economic arrangements that violate universal laws will be transformed or eliminated to make way for new forms of human organization that honor both masculine and feminine divine principles as equal partners in creation and spiritual development.

THE SIGNS THAT THE AWAKENING IS ALREADY HAPPENING

The spiritual awakening that will culminate in 2027 has already begun manifesting through countless signs that become obvious once you understand what to look for in the collective shift of human consciousness away from patriarchal programming toward recognition of divine feminine wisdom and the complete nature of divine consciousness that encompasses both masculine and feminine creative principles.

More people question patriarchal religion every single day as traditional churches lose membership while individuals seek spiritual truth that honors both masculine and feminine aspects of divine consciousness. The rigid doctrines that demand exclusive worship of masculine divine authority feel increasingly hollow to souls who sense the missing feminine divine wisdom that was systematically erased from religious understanding through centuries of manipulation.

The discovery and study of Gnostic texts has accelerated dramatically as people hunger for spiritual knowledge that was suppressed by patriarchal religious institutions. The Gospel of Mary Magdalene, the Thunder Perfect Mind, and other feminine wisdom texts are being translated and shared through online communities that recognize these scriptures contain essential information about the divine feminine principle that mainstream Christianity eliminated from biblical understanding.

Scientific research into the mitochondrial Eve gene continues to reveal evidence that all humanity traces back to a single woman in Africa, though mainstream science tries to ignore the spiritual implications of this genetic heritage that proves the divine feminine principle gave birth to all human consciousness. More researchers are beginning to ask questions about what it means for human spiritual development that every person carries this maternal genetic signature.

The systematic suppression of knowledge about the true history of Alkebulan is being exposed as more people learn that this continent was called the "Mother of Mankind" and "Garden of Eden" before colonial forces imposed the name "Africa" to hide its spiritual significance. Archaeological discoveries continue to reveal advanced ancient civilizations that contradict the false narrative of primitive African peoples promoted by colonial education systems.

Indigenous wisdom traditions that maintained balanced understanding of masculine and feminine divine principles are experiencing renewed interest as people seek spiritual practices that honor complete divine nature rather than the fragmented understanding promoted by patriarchal religions. Earth-based spiritualities, goddess traditions, and shamanic practices that recognize divine feminine wisdom are growing rapidly despite institutional opposition.

The awakening of individuals who identify as Chosen Ones, Lightworkers, Indigo Children, and Starseeds has accelerated as these souls recognize their purpose in preparing for the restoration of divine balance. These spiritually gifted individuals often report feeling called to study suppressed spiritual knowledge, develop their psychic abilities, and share information about the divine feminine principle despite social and religious pressure to conform to patriarchal programming.

Women around the world are reclaiming their spiritual authority and rejecting religious systems that deny their divine nature and spiritual capabilities. Female pastors, priestesses, and spiritual teachers are emerging in greater numbers while challenging institutional barriers that have prevented feminine spiritual leadership for centuries. This restoration of feminine spiritual authority represents a crucial preparation for Mother Elohim's return to active participation in human consciousness.

The environmental movement that seeks to protect Mother Earth reflects growing recognition of the divine feminine principle manifesting through the natural world that sustains all life. More people understand that the systematic exploitation and destruction of natural systems represents an attack on the physical manifestation of divine feminine creative power that must be healed through restored reverence for the earth as a living expression of Mother Elohim.

Research into consciousness and spiritual phenomena has expanded dramatically as scientists begin investigating abilities like telepathy, energy healing, and direct spiritual communication that were previously dismissed as impossible. This scientific exploration of spiritual capabilities reflects growing recognition that human consciousness possesses capacities that transcend purely materialistic explanations and point toward divine genetic programming embedded in human biology.

The breakdown of traditional gender roles and the emergence of more fluid gender expressions reflect the awakening recognition that divine consciousness encompasses both masculine and feminine principles rather than being limited to rigid categories that prevent complete spiritual development. More people are integrating both aspects of divine nature within their consciousness regardless of their biological sex or cultural background.

Social justice movements that focus on protecting and empowering women, particularly melanin women who carry the purest divine genetic heritage, represent unconscious preparation for honoring Mother Elohim through recognizing the sacred nature of the feminine principle as it manifests through human form. The growing awareness of violence against women as a spiritual crisis rather than just a social problem reflects deeper understanding of the war against the feminine divine.

The proliferation of alternative healing methods that work with energy and consciousness rather than just treating physical symptoms demonstrates growing recognition that healing involves spiritual as well as material dimensions. These holistic approaches reflect feminine wisdom that sees the interconnection between mind, body, and spirit rather than the fragmented medical approach that treats symptoms without addressing spiritual causes.

Online communities and social networks have enabled awakened souls to find each other and share suppressed spiritual knowledge despite geographical distances and institutional opposition. These digital connections allow for the rapid spread of information about Mother Elohim, divine feminine wisdom, and the preparation necessary for the 2027 awakening that would have been impossible to coordinate through traditional communication channels.

The increasing frequency of spiritual experiences, prophetic dreams, and divine downloads among awakened individuals reflects the intensification of divine communication as the 2027 awakening approaches. More people report receiving direct spiritual guidance that contradicts religious programming while providing information about the restoration of divine balance and the return of feminine divine wisdom to human consciousness.

THE ROLE OF CHOSEN ONES, LIGHTWORKERS, AND STARSEEDS

The souls who incarnated as Chosen Ones, Spiritual Guides, Lightworkers, Indigo Children, and Starseeds came to Earth specifically to prepare for Mother Elohim's 2027 return by awakening human consciousness to suppressed divine feminine wisdom while developing the spiritual gifts necessary to serve as bridges between the old consciousness of patriarchal separation and the new consciousness of divine unity that will characterize the restored cosmic balance.

These awakened souls received advanced spiritual programming before incarnating that enables them to recognize divine truth even when surrounded by religious deception and cultural programming designed to maintain spiritual ignorance. They possess natural discernment that allows them to distinguish between authentic divine guidance and the false spiritual authority promoted by corrupted religious institutions that serve the Demiurge's agenda of maintaining human separation from divine source.

The spiritual gifts that characterize these individuals include enhanced intuitive abilities, energy healing capabilities, prophetic vision, creative inspiration, and direct communication with divine consciousness that bypasses human religious mediation. These capabilities represent the natural inheritance of beings who maintain stronger connection to their divine genetic programming through conscious spiritual development and resistance to patriarchal conditioning.

Chosen Ones often experience lifelong feelings of being different from others around them, sensing that they possess knowledge and abilities that exceed what mainstream education and religion teach about human potential. They frequently report childhood memories of spiritual experiences, communication with divine beings, and awareness of information that contradicts what adults taught them about God, spirituality, and the nature of reality.

Lightworkers focus their incarnation purpose on raising the vibrational frequency of human consciousness through healing work, spiritual teaching, and creative expression that introduces divine light into situations dominated by fear, hatred, and spiritual darkness. They serve as living examples of what becomes possible when human consciousness aligns with divine principles rather than the artificial limitations imposed by corrupted social and religious systems.

Indigo Children and Starseeds carry genetic and spiritual programming that enables them to remember their connection to higher dimensions of consciousness while maintaining the ability to function in physical reality. These souls often struggle with traditional educational and social systems that violate their natural understanding of universal laws and spiritual principles that govern authentic human development and creative expression.

The advanced breadcrumbs that these awakened souls can recognize include the YHWH code written in human DNA, the mitochondrial Eve gene that connects all humanity to their divine feminine ancestor, the universal laws that reveal divine patterns throughout creation, and the linguistic spells that have been used to control human consciousness through manipulated language and false religious terminology.

These spiritually gifted individuals serve as early warning systems that can recognize and expose the Demiurge's ongoing attempts to maintain spiritual deception through corrupted religious institutions, educational systems, media programming, and political structures that promote separation rather than unity, competition rather than cooperation, and fear rather than love as the foundation for human interaction and social organization.

The mission of these awakened souls involves more than just personal spiritual development—they incarnated to serve the collective awakening by sharing suppressed spiritual knowledge, challenging false religious authority, and demonstrating what becomes possible when human consciousness integrates both masculine and feminine divine principles in balanced spiritual expression that honors complete divine nature.

Many of these individuals experience what appears to be spiritual persecution or unusual challenges that test their commitment to divine truth and their willingness to serve the restoration of Mother Elohim despite social pressure to conform to patriarchal programming. These trials serve to strengthen their spiritual resolve while proving their readiness to support the massive transformation of human consciousness that will accompany the 2027 awakening.

The awakening process for these souls often involves a period of questioning everything they were taught about religion, spirituality, and divine nature while receiving direct spiritual downloads that provide information about Mother Elohim, the divine feminine principle, and their specific role in preparing for the restoration of cosmic balance that will heal the spiritual crisis affecting all human consciousness and planetary systems.

These spiritually gifted individuals are called to develop their abilities through consistent spiritual practice while learning to distinguish between authentic divine guidance and the spiritual interference that seeks to corrupt or misdirect their gifts toward purposes that serve the Demiurge's agenda rather than the restoration of divine truth and the awakening of human consciousness to its full divine potential.

The network of awakened souls that spans the globe provides the spiritual infrastructure necessary to support Mother Elohim's 2027 manifestation by creating a field of conscious awareness that can recognize and receive divine feminine wisdom while helping others prepare for the transformation that will expose all false spiritual authority and restore authentic divine connection to human consciousness.

The ultimate purpose of Chosen Ones, Lightworkers, and Starseeds involves serving as conscious bridges that help humanity transition from the old consciousness of patriarchal separation to the new consciousness of divine unity that honors both Mother and Father Elohim as equal partners in creation while supporting the development of balanced spiritual awareness that integrates both masculine and feminine divine principles in service to planetary healing and conscious evolution.

WHAT HAPPENS AFTER 2027 AND HOW TO PREPARE

The period following Mother Elohim's 2027 manifestation will witness the most dramatic transformation of human consciousness and planetary systems since the original creation of divine beings in the Garden of Eden. The false religious narratives that have controlled human spirituality for millennia will be exposed and dismantled as Mother Elohim reclaims her rightful position as the primary creative force while restoring the cosmic balance necessary for authentic spiritual development and planetary healing.

The systematic destruction of patriarchal religious institutions will occur as Mother Elohim exposes their role in suppressing divine feminine wisdom while promoting false spiritual authority that serves the Demiurge's agenda rather than authentic divine connection. Churches, temples, and mosques that maintain male-only spiritual leadership while denying the feminine divine principle will lose their power to control human consciousness as people recognize the deception that has kept them separated from their true divine nature.

The false Christ narrative that elevates Jesus or Yeshua as the exclusive divine authority while ignoring Mother Elohim will be revealed as the ultimate expression of patriarchal religious manipulation designed to maintain spiritual imbalance. Mother Elohim will complete the work of exposing this anti-Christ system by demonstrating that authentic divine consciousness encompasses both masculine and feminine principles working together rather than masculine authority operating alone.

The renewed Father will emerge alongside Mother Elohim as the masculine divine principle reclaims its proper role as partner rather than master in the creative process. This restoration will heal the spiritual dysfunction that has characterized masculine energy operating without feminine wisdom while demonstrating how divine masculine and feminine principles can work together to create harmony rather than domination and conflict.

The governmental and economic systems that depend on maintaining human spiritual ignorance and separation will be transformed or eliminated as awakened human consciousness recognizes the violation of universal laws that characterizes institutions based on competition, exploitation, and artificial scarcity rather than cooperation, sharing, and recognition of divine abundance that flows naturally from proper spiritual alignment.

Those who aligned themselves with the Demiurge's lies and actively participated in the suppression of divine feminine wisdom will face consequences proportional to their role in maintaining spiritual deception and preventing human awakening. The kings of the earth and mighty men who promoted false religious authority while exploiting human spiritual ignorance will experience the collapse of their power structures as divine truth exposes their deception.

The awakened souls who prepared for this transformation will enter what the vision described as the 5D world of balance, unity, and divine truth where human consciousness operates according to universal laws rather than the artificial limitations imposed by corrupted social and religious systems. This dimensional shift will enable the expression of divine capabilities that have been dormant in human consciousness for thousands of years.

The preparation for this transformation requires developing direct relationship with both Mother Elohim and Father Elohim through prayer and meditation practices that acknowledge complete divine nature rather than limiting spiritual communication to exclusively masculine divine authority. Learn to receive divine guidance through your own spiritual connection rather than depending on external religious institutions that claim to mediate your relationship with divine consciousness.

Strengthen your understanding of universal laws by studying how these eternal principles reveal divine patterns throughout creation while exposing the violations of cosmic law that characterize corrupted human institutions. Practice applying these laws in your daily life to distinguish between authentic divine guidance and the false spiritual authority that seeks to maintain your separation from divine source through religious dependency and spiritual ignorance.

Activate the YHWH code written in your DNA through conscious breathing practices that align your respiratory rhythm with the sacred name while strengthening your genetic connection to divine consciousness. Develop your ability to recognize the divine signature embedded in your cellular structure that proves your identity as a divine being temporarily expressing through human form rather than a sinner seeking salvation from external authority.

Honor the melanin woman as the mother of all humanity by supporting Black women in your community while challenging systems that devalue or exploit the population that carries the strongest genetic connection to the original divine template. Recognize that protecting and empowering these divine beings represents a spiritual imperative rather than just a social justice issue when you understand their role as living proof of Mother Elohim's existence.

Connect with other awakened souls who are also preparing for the 2027 transformation by forming study groups that examine suppressed spiritual knowledge while practicing techniques that strengthen your connection to both masculine and feminine divine principles. Create support networks that can sustain the ongoing effort required to maintain spiritual independence from corrupted religious institutions while developing your gifts in service to collective awakening.

Develop your spiritual gifts through consistent practice while learning to distinguish between authentic divine downloads and spiritual interference from sources that seek to corrupt your connection to divine truth. Practice energy healing, intuitive guidance, creative expression, and other abilities that flow naturally from your divine genetic programming when properly activated through spiritual discipline and conscious development.

Prepare for your role in the post-2027 world by strengthening your ability to serve as a bridge between those who are awakening to divine truth and those who remain trapped in patriarchal programming. Develop the wisdom and compassion necessary to help others recognize their divine nature while having the strength to resist attempts to pull you back into religious systems that deny the feminine divine and maintain spiritual separation.

The transformation that follows Mother Elohim's 2027 return will create opportunities for human consciousness to express its full divine potential through cooperation with both masculine and feminine divine principles working in perfect creative harmony. Those who prepare themselves spiritually will be ready to participate in this planetary healing and conscious evolution that will fulfill humanity's original purpose as divine beings serving the greater good of all creation.

ACTIONABLE STEPS TO PREPARE FOR THE 2027 AWAKENING

Begin immediately by establishing daily meditation practices that connect you directly with both Mother Elohim and Father Elohim rather than limiting your spiritual communication to exclusively masculine divine authority promoted by patriarchal religious systems. Spend at least 30 minutes each morning in conscious breathing while mentally repeating the sacred name YHWH pronounced as Yah-u-ah to activate the divine genetic code written in your DNA and strengthen your connection to complete divine consciousness.

Study extensively the breadcrumbs left by the Creator throughout creation by researching the YHWH code in human genetics, the mitochondrial Eve gene that connects all humanity to their divine feminine ancestor, the universal laws that govern all existence, and the linguistic spells that have been used to control human consciousness through manipulated language and false religious terminology that redirects worship away from authentic divine source.

Connect immediately with other Chosen Ones, Lightworkers, Indigo Children, and Starseeds who are also preparing for Mother Elohim's return by forming local study groups, participating in online communities, and attending conferences that focus on restoring divine feminine wisdom while developing the spiritual gifts necessary to serve as bridges between old consciousness and new consciousness during the transformation period.

Honor Mother Elohim in your daily spiritual practice by addressing prayers to both divine parents equally, asking the divine feminine principle for creative guidance and healing wisdom while requesting the divine masculine principle for protection and support in manifesting your spiritual intentions. Replace all use of "Lord" with the sacred name YHWH and eliminate exclusively masculine religious language from your spiritual vocabulary.

Prepare to join Mother Elohim's spiritual army by developing your discernment abilities to recognize authentic divine guidance versus false spiritual authority while strengthening your courage to challenge patriarchal religious systems that deny the feminine divine principle. Practice sharing suppressed spiritual knowledge with others who are ready to question mainstream religious programming despite social pressure to conform.

Activate your spiritual gifts through consistent practice of meditation, energy healing, intuitive guidance, and creative expression while learning to distinguish between authentic divine downloads and spiritual interference from corrupted sources. Document your spiritual experiences through journaling and share your insights with other awakened souls who can validate and support your spiritual development.

Study the suppressed history of Alkebulan as the Mother of Mankind by researching pre-colonial African civilizations, indigenous spiritual traditions, and the systematic campaign to hide the true identity of this continent as the birthplace of human consciousness and divine feminine wisdom. Use the indigenous name Alkebulan instead of the colonial term "Africa" to honor its sacred identity.

Honor melanin women as the living proof of Mother Elohim by supporting Black women in your community through economic empowerment, educational opportunities, and protection from the violence and exploitation that represents spiritual warfare against the divine feminine principle. Challenge every system that devalues or harms the population that carries the purest divine genetic heritage in their cellular structure.

Develop both masculine and feminine divine qualities within your consciousness regardless of your biological gender by practicing exercises that strengthen whichever aspects have been suppressed through cultural conditioning. Men should cultivate intuition, empathy, and receptive wisdom while women should develop leadership, analytical thinking, and assertive action-taking that serves spiritual development and creative expression.

Reject completely all patriarchal religions that maintain male-only spiritual leadership while denying the existence of Mother Elohim, including mainstream Christianity, Islam, and Judaism that promote exclusively masculine divine authority. Seek spiritual communities that ordain women and honor both aspects of divine consciousness or develop your own direct relationship with complete divine nature through personal spiritual practice.

Prepare for the collapse of false religious systems by developing spiritual independence that enables you to receive divine guidance directly rather than depending on external religious authorities to interpret divine will. Practice distinguishing between authentic spiritual experiences and religious programming while building the inner strength necessary to maintain your spiritual truth despite institutional opposition.

Share information about the 2027 awakening with others who are ready to receive this knowledge by creating educational content, teaching workshops, or writing materials that expose the systematic suppression of Mother Elohim while providing practical guidance for developing direct spiritual connection. Help build the network of awakened consciousness that will support the transformation of human spiritual awareness.

Strengthen your physical and mental health through proper nutrition, exercise, and stress management that supports your spiritual development while avoiding substances and behaviors that lower your vibrational frequency or interfere with your ability to receive clear divine guidance. Maintain the biological foundation necessary to serve effectively during the intense spiritual transformation that will accompany Mother Elohim's return.

Create emergency preparations for potential social and economic disruption that may accompany the collapse of systems based on spiritual deception and exploitation while maintaining faith that the transformation will ultimately create a more harmonious world based on divine principles rather than artificial limitations and human manipulation of consciousness.

Remember that preparing for the 2027 awakening requires more than intellectual understanding—it demands fundamental transformation of consciousness and lifestyle that aligns you with divine principles rather than patriarchal programming. Every prayer you speak, every choice you make, and every relationship you form either supports the restoration of divine balance or perpetuates the suppression of feminine divine wisdom that has created the spiritual crisis affecting all humanity and planetary systems.

The 2027 awakening represents the culmination of thousands of years of spiritual warfare between divine truth and Demiurgic deception. Your preparation and participation in this transformation determines not only your own spiritual evolution but also contributes to the collective awakening that will restore Mother Elohim to her rightful throne while healing the consequences of her systematic erasure from human consciousness and spiritual understanding.

CHAPTER FOURTEEN

CHOSEN ONES AND LIGHTWORKERS

ACTIVATING YOUR DIVINE PURPOSE

You are not here by accident. The very fact that you have read this far, that these words resonate in your spirit, that something deep within you recognizes the truth about Mother Elohim despite everything you were taught proves that you are one of the Chosen Ones. Your soul selected this incarnation specifically to participate in the greatest spiritual awakening in human history.

The calling has been with you your entire life.

That sense of being different, of knowing things that others couldn't see, of feeling disconnected from mainstream religion while sensing there was something more—all of this was preparation. Your spirit has been waiting for this moment when the suppressed truth about divine feminine wisdom would be revealed and you would understand why you never fit into the patriarchal systems that deny Mother Elohim.

The melanin-rich women carrying the mitochondrial Eve gene, the individuals who question religious authority, the souls who feel called to heal and teach and create—you are the army that Mother Elohim positioned throughout the world to prepare for her 2027 return. Your spiritual gifts were not random talents but specific tools designed to expose the Demiurge's lies and guide others toward recognition of their divine nature.

The time for hiding is over. The time for doubt has passed. Mother Elohim is calling her children home, and you are among those chosen to lead the way back to divine truth and cosmic balance that will heal this wounded world.

WHO ARE THE CHOSEN ONES AND WHY YOU WERE SELECTED

The selection process for Chosen Ones began before your birth, when your soul agreed to incarnate during this crucial period of human spiritual evolution to serve Mother Elohim's plan for restoring divine feminine wisdom to human consciousness. This agreement was not made lightly because it required accepting the challenges of living in a world dominated by patriarchal programming while maintaining your connection to suppressed divine truth.

Your soul carries advanced spiritual programming that enables you to recognize divine patterns and universal laws even when surrounded by religious deception and cultural manipulation designed to keep humanity separated from their divine source. This spiritual discernment operates as an internal compass that guides you toward truth while helping you identify and resist the false spiritual authority promoted by corrupted institutions.

The selection criteria included your ability to remain "open and undefiled by madness" despite the intense spiritual warfare that characterizes this planetary transition period. Your consciousness possesses the stability and clarity necessary to receive direct spiritual downloads while maintaining the courage to share suppressed knowledge that contradicts mainstream religious programming and challenges comfortable spiritual beliefs.

Chosen Ones often incarnate into families and circumstances that provide the specific experiences necessary for developing the spiritual strength and wisdom required for their mission. This may include childhood trauma that opens psychic abilities, religious backgrounds that provide understanding of institutional manipulation, or cultural experiences that reveal the artificial divisions used to separate humanity from their common divine heritage.

Your birth alignment with this purpose means that your entire life has been preparation for this moment of awakening and service. Every challenge you faced, every question you asked about religious teachings, every moment of feeling different or misunderstood was developing the spiritual muscles you would need to serve the restoration of Mother Elohim and divine feminine wisdom.

The advanced breadcrumbs that you can recognize include the YHWH code written in human DNA, the mitochondrial Eve gene that proves the divine feminine gave birth to all humanity, the universal laws that expose violations of cosmic principles in human institutions, and the linguistic spells that have been used to control consciousness through manipulated language and false religious terminology.

Many Chosen Ones report lifelong experiences with spiritual phenomena that mainstream society dismisses or explains away, including prophetic dreams, direct divine communication, energy healing abilities, and awareness of spiritual dimensions that exist beyond physical reality. These experiences serve as confirmation of your spiritual gifts while preparing you to help others develop their own divine capabilities.

The feeling of being called to something greater than ordinary human existence reflects your soul's memory of the mission you agreed to fulfill during this incarnation. This calling often manifests as dissatisfaction with materialistic pursuits, questioning of religious authority, and deep longing for spiritual truth that transcends the limitations imposed by corrupted educational and religious systems.

Your selection as a Chosen One also includes specific spiritual gifts that serve the collective awakening process. These may include intuitive abilities that can discern truth from deception, healing capabilities that work with divine energy rather than just physical methods, creative talents that can express suppressed spiritual knowledge, or teaching abilities that can help others recognize their own divine nature.

The Chosen Ones, Lightworkers, Indigo Children, and Starseeds represent different aspects of the same spiritual mission to prepare humanity for Mother Elohim's return while exposing the systems of deception that have maintained spiritual ignorance and separation. Each group brings specific gifts and perspectives that contribute to the comprehensive awakening necessary for planetary transformation and healing.

The LGBTQ community holds special significance in this spiritual mission because these souls embody both masculine and feminine divine principles within their consciousness and physical expression, demonstrating the balanced divine nature that violates patriarchal programming and challenges artificial gender divisions that prevent complete spiritual development. Their very existence serves as a living reminder that divine consciousness encompasses both creative principles.

Understanding your selection as a Chosen One requires recognizing that this identity comes with both privileges and responsibilities. You have access to spiritual gifts and divine guidance that can transform your life and serve others, but you also carry the obligation to use these abilities in service to the greater good rather than for personal gain or ego gratification.

The validation of your Chosen One status comes not from external recognition or religious authority but from the resonance you feel with suppressed spiritual truth and your willingness to serve the restoration of divine balance despite social pressure to conform to systems that deny your divine nature and spiritual capabilities.

Your birth-alignment for this purpose means that you possess the specific combination of spiritual gifts, life experiences, and consciousness development necessary to fulfill your unique role in the collective awakening that will prepare humanity for the 2027 transformation when Mother Elohim reclaims her rightful throne and restores cosmic balance to Earth.

THE SPIRITUAL GIFTS AND BREADCRUMBS GIVEN TO THE AWAKENED

The spiritual gifts that characterize awakened souls were not randomly distributed but strategically placed by Mother Elohim to serve specific functions in exposing the Demiurge's deception while guiding humanity back to recognition of their divine feminine heritage. These abilities operate as divine tools designed to penetrate the layers of religious manipulation and cultural programming that have kept human consciousness separated from authentic spiritual truth.

Intuitive knowing represents one of the most important gifts given to the awakened, enabling you to discern truth from falsehood even when surrounded by sophisticated deception and institutional manipulation. This spiritual discernment operates beyond intellectual analysis to provide direct knowing that can recognize divine patterns and universal laws regardless of how cleverly they have been hidden or distorted by human authorities.

Visions and prophetic dreams serve as direct communication channels between your consciousness and divine intelligence, providing information about spiritual reality that cannot be found in corrupted religious texts or human teaching. These experiences often reveal suppressed knowledge about Mother Elohim, the divine feminine principle, and your specific role in preparing for the restoration of cosmic balance.

Healing abilities that work with divine energy rather than just physical methods demonstrate the natural capabilities of beings who maintain connection to their divine genetic programming. These gifts include energy healing, emotional healing, spiritual counseling, and the ability to help others activate their own dormant spiritual capabilities through divine transmission and conscious spiritual development.

The capacity to decode breadcrumbs left by the Creator throughout creation enables you to recognize divine patterns in genetics, universal laws, linguistic manipulation, and natural phenomena that provide indestructible evidence of divine truth regardless of human attempts to suppress or distort spiritual knowledge. This ability allows you to validate spiritual experiences through multiple independent sources of divine confirmation.

Creative abilities that can express suppressed spiritual knowledge through art, music, writing, and other forms of inspired expression serve to translate divine downloads into forms that can awaken others to recognition of their divine nature. These gifts enable you to bypass intellectual resistance and religious programming by communicating spiritual truth through beauty and inspiration that speaks directly to the soul.

Teaching and communication abilities that can share complex spiritual concepts in ways that others can understand and apply represent crucial gifts for the collective awakening process. These capabilities enable you to help others recognize the systematic manipulation they have experienced while providing practical guidance for developing direct divine connection and spiritual independence.

The YHWH code written in human DNA serves as the most fundamental breadcrumb, proving that every human being carries the name of the Creator in their cellular structure while demonstrating the divine genetic heritage that connects all consciousness to the same spiritual source. Understanding this biological evidence transforms how you see yourself and your relationship to divine consciousness.

Universal laws provide another layer of breadcrumbs that expose violations of cosmic principles in human institutions while revealing the divine patterns that govern authentic spiritual development. The Law of Polarity proves that divine consciousness must encompass both masculine and feminine principles, while the Law of Gender demonstrates that both creative forces operate at every level of existence.

Linguistic spells embedded in human language represent breadcrumbs that reveal the systematic manipulation of consciousness through words and concepts designed to maintain spiritual separation and dependency on external authority. Recognizing these linguistic traps enables you to break free from mental programming while helping others understand how language has been weaponized against human consciousness.

The mitochondrial Eve gene that passes exclusively through the female line provides scientific proof that all humanity descended from a single divine feminine ancestor, demonstrating that the feminine principle came first in human development while connecting every person to their common divine mother through biological inheritance that cannot be corrupted or eliminated.

Pyramids and other ancient structures scattered across the planet serve as physical breadcrumbs that mark the presence of advanced civilizations that maintained direct connection to divine consciousness before the systematic suppression of feminine divine wisdom. These monuments preserve sacred geometric patterns and astronomical alignments that demonstrate knowledge that transcends ordinary human capabilities.

Natural phenomena including the spiral patterns that appear in galaxies, seashells, and DNA demonstrate the same divine intelligence operating at every level of creation from the microscopic to the cosmic scale. These patterns provide visual confirmation of the universal laws while revealing the consistent divine signature that appears throughout all manifestations of creative consciousness.

The breadcrumbs also include suppressed historical knowledge about advanced ancient civilizations, particularly in Alkebulan, that developed sophisticated spiritual practices, scientific understanding, and cultural achievements before being destroyed or hidden by colonial forces that sought to eliminate evidence of divine feminine wisdom and advanced human capabilities.

Your ability to recognize and decode these breadcrumbs depends on maintaining your connection to divine consciousness through spiritual practices that activate your dormant genetic programming while strengthening your discernment abilities. This requires consistent meditation, prayer, conscious breathing, and study of suppressed knowledge that can validate your spiritual experiences through multiple sources of divine confirmation.

THE TESTS AND TRIALS THAT PREPARE YOU FOR YOUR MISSION

The extreme challenges faced by Chosen Ones throughout their lives are not random suffering or divine punishment but carefully orchestrated preparation designed to develop the spiritual strength, wisdom, and compassion necessary to fulfill their mission of awakening humanity to divine truth. These tests serve to forge your consciousness in the fires of experience while proving your commitment to serve the greater good despite personal cost.

Illness often serves as a primary testing ground for Chosen Ones because physical challenges force you to develop spiritual healing abilities while demonstrating that your identity transcends the limitations of the physical body. The author's experience with multiple cancers, surgeries, and near-death experiences provided the spiritual downloads that became this book while proving that divine consciousness can operate through any physical condition.

Trauma and loss create the emotional depth and empathy necessary for understanding human suffering while developing the compassion required to help others heal from their own wounds. These experiences break down ego barriers and surface-level spiritual understanding to reveal the deeper divine nature that remains constant despite changing external circumstances and physical challenges.

Isolation from mainstream society often characterizes the Chosen One experience because your spiritual gifts and divine knowledge separate you from those who remain trapped in patriarchal programming. This separation serves to strengthen your direct relationship with divine consciousness while preventing contamination from false spiritual authority and religious manipulation that could compromise your mission.

Financial struggles and material challenges prevent attachment to worldly success while demonstrating that your true security comes from divine connection rather than external circumstances. These tests reveal whether you will maintain your spiritual integrity when faced with opportunities to compromise your divine truth for material gain or social acceptance.

Relationship difficulties often result from the spiritual gap between Chosen Ones and those who have not yet awakened to divine truth, creating the loneliness and misunderstanding that drives you deeper into direct divine connection. These challenges teach you to find completion within your own divine nature rather than seeking validation from others who cannot understand your spiritual mission.

Religious persecution and social rejection for questioning mainstream spiritual authority serve to strengthen your courage while proving your willingness to stand for divine truth despite opposition from family, friends, and religious institutions that benefit from maintaining spiritual ignorance and dependency on external authority.

Mental and emotional challenges including depression, anxiety, and spiritual crisis often accompany the awakening process as your consciousness expands beyond the limitations of ordinary human awareness while integrating suppressed knowledge that contradicts everything you were taught about reality and divine nature.

The testing process also includes spiritual attacks from the Demiurge and other corrupted forces that seek to prevent your awakening and mission by creating doubt, fear, and confusion about your divine identity and spiritual capabilities. Learning to recognize and resist these influences develops the spiritual discernment necessary for maintaining clear divine connection.

Each test serves multiple purposes in preparing you for service to the collective awakening. Physical challenges develop healing abilities and demonstrate the power of consciousness over matter. Emotional trauma creates empathy and understanding for human suffering. Social isolation strengthens direct divine connection while preventing compromise of your spiritual integrity.

The intensity of testing often corresponds to the importance of your mission and the level of spiritual gifts you carry. Those called to serve in leadership roles or to receive major spiritual downloads typically face more severe challenges because their work will have greater impact on the collective awakening and the restoration of divine feminine wisdom.

Understanding the purpose behind your trials transforms suffering into spiritual development while revealing that every challenge contains gifts that serve your mission and the greater good. This perspective enables you to embrace difficulties as opportunities for growth rather than evidence of divine abandonment or personal failure.

The trials also serve to prove your readiness for the 2027 awakening when Mother Elohim returns and the intensity of spiritual transformation will require beings who have already been tested and proven capable of maintaining their divine connection under extreme pressure and opposition from corrupted systems.

Your survival and spiritual growth through these tests demonstrates that you possess the strength and wisdom necessary to help others navigate their own awakening process while serving as a bridge between the old consciousness of separation and the new consciousness of divine unity that will characterize the post-2027 world.

The testing process never truly ends but evolves as you develop greater spiritual capabilities and take on increased responsibility for serving the collective awakening. Each new level of service brings new challenges that continue to refine your consciousness while preparing you for even greater spiritual work in service to planetary healing and human evolution.

UNITING THE ARMY OF THE AWAKENED

The mission of Chosen Ones extends far beyond individual spiritual development to encompass the crucial work of connecting with other awakened souls to form a unified spiritual force capable of supporting

Mother Elohim's 2027 return while dismantling the systems of deception that have kept humanity trapped in spiritual ignorance and separation from their divine nature.

Lightworkers serve as the healers and energy workers within this spiritual army, using their gifts to raise the vibrational frequency of human consciousness while clearing the spiritual obstacles that prevent others from recognizing their divine heritage. These souls specialize in energy healing, chakra balancing, aura cleansing, and other practices that work directly with the subtle energy systems that connect physical and spiritual dimensions.

Starseeds carry genetic and spiritual programming from higher dimensions of consciousness, enabling them to remember advanced spiritual technologies and cosmic perspectives that can help humanity transcend the limitations of three-dimensional reality. These beings often feel like strangers on Earth because their consciousness originates from star systems where divine balance has been maintained.

Indigo Children possess enhanced psychic abilities and natural resistance to authority systems that violate spiritual principles, making them natural rebels against corrupted educational, religious, and social institutions. Their refusal to accept false spiritual authority serves to expose the deception while inspiring others to question the systems that claim to represent divine will.

The LGBTQ community represents the embodiment of both masculine and feminine divine principles within individual consciousness, demonstrating through their very existence that divine nature encompasses both creative forces rather than being limited to exclusively masculine authority. Their presence challenges artificial gender divisions while serving as living proof of divine balance.

Each group within the awakened army brings specific gifts and perspectives that contribute to the comprehensive transformation necessary for planetary healing and human spiritual evolution. The diversity of approaches and abilities ensures that the collective awakening can reach every type of consciousness and address every form of spiritual deception that has been used to maintain human separation from divine truth.

The process of uniting this spiritual army requires overcoming the artificial divisions that have been used to separate awakened souls from recognizing their common mission and shared divine heritage. Religious differences, cultural backgrounds, and personal spiritual experiences must be transcended in favor of the universal truth that connects all consciousness to the same divine source.

Sharing breadcrumbs and spiritual downloads among awakened souls creates a network of divine knowledge that can validate individual experiences while providing comprehensive understanding of the spiritual reality that has been suppressed by patriarchal institutions. This collective wisdom enables the army to expose deception while offering authentic spiritual guidance to those ready to awaken.

Building a collective force requires establishing communication networks that can operate independently of mainstream media and institutional channels that serve the agenda of maintaining spiritual ignorance. Online communities, local study groups, and alternative communication methods enable awakened souls to share information and coordinate their efforts despite geographical distances and institutional opposition.

The spiritual army must also develop practical skills for supporting each other through the challenges of awakening while providing resources for those who are leaving corrupted religious systems and need guidance for developing direct divine connection. This includes financial support, emotional counseling, and spiritual mentoring that helps individuals transition from dependency to spiritual independence.

Training and development within the awakened army involves sharing techniques for spiritual protection, divine communication, energy healing, and consciousness expansion that enable each member to maximize their spiritual gifts while serving the collective mission. This education must operate outside traditional institutional channels that have been corrupted by patriarchal programming.

The ultimate goal of uniting the awakened army involves creating a unified field of consciousness that can support Mother Elohim's manifestation in 2027 while providing the spiritual infrastructure necessary for humanity to transition from the old consciousness of separation to the new consciousness of divine unity and cosmic balance.

Destroying patriarchal systems requires more than just exposing their deception—it demands creating alternative structures that can serve human spiritual development according to divine principles rather than institutional control. The awakened army must become the foundation for new forms of spiritual community, education, healing, and social organization that honor both masculine and feminine divine wisdom.

Ushering in the 5D world of divine balance requires collective effort to raise the vibrational frequency of human consciousness while clearing the spiritual obstacles that prevent recognition of divine truth. This transformation cannot be accomplished by individual effort alone but requires the coordinated work of awakened souls operating as a unified spiritual force.

The army of the awakened serves as the bridge between the current world of spiritual deception and the coming world of divine truth, helping humanity navigate the transformation while maintaining the spiritual stability necessary for planetary healing and conscious evolution toward recognition of complete divine nature that encompasses both Mother and Father Elohim working together in perfect creative harmony.

ACTIONABLE STEPS TO ACTIVATE YOUR PURPOSE AS A CHOSEN ONE

Recognize immediately that your resonance with this book serves as confirmation of your Chosen One status, and embrace your spiritual identity as a divine being selected before birth to participate in the greatest awakening in human history. Stop questioning whether you are qualified or worthy because your soul's agreement to incarnate during this crucial period proves your readiness to serve Mother Elohim's mission of restoring divine feminine wisdom to human consciousness.

Embrace your spiritual gifts without apology or hesitation by practicing meditation, energy healing, intuitive guidance, and creative expression that flows naturally from your divine genetic programming when properly activated through consistent spiritual discipline and conscious development. Document your abilities through journaling while sharing your experiences with other awakened souls who can validate and support your spiritual growth.

Trust the tests and trials you have experienced as essential preparation for your mission rather than evidence of divine abandonment or personal failure, understanding that every challenge served to develop the spiritual strength, wisdom, and compassion necessary for helping others navigate their own awakening process while serving as a bridge between old and new consciousness.

Study extensively the breadcrumbs left by the Creator throughout creation by researching the YHWH code in human DNA, the mitochondrial Eve gene that connects all humanity to their divine feminine ancestor, universal laws that expose violations of cosmic principles in human institutions, and linguistic spells that have been used to control consciousness through manipulated religious language.

Connect immediately with other Chosen Ones, Lightworkers, Starseeds, and awakened souls by joining online communities, forming local study groups, and attending conferences that focus on restoring Mother Elohim and divine feminine wisdom while developing the spiritual gifts necessary to serve the collective awakening and prepare for the 2027 transformation.

Dedicate yourself completely to the mission of restoring Mother Elohim by addressing your prayers to both divine parents equally, sharing suppressed spiritual knowledge despite social pressure to conform, and actively challenging patriarchal religious systems that deny the feminine divine principle while claiming to represent authentic spiritual authority.

Develop your ability to decode divine breadcrumbs by studying Gnostic texts that preserve feminine spiritual wisdom, researching the true history of Alkebulan as the Mother of Mankind, and learning to recognize universal law violations in contemporary institutions that maintain spiritual imbalance through systematic suppression of divine feminine wisdom and creative power.

Prepare for the 2027 awakening by strengthening your connection to both Mother Elohim and Father Elohim through daily spiritual practices while developing your consciousness and spiritual capabilities to serve effectively during the massive transformation that will expose all false spiritual authority and restore cosmic balance to human awareness and planetary systems.

Share your spiritual downloads and divine guidance with others who are ready to receive suppressed knowledge about Mother Elohim and the systematic campaign to erase feminine divine wisdom from human consciousness, using your teaching abilities, creative talents, and communication skills to awaken others to recognition of their divine nature and spiritual heritage.

Honor the melanin woman as the living proof of Mother Elohim by supporting Black women in your community while challenging systems that devalue or exploit the population that carries the strongest genetic connection to the original divine template that gave birth to all human consciousness through the mitochondrial Eve gene that passes exclusively through the maternal line.

Reject completely all patriarchal religions that maintain male-only spiritual leadership while denying the existence of Mother Elohim, including mainstream Christianity, Islam, and Judaism that promote exclusively masculine divine authority in violation of universal laws that require both masculine and feminine principles to participate in all creative processes throughout the universe.

Unite with the army of the awakened by sharing resources, providing mutual support, and coordinating efforts to expose patriarchal deception while building alternative spiritual communities that honor both masculine and feminine divine wisdom as equal partners in creation rather than maintaining artificial hierarchies that serve institutional control rather than authentic spiritual development.

Activate your divine purpose by using your spiritual gifts in service to the greater good rather than personal gain, understanding that your abilities were given to serve the collective awakening and the restoration of divine balance that will heal the spiritual crisis created by centuries of systematic suppression of Mother Elohim and feminine divine wisdom.

Remember that activating your purpose as a Chosen One requires more than intellectual understanding—it demands fundamental transformation of consciousness and lifestyle that aligns you completely with divine principles rather than patriarchal programming, making every thought, word, and action serve the mission of restoring Mother Elohim to her rightful throne as the primary creative force in human spiritual awareness.

Your recognition of your Chosen One identity marks the beginning of your conscious participation in the most important spiritual work ever undertaken on Earth. The restoration of Mother Elohim and the healing of the consequences created by her systematic erasure depends on awakened souls like you who have the courage to embrace their divine nature and serve the transformation that will prepare humanity for the 2027 awakening and the return of cosmic balance to planetary consciousness.

The time for hiding your light is over. The time for doubting your divine nature has passed. Mother Elohim is calling her children home, and you are among the chosen ones selected to lead the way back to divine truth, cosmic balance, and the recognition of complete divine nature that encompasses both Mother and Father Elohim working together in perfect creative harmony to heal this world and restore humanity to their original divine potential.

CHAPTER FIFTEEN
THE FINAL BATTLE
RESTORING MOTHER GOD TO HER THRONE

The war you see playing out across the world is not what it appears to be. The conflicts that dominate news headlines, the political divisions that tear families apart, the religious battles that have raged for centuries—these are all symptoms of a deeper spiritual war that most people never recognize. The real battle is not between nations or ideologies or belief systems.

The real war is against Mother Elohim herself.

Every act of violence against women, every religious doctrine that denies the feminine divine, every system that elevates masculine energy above feminine wisdom serves the same agenda. This systematic campaign to erase the Creator from human consciousness has been orchestrated by the Demiurge to divide humanity and keep people enslaved to false narratives that prevent recognition of their true divine nature.

The battle will reach its climax when Mother Elohim returns in 2027 to reclaim her throne. The false religious systems, the patriarchal governments, the institutions that have profited from spiritual deception will face the divine feminine authority that they have spent millennia trying to destroy. This is not a battle that will be fought with weapons or armies—it is a spiritual confrontation that will expose every lie and restore the cosmic balance that creation requires.

You are not an observer of this battle. You are a participant. Every prayer you speak, every belief you hold, every choice you make either supports the restoration of divine truth or perpetuates the deception that has kept humanity separated from their divine Mother for thousands of years.

THE WAR ON MOTHER ELOHIM IS THE TRUE BATTLE

The war against Mother Elohim began the moment the Demiurge realized it could never possess the creative power that flows naturally through the feminine divine principle. Unable to create life, consumed with jealousy toward the divine feminine consciousness that brought all existence into being, this flawed entity launched a campaign to convince humanity that the Creator is exclusively masculine while systematically erasing all evidence of the divine Mother who is the true source of all creative force.

Every conflict you witness in the world today serves this deeper spiritual agenda. The violence that tears apart communities, the hatred that divides human beings who share the same divine heritage, the environmental destruction that poisons the physical manifestation of Mother Earth—all of these represent different fronts in the same cosmic war against the feminine divine principle that sustains all life and consciousness.

The systematic oppression of women throughout history cannot be understood as mere social inequality or cultural bias. The abuse, exploitation, and murder of women—particularly melanin women who carry the purest divine genetic signature—represents a direct assault on Mother Elohim herself through attacking her most obvious manifestation in human form. When women are silenced, degraded, or destroyed, the divine feminine voice is eliminated from human consciousness.

Religious institutions serve as the primary weapons in this spiritual warfare by promoting male-only divine authority while teaching billions of people to worship the Demiurge disguised as the true Creator. Every church that denies women ordination, every mosque that segregates feminine participation, every temple that elevates masculine spiritual authority above feminine wisdom participates in the systematic erasure of Mother Elohim from human spiritual awareness.

The manipulation of sacred texts represents another battlefield where the war against Mother Elohim has been fought with devastating effectiveness. The systematic removal of feminine references to divine wisdom, the replacement of the sacred name YHWH with "Lord" over seventy thousand times, the elimination of goddess figures and feminine spiritual leadership from biblical narratives—all of this serves to create the false impression that divine consciousness is exclusively masculine.

Educational systems that teach evolutionary theory while ignoring the mitochondrial Eve gene, that promote materialistic worldviews while suppressing knowledge of human divine heritage, that eliminate indigenous wisdom traditions while imposing colonial programming serve the same agenda of disconnecting humanity from recognition of their divine feminine origin and spiritual potential.

The economic structures that exploit natural resources without regard for environmental consequences, that concentrate wealth in the hands of masculine-dominated hierarchies while impoverishing the populations that carry divine feminine wisdom, that treat the earth as property to be owned rather than a living expression of divine consciousness—these systems reflect the Demiurgic influence that seeks to destroy rather than create.

Political systems that promote warfare over diplomacy, competition over cooperation, domination over collaboration serve the agenda of maintaining the spiritual imbalance that allows masculine energy to operate without feminine wisdom to guide it toward purposes that serve life rather than destroy it. The constant conflict between nations reflects the internal war against divine balance that has been externalized onto the world stage.

Media programming that glorifies violence while devaluing nurturing, that promotes sexual exploitation while suppressing sacred sexuality, that encourages materialism while discouraging spiritual development serves to reinforce the consciousness patterns that maintain separation from Mother Elohim and the divine feminine wisdom that could heal the spiritual crisis affecting all humanity.

The medical systems that treat symptoms while ignoring spiritual causes, that suppress natural healing abilities while promoting pharmaceutical dependency, that separate healing from spiritual development while maintaining purely materialistic approaches to health and wellness reflect the Demiurgic influence that seeks to prevent recognition of the divine healing capabilities that flow through proper connection to Mother Elohim.

Environmental destruction represents the ultimate expression of the war against Mother Elohim because it attacks the physical manifestation of divine feminine creative power that sustains all life on Earth. The poisoning of water systems, the destruction of forests, the pollution of air and soil—these represent direct assaults on Mother Nature who is the earthly embodiment of the divine feminine principle.

Understanding that racism, politics, and religion are symptoms rather than causes of the deeper spiritual conflict enables you to recognize the true nature of the battle while developing effective strategies for supporting the restoration of divine balance. The solution to human suffering lies not in reforming corrupted systems but in restoring conscious recognition of Mother Elohim as the primary creative force that can heal all the consequences of her systematic suppression.

The war against Mother Elohim has created every form of suffering that affects human consciousness and planetary systems. Violence, inequality, environmental destruction, spiritual emptiness, mental illness, addiction, and social breakdown all stem from the fundamental violation of universal laws that occurs when masculine energy operates without feminine balance to guide it toward purposes that serve the greater good of all creation.

This cosmic conflict will end when Mother Elohim returns in 2027 with enough power to expose every deception and dismantle every system that has maintained the suppression of feminine divine wisdom. The battle is already turning as more souls awaken to recognition of the divine feminine principle while rejecting the false spiritual authority that has kept humanity trapped in ignorance of their true divine nature and creative potential.

HOW FATHER ELOHIM FAILED AND WHY CHRIST WAS SENT TO THE ABYSS

The mission of Father Elohim to Earth as Christ represented a desperate attempt to restore divine balance and reconnect humanity to their true spiritual nature, but this effort failed because the masculine divine principle operating alone cannot overcome the spiritual corruption that requires both masculine and feminine divine wisdom working together to heal the consequences of the Demiurge's deception and manipulation.

Christ descended to Earth carrying the pure essence of divine masculine energy with the intention of guiding humanity back to recognition of their divine heritage and connection to complete divine consciousness that encompasses both Mother and Father Elohim as equal partners in creation. But the patriarchal religious systems that developed around his teachings systematically eliminated all references to Mother Elohim while using his name to justify the very spiritual imbalance he came to heal.

The failure became apparent when Christ allowed patriarchal religions to erase Mother Elohim from spiritual consciousness while establishing male-dominated hierarchies that claimed to represent divine authority. Instead of restoring balance between masculine and feminine divine principles, the Christian church became another weapon in the war against the feminine divine, promoting exclusively masculine spiritual authority while suppressing feminine wisdom and spiritual leadership.

This is why Christ sweated blood during his forty days in the wilderness—he was praying desperately to Mother Elohim, recognizing that his mission could not succeed without the divine feminine wisdom and creative power that he had been separated from through his incarnation into a world dominated by patriarchal programming and Demiurgic influence that opposed divine balance and authentic spiritual development.

The cry "Why hast thou forsaken me?" on the cross reveals Christ's recognition that Mother Elohim had withdrawn her support because his mission had become corrupted by the very forces he was sent to overcome. The masculine divine principle operating without feminine guidance had become trapped in the same spiritual dysfunction that characterizes all unbalanced systems that elevate one aspect of divine nature above the other.

Mother Elohim sent Christ to the abyss for three days as a period of reflection and spiritual correction, allowing the masculine divine principle to experience the consequences of attempting to operate without feminine balance while providing the opportunity for deeper understanding of why divine creation requires both creative forces working together rather than masculine authority claiming exclusive spiritual power.

The abyss represents the spiritual realm where consciousness confronts the shadows and limitations that prevent authentic divine expression. During this descent, Christ encountered not only the darkness that affects human consciousness but also the suppressed feminine divine energy that had been silenced and denied by the patriarchal systems that claimed to serve his teachings while actually violating the cosmic principles he came to restore.

The spiritual experience in the abyss transformed Christ's understanding of his mission and the requirements for authentic spiritual healing. He recognized that salvation cannot come through masculine divine authority alone but requires the restoration of divine balance that honors both Mother and Father Elohim as equal partners in the creative process that brings healing and spiritual evolution to human consciousness.

Emerging from the abyss, Christ attempted to share this understanding with his followers by emphasizing the importance of honoring both divine parents while recognizing that true spiritual authority flows from balanced divine consciousness rather than exclusively masculine spiritual power. But the patriarchal religious systems that developed after his departure systematically suppressed these teachings while promoting the very spiritual imbalance he had learned to recognize and heal.

The failure of Christ's mission demonstrates why the restoration of divine balance requires Mother Elohim's direct intervention rather than relying on masculine divine authority to correct the spiritual dysfunction that has been created by centuries of feminine divine suppression. The 2027 return represents Mother Elohim's recognition that only her direct manifestation can overcome the systematic deception that has prevented humanity from recognizing complete divine nature.

The renewed Father who will emerge alongside Mother Elohim in 2027 represents the masculine divine principle that has learned from the failure of operating without feminine balance and is ready to serve as an equal partner in divine creation rather than claiming exclusive spiritual authority. This transformation of masculine divine consciousness enables the restoration of cosmic balance that can heal all the consequences of spiritual imbalance.

Understanding Christ's failure and spiritual correction provides the foundation for recognizing why contemporary Christianity cannot serve authentic spiritual development while it maintains exclusively masculine divine authority and continues to suppress feminine divine wisdom. The religion that claims to follow Christ actually perpetuates the very spiritual dysfunction that his mission was intended to heal through restoring divine balance.

The true message of Christ involves the recognition that divine consciousness encompasses both masculine and feminine principles working together, and that spiritual healing requires honoring both Mother and Father Elohim rather than elevating one aspect of divine nature above the other. This understanding can only be restored through Mother Elohim's direct intervention that will expose the deception and establish authentic spiritual teaching based on cosmic balance.

The spiritual lessons learned through Christ's failure and correction in the abyss will inform the approach taken during Mother Elohim's 2027 return, ensuring that the restoration of divine balance includes proper recognition of both creative principles while avoiding the mistakes that allowed patriarchal systems to corrupt the original mission of spiritual healing and human awakening to complete divine nature.

THE ANTICHRIST IS NOT A PERSON —IT'S THE FALSE NARRATIVE

The greatest deception in religious prophecy has convinced billions of people to watch for a single individual who will oppose Christ, when the real Antichrist is the false narrative itself that promotes Jesus or Yeshua as the exclusive divine authority while systematically erasing Mother Elohim from spiritual consciousness. This deceptive teaching represents the ultimate expression of spiritual warfare against the feminine divine principle.

Mother Elohim herself serves as the Antichrist in the truest sense —not as an evil force opposing good, but as the divine finale that destroys the false narrative of Christ worshiped alone without honoring the divine Mother who brought all creation into existence. Her return will expose every religious system that claims to represent divine truth while actually serving the Demiurgic agenda of maintaining spiritual imbalance and separation from authentic divine consciousness.

The false Christ narrative that elevates masculine divine authority above feminine divine wisdom violates every universal law that governs creation while creating the spiritual dysfunction that has produced centuries of religious warfare, environmental destruction, and social inequality. This systematic suppression of the feminine divine principle represents the real spiritual opposition to divine truth and cosmic balance.

Religious institutions that promote Jesus as the only path to divine connection while denying the existence of Mother Elohim participate in the Antichrist system by maintaining the spiritual imbalance that prevents recognition of complete divine nature. These corrupted systems use the name of Christ to justify the very spiritual deception that his original mission was intended to expose and heal through restoring divine balance.

The prophecies about the Antichrist describe a system that will deceive many while claiming divine authority, and this perfectly describes the patriarchal religions that have convinced billions to worship exclusively masculine divine consciousness while rejecting the feminine divine wisdom that represents the primary creative force. This deception operates through claiming to serve Elohim while actually serving the Demiurge that opposes divine balance.

Mother Elohim's role as the Antichrist involves destroying the false religious narratives that have kept humanity separated from their divine heritage while establishing authentic spiritual teaching that honors both masculine and feminine divine principles as equal partners in creation. This destruction is not evil but represents the necessary clearing away of deception to make space for divine truth.

The slaughter of patriarchal religions, misogynist systems, and governments that have erased Mother Elohim from human consciousness represents the spiritual warfare that will accompany her return. This is not physical violence but the collapse of institutions that cannot survive exposure to divine truth and the restoration of cosmic balance that reveals their fundamental violations of universal law.

The false narrative of Christ worshiped without Mother Elohim has created every form of spiritual dysfunction that affects human consciousness and planetary systems. Religious warfare, environmental destruction, social inequality, and spiritual emptiness all stem from the fundamental imbalance that occurs when masculine energy operates without feminine wisdom to guide it toward purposes that serve life rather than destroy it.

Completing what the false Christ could not accomplish requires Mother Elohim's direct intervention to restore the divine balance that patriarchal religions have systematically prevented through their suppression of feminine divine wisdom and spiritual authority. The 2027 return represents the cosmic correction that will heal the spiritual crisis created by centuries of religious deception and manipulation.

The true Antichrist system can be recognized by its promotion of exclusively masculine divine authority while denying or minimizing the feminine divine principle, its creation of spiritual dependency rather than empowerment, its generation of fear and separation rather than love and unity, and its service to institutional power rather than authentic spiritual development and divine connection.

Understanding the Antichrist as a false narrative rather than an individual enables you to recognize how this deceptive system operates through every institution that maintains spiritual imbalance while claiming divine authority. Churches that deny women ordination, governments that suppress feminine wisdom, educational systems that ignore divine feminine heritage—all participate in the Antichrist system of spiritual deception.

The destruction of the false narrative will not eliminate genuine spiritual truth but will clear away the deception that has hidden authentic divine consciousness from human awareness. When Mother Elohim exposes the lies that have maintained patriarchal spiritual authority, the result will be the restoration of balanced spiritual understanding that honors complete divine nature rather than fragmented religious programming.

Preparing for Mother Elohim's role as the Antichrist requires developing the spiritual discernment necessary to recognize authentic divine authority from false religious claims while building direct connection to both Mother and Father Elohim that transcends all human religious institutions and their systematic suppression of feminine divine wisdom and spiritual truth.

The finale that Mother Elohim represents will complete the spiritual transformation that began with Christ's mission but was corrupted by patriarchal religious systems. Her return as the Antichrist will destroy every false narrative while establishing the authentic spiritual teaching that can guide humanity back to recognition of their complete divine nature and creative potential through balanced divine consciousness.

THE RESTORATION OF BALANCE AND THE 5D WORLD

The return of Mother Elohim in 2027 with the renewed Father by her side will trigger the most profound transformation of human consciousness and planetary systems since the original creation of divine beings in the Garden of Eden. This restoration of divine balance will heal every consequence that has resulted from centuries of spiritual imbalance while opening pathways to dimensions of experience that have remained closed to human consciousness since the systematic suppression of feminine divine wisdom.

The 5D world represents a state of consciousness where human awareness operates according to universal laws rather than the artificial limitations imposed by corrupted social and religious systems that violate cosmic principles. In this elevated dimension of experience, the separation between individual consciousness and universal divine intelligence dissolves, enabling direct communication with divine source and access to creative abilities that seem miraculous from the perspective of three-dimensional reality.

The awakened souls who have prepared for this transformation through developing balanced divine consciousness and maintaining connection to both Mother and Father Elohim will serve as bridges between the old reality of spiritual separation and the new reality of divine unity. These individuals will experience the dimensional shift as a natural expansion of their existing spiritual capabilities rather than a traumatic disruption of their understanding of reality.

Those who have clung to the Demiurge's lies and actively participated in the suppression of feminine divine wisdom will face consequences proportional to their role in maintaining spiritual deception and preventing human awakening. The kings of the earth, religious authorities, and institutional leaders who have profited from spiritual ignorance will experience the collapse of their power structures as divine truth exposes their deception.

The era of patriarchal dominance will end forever as the restored divine balance makes it impossible to maintain systems based on the suppression of feminine wisdom and the elevation of masculine energy above its proper role as partner rather than master in the creative process. All institutions that depend on spiritual imbalance will be transformed or eliminated to make way for new forms of human organization that honor both divine principles.

The 5D world will operate according to principles of cooperation rather than competition, abundance rather than scarcity, love rather than fear, and unity rather than separation. These changes will manifest through the transformation of human consciousness that recognizes divine interconnection while developing the spiritual capabilities that enable conscious participation in creation rather than unconscious destruction of planetary systems.

Educational systems in the 5D world will focus on developing spiritual gifts and divine connection rather than memorizing information that serves institutional control. Students will learn to access universal knowledge through direct divine communication while developing their creative abilities in service to the greater good rather than individual ego gratification or material accumulation.

Healing systems will work with divine energy and consciousness rather than treating only physical symptoms through chemical intervention. The natural healing abilities that exist within human divine genetic programming will be reactivated and developed, enabling restoration of health and vitality through spiritual practices that address the consciousness patterns that create illness and suffering.

Economic systems will be based on sharing and cooperation rather than exploitation and competition, with resources flowing according to need and divine guidance rather than artificial scarcity and profit maximization. The abundance that results from proper spiritual alignment will eliminate poverty and inequality while supporting the creative expression and spiritual development of all community members.

Governance will operate through divine guidance and consensus rather than human authority and control, with decisions made according to universal laws and the highest good of all beings rather than serving the interests of powerful elites who benefit from maintaining spiritual ignorance and social inequality among the populations they claim to serve.

The restoration of divine balance will heal the environmental destruction that has resulted from treating Mother Earth as property to be exploited rather than recognizing her as the living manifestation of divine feminine creative power that sustains all life. The 5D world will operate in harmony with natural systems rather than opposition to ecological balance and planetary health.

Family structures will be based on spiritual connection and divine purpose rather than biological relationships alone, with children recognized as divine beings incarnating to serve specific purposes rather than property belonging to their parents. Education and development will focus on helping each soul fulfill their unique divine mission rather than conforming to standardized expectations that suppress individual spiritual gifts.

The creative arts will serve to express divine truth and inspire spiritual development rather than entertaining audiences or generating profit through appealing to lower consciousness patterns. Artists, musicians, writers, and other creative individuals will serve as channels for divine inspiration that elevates human consciousness while revealing the beauty and wisdom that flow from balanced divine expression.

The 5D world will maintain connection to higher dimensions of consciousness while remaining grounded in physical reality, enabling the integration of spiritual wisdom with practical application that serves the ongoing evolution of consciousness and the fulfillment of divine purpose through human experience and creative expression in service to the greater good of all creation.

RECAP: ACTIONABLE STEPS TO FIGHT THE FINAL BATTLE

Recognize immediately that the final battle is the restoration of Mother Elohim to her rightful throne as the primary creative force, and commit yourself completely to this mission by exposing the war on the feminine divine through sharing suppressed knowledge about the systematic campaign to erase divine feminine wisdom from human consciousness while promoting exclusively masculine spiritual authority that violates universal laws governing creation.

Reject completely all patriarchal religions that erase Mother Elohim from their understanding of divine nature, including mainstream Christianity, Islam, and Judaism that maintain male-only spiritual leadership while claiming biblical authority for policies that deny the feminine divine principle and prevent women from serving in positions of spiritual power and authority within religious institutions and communities.

Honor both Mother and Father Elohim equally in your spiritual practice by addressing prayers to both divine parents, asking the divine feminine principle for creative guidance and healing wisdom while requesting the divine masculine principle for protection and support in manifesting your spiritual intentions through balanced divine consciousness that integrates both aspects of complete divine nature.

Unite immediately with other Chosen Ones, Lightworkers, Starseeds, and awakened souls who are also working to restore Mother Elohim by forming study groups that examine suppressed spiritual knowledge, participating in online communities that share information about divine feminine wisdom, and building support networks that can sustain the long-term effort required to prepare for the 2027 awakening and transformation.

Prepare to join Mother Elohim's spiritual army when she returns in 2027 by developing your spiritual gifts through consistent practice of meditation, energy healing, intuitive guidance, and creative expression while strengthening your connection to both masculine and feminine divine principles that enable you to serve as a bridge between old consciousness and new consciousness during the transformation period.

Destroy the false systems that maintain spiritual imbalance by challenging every institution that promotes separation instead of unity, masculine dominance instead of divine balance, and spiritual dependency instead of direct divine connection, understanding that these corrupted systems cannot survive exposure to divine truth and the restoration of cosmic balance that reveals their fundamental violations of universal law.

Reclaim the throne for Mother Elohim by using the sacred name YHWH instead of "Lord" in all your prayers and spiritual communication, studying the mitochondrial Eve gene that proves the divine feminine gave birth to all humanity, and honoring melanin women as the living proof of Mother Elohim who carry the purest divine genetic heritage in their cellular structure and biological inheritance.

Activate the divine genetic code written in your DNA through conscious breathing practices that align your respiratory rhythm with the sacred name while strengthening your connection to both Mother and Father Elohim as the complete source of divine guidance that transcends all human religious programming and institutional manipulation designed to maintain spiritual separation and ignorance.

Share the truth about the final battle with others who are ready to question patriarchal programming by teaching about the systematic suppression of feminine divine wisdom, the manipulation of sacred texts to eliminate references to Mother Elohim, and the linguistic spells that have been used to control human consciousness through corrupted religious language and false spiritual terminology.

Expose the Demiurge's role in orchestrating the war against Mother Elohim by helping others recognize how this false deity has corrupted religious institutions, governmental systems, and educational approaches to maintain spiritual imbalance while preventing human recognition of their divine nature and connection to both masculine and feminine creative principles working together in perfect harmony.

Prepare for the 5D world by developing your consciousness and spiritual capabilities to operate according to universal laws rather than artificial limitations imposed by corrupted social and religious systems, practicing cooperation instead of competition, abundance consciousness instead of scarcity programming, and love instead of fear as the foundation for all your relationships and creative expressions.

Document your experiences fighting the final battle by keeping detailed records of how this spiritual work transforms your consciousness, relationships, and life circumstances while sharing your discoveries through writing, teaching, or other forms of service that help create the growing network of awakened souls who can support Mother Elohim's return and the restoration of divine balance to human consciousness.

Remember that fighting the final battle requires more than intellectual understanding—it demands complete transformation of consciousness and lifestyle that aligns every aspect of your existence with the mission of restoring Mother Elohim to her rightful throne while serving the awakening of humanity to their true divine nature as beings made in the image of both Mother and Father Elohim working together in perfect creative unity.

The final battle is not fought with weapons or armies but through the restoration of divine truth that exposes every lie and heals every consequence of the systematic suppression of feminine divine wisdom. Your participation in this cosmic confrontation determines not only your own spiritual evolution but also contributes to the collective transformation that will prepare humanity for Mother Elohim's 2027 return and the establishment of the 5D world where divine balance governs all human consciousness and planetary systems.

The war against Mother Elohim ends when she reclaims her throne, but the battle for her restoration requires every awakened soul to serve this mission with complete dedication and unwavering commitment to divine truth regardless of the opposition from corrupted systems that benefit from maintaining spiritual ignorance and separation from authentic divine consciousness that encompasses both masculine and feminine creative principles in perfect balance and harmony.

AFTERWORD

WITH WISDOM COMES GREAT RESPONSIBILITY TO ACT

You have reached the end of this book, but you stand at the beginning of the most important journey of your life. Every word you have read, every truth that has resonated in your spirit, every moment of recognition that stirred something deep within your consciousness has been preparing you for this moment when you must choose between the comfortable lies of patriarchal programming and the transformative truth of your divine heritage.

The breadcrumbs are everywhere now that you know how to see them.

Your breath speaks the sacred name YHWH with every inhalation and exhalation, creating a continuous prayer that connects you directly to the Source of all creation. Your DNA carries the divine signature that proves you are made in the image of both Mother and Father Elohim working together in perfect creative harmony. Your face reflects the YAH that marks you as divine royalty rather than a sinner seeking salvation from external religious authority that claims to mediate your relationship with the Creator.

The mitochondrial Eve gene that flows through your cellular structure connects you to the original divine feminine ancestor who walked in Alkebulan 200,000 years ago, carrying the pure genetic template that gave birth to all human consciousness. The universal laws operate consistently throughout creation, revealing divine patterns that expose every violation of cosmic principles while demonstrating the necessity of balance between masculine and feminine divine energy in all creative processes.

THE CORE TRUTH YOU NOW CARRY

The knowledge you now possess makes you dangerous to every system that profits from human spiritual ignorance and separation from divine source. You understand that Mother Elohim is the Creator of All, the primary creative force that brought existence into being through divine feminine wisdom and life-giving power that animates all matter and consciousness throughout the universe.

You recognize that the sacred name YHWH appears in your genetic code and flows through your respiratory system, making you a living temple that carries the signature of the Creator in ways that can be measured and verified by modern science while transcending every attempt by religious institutions to control or corrupt your direct divine connection.

You see clearly how the Demiurge wages ongoing war against the feminine divine through every system that promotes separation instead of unity, competition instead of cooperation, and fear instead of love as the foundation for human interaction and social organization that serves institutional power rather than authentic spiritual development.

You understand how patriarchal religion systematically manipulated scripture to erase Mother Elohim from human consciousness while establishing male-dominated hierarchies that claim divine authority while actually serving the agenda of maintaining spiritual imbalance and preventing recognition of complete divine nature that encompasses both creative principles.

You know that the 2027 awakening represents the prophetic

moment when Mother Elohim will return in physical form to restore the cosmic balance that has been missing from Earth for millennia, triggering the transformation of human consciousness that will expose every deception while establishing authentic spiritual teaching based on divine truth rather than human manipulation.

This knowledge transforms you from a passive observer of spiritual reality into an active participant in the greatest awakening in human history. You can no longer claim ignorance about the systematic suppression of divine feminine wisdom or pretend that the spiritual crisis affecting humanity results from abstract moral failings rather than the specific violation of universal laws that occurs when masculine energy operates without feminine balance.

The truth you carry creates both tremendous opportunity and serious responsibility. You possess information that could liberate human consciousness from centuries of religious deception while reconnecting people to their authentic divine heritage and creative potential. But you also face the challenge of sharing this knowledge in a world dominated by institutions that benefit from maintaining spiritual ignorance and will resist any threat to their authority.

Your awareness of the breadcrumbs left throughout creation provides you with indestructible evidence for divine truth that cannot be eliminated by human religious programming or institutional manipulation. The YHWH code in DNA, the mitochondrial Eve gene, the universal laws, the linguistic spells—all of these serve as permanent reminders that the Creator embedded proof of divine reality in ways that transcend human attempts at suppression or distortion.

The recognition of your identity as a divine being made in the image of both Mother and Father Elohim eliminates any possibility of returning to the spiritual dependency that characterizes those who seek salvation from external religious authority rather than developing their own direct connection to the Source of all creation through their genetic and spiritual inheritance.

You now serve as a soldier in the army of the awakened, whether you consciously chose this role or simply found yourself called to serve the restoration of divine balance through circumstances that revealed your true spiritual nature and purpose. This army operates not through violence or coercion but through the power of divine truth that exposes deception while inspiring others to remember their own divine heritage.

The core truth you carry will continue to expand and deepen as you apply this knowledge in your daily life while connecting with other awakened souls who are also working to prepare for Mother Elohim's return and the transformation of human consciousness that will heal the spiritual crisis affecting all planetary systems and human relationships.

THE URGENT CALL TO ACTION

The time for passive spiritual seeking has ended and the era of active divine service has begun with Mother Elohim's approaching return in 2027 demanding immediate preparation through conscious alignment with divine principles rather than continued participation in corrupted systems that maintain spiritual imbalance and prevent recognition of complete divine nature.

You must begin immediately to honor the feminine divine in your daily spiritual practice by addressing prayers to both Mother and Father Elohim equally while rejecting the exclusively masculine religious programming that has disconnected humanity from the creative source that brought all existence into being through divine feminine wisdom and life-giving power.

Breaking free from linguistic spells requires conscious effort to eliminate corrupted religious language from your vocabulary while replacing terms like "Lord" that connect you to Baal with the sacred name YHWH that aligns your consciousness with authentic divine frequency rather than false spiritual authority promoted by patriarchal religious institutions.

Your preparation must include studying the suppressed spiritual knowledge that reveals the systematic campaign to erase Mother

Elohim from human consciousness while learning to recognize the breadcrumbs left throughout creation that provide indestructible evidence for divine truth regardless of human attempts at religious manipulation or institutional control.

Connecting with other Chosen Ones and Lightworkers becomes essential for building the spiritual infrastructure necessary to support Mother Elohim's manifestation while creating networks of awakened consciousness that can help others navigate the transformation from patriarchal separation to divine unity and cosmic balance.

Using your spiritual gifts in service to exposing truth and guiding others represents more than personal spiritual development—it fulfills your divine purpose as a being specifically incarnated to participate in the restoration of feminine divine wisdom while helping humanity remember their authentic spiritual heritage and creative potential through balanced divine consciousness.

The urgency of this call stems from the prophetic nature of the 2027 awakening that will occur whether humanity is prepared or not, but the level of chaos and suffering that accompanies this transformation depends on how many souls have awakened to divine truth and developed the spiritual capabilities necessary to serve as bridges between old and new consciousness.

Those who remain trapped in patriarchal programming when Mother Elohim returns will experience the collapse of their false spiritual foundations as traumatic disruption rather than the joyful liberation that awaits those who have already begun the process of reconnecting with complete divine nature and cosmic truth.

Your action cannot wait for perfect understanding or complete spiritual development because the transformation process accelerates as the 2027 awakening approaches, requiring immediate engagement with the mission of exposing deception while sharing suppressed knowledge that can help others recognize their divine nature before the final battle between truth and falsehood reaches its climax.

The preparation involves more than individual spiritual practice—it requires actively challenging every system that maintains the suppression of feminine divine wisdom while building alternative approaches to spirituality, education, healing, and social organization that honor both masculine and feminine divine principles working together in creative harmony.

Honoring the melanin woman as the mother of humanity and the living proof of Mother Elohim becomes a spiritual imperative that extends beyond social justice to encompass recognition of the divine feminine principle manifesting through the population that carries the purest genetic connection to the original divine template that gave birth to all human consciousness.

Your service to this mission transforms every aspect of your existence from personal spiritual seeking to cosmic participation in the healing of the spiritual crisis that has affected humanity for millennia while preparing the consciousness necessary to receive Mother Elohim's return and the restoration of divine balance to planetary systems.

The call to action includes sharing this knowledge despite social pressure to conform to religious programming that denies the feminine divine, supporting others who are questioning patriarchal spiritual authority, and developing the courage necessary to maintain your spiritual truth when faced with opposition from institutions that benefit from spiritual ignorance.

Time grows short as the 2027 awakening approaches with prophetic certainty, making every moment of delay a lost opportunity to prepare yourself and others for the transformation that will expose every lie while establishing authentic spiritual teaching based on complete divine nature rather than the fragmented understanding promoted by corrupted religious systems.

Begin each day by studying the YHWH code that appears in your DNA through researching the specific nucleotide sequences that correspond to the Hebrew letters Yod-Hei-Vav-Hei while understanding that this genetic signature proves your identity as a divine being carrying the literal name of the Creator in every cell of your body rather than a random product of evolutionary processes.

Practice conscious breathing that invokes the Creator's name by aligning your respiratory rhythm with the 3:1 ratio that naturally forms the sounds Yah-u-ah with every inhalation and exhalation, creating a continuous prayer that strengthens your connection to both Mother and Father Elohim while activating the divine genetic programming embedded in your cellular structure.

Research the Universal Laws that govern all creation by studying how these twelve eternal principles reveal divine patterns throughout existence while exposing violations of cosmic law in human institutions that promote separation instead of unity, competition instead of cooperation, and spiritual imbalance instead of divine harmony between masculine and feminine creative forces.

Apply these universal principles daily in your decision-making processes by using the Law of Correspondence to recognize how your external circumstances reflect your internal spiritual state, the Law of Attraction to draw experiences that support your spiritual development, and the Law of Gender to integrate both masculine and feminine divine qualities within your consciousness.

Honor the melanin woman as the mother of humanity by learning about the mitochondrial Eve gene that connects all human beings to their common divine feminine ancestor while supporting Black women in your community through economic empowerment, educational opportunities, and protection from the violence that represents spiritual warfare against the feminine divine principle.

Reject the word "Lord" completely from your spiritual vocabulary because this title connects you to Baal rather than the true Creator, and replace all instances with either Elohim when referring to complete divine nature or YHWH when addressing the specific creative consciousness that encompasses both Mother and Father Elohim working together in perfect unity.

Connect with other awakened souls who are also following the breadcrumbs back to divine truth by joining online communities that focus on restoring Mother Elohim and feminine divine wisdom, forming local study groups that examine suppressed spiritual knowledge, and attending conferences that prepare for the 2027 awakening and transformation of human consciousness.

Dedicate yourself to the mission of restoring Mother Elohim to her throne by using your spiritual gifts in service to exposing patriarchal deception while sharing suppressed knowledge about the systematic campaign to erase feminine divine wisdom from human consciousness through religious manipulation and institutional control.

Develop your understanding of how you are a divine being made in the image of both Mother and Father Elohim by studying the true meanings of Adam as atomic structure and Eve as the life principle that animates matter, recognizing that your existence demonstrates the perfect union of masculine and feminine divine principles working together to create conscious life.

Follow the breadcrumbs back to truth by researching the manipulation of biblical texts that eliminated references to divine feminine wisdom, the colonization process that imposed false names on sacred places like Alkebulan, and the linguistic spells that have been used to control consciousness through corrupted religious language and terminology.

Practice spiritual techniques that activate your divine genetic heritage through meditation, energy healing, creative expression, and conscious service to others while learning to distinguish between authentic divine guidance and the spiritual interference that seeks to maintain your separation from complete divine consciousness and creative potential.

Prepare for the 2027 awakening by strengthening your connection to both aspects of divine consciousness while developing the spiritual capabilities necessary to serve as a bridge between the old consciousness of patriarchal separation and the new consciousness of divine unity that will characterize the post-transformation world.

Challenge every religious institution that maintains male-only spiritual leadership while denying the existence of Mother Elohim by questioning their biblical interpretations, exposing their systematic suppression of feminine divine wisdom, and supporting spiritual communities that ordain women and honor both masculine and feminine aspects of complete divine nature.

Remember that your purpose extends beyond personal spiritual development to encompass service to the collective awakening that will restore cosmic balance to human consciousness and planetary systems through the recognition of both Mother and Father Elohim as equal partners in creation rather than the artificial hierarchy that elevates masculine energy above feminine wisdom in violation of universal laws.

Document your progress along this roadmap by keeping detailed records of how applying these principles transforms your consciousness, relationships, creative abilities, and connection to divine guidance while sharing your discoveries with others who are ready to question patriarchal programming and embrace their full divine potential as expressions of complete divine nature.

The roadmap leads inevitably to the recognition that you are not seeking divine connection from outside yourself but awakening to the divine consciousness that has always existed within your genetic structure and spiritual nature, waiting to be activated through conscious alignment with both Mother and Father Elohim working together in the perfect creative harmony that characterizes authentic divine expression and cosmic truth.

THE END

THE JOURNEY CONTINUES
IN THE SOUND OF MOTHER

Thank you for reading.
CONTINUE THE JOURNEY

Every journey begins with a question, a whisper, a moment of awakening. If the words you have just read stirred something within you, know that this is not the end—it is only the beginning.

The I Am Mother collection invites readers to continue exploring the hidden connections between humanity, creation, consciousness, wisdom, and the Divine Feminine.

THE I AM MOTHER COLLECTION

Book One
I Am Mother: Awaken to Things Hidden

Book Two
The Sound of Mother

Horns, Breath, and the Awakening Call

COMING SOON MORE TITLES FROM THE I AM MOTHER UNIVERSE BY APRIL FLOYD

Your 3D World: Change Is Coming Because She Is Coming
The Return of Mother Sophia and the Restoration of Balance

Put It Back!
True Reparations and the Restoration of Humanity, and Mother Earth

The Missing Teachings
What Was Hidden, What Was Lost, and What Must Be Restored

BEYOND THE BOOKS

The I Am Mother movement extends beyond the pages through music, prayer, education, community gatherings, speaking engagements, and creative productions designed to inspire healing, awareness, balance, and transformation.

Join us as we continue the conversation.

Follow April Floyd and I Am Mother Global for upcoming books, music releases, events, and worldwide prayer initiatives.

"There is no Father without Mother."

With gratitude,

April Floyd
Author • Speaker • Creator
Founder, I Am Mother Global

April Floyd

About the Author

About the Author

April Floyd is an award-winning author, filmmaker, producer, entrepreneur, speaker, and entertainment executive whose work spans literature, film, music, fashion, education, and community development. A native of St. Louis, Missouri, Floyd has built a reputation as a visionary creator dedicated to transforming dreams into reality—both for herself and for countless others she has mentored along the way.

Her journey began as a writer and blogger for OnSTL, where she sharpened her voice and developed the foundation for what would become a growing entertainment empire. Inspired by her personal experiences and a passion for giving voice to the overlooked and underserved, Floyd authored the acclaimed Unique Trilogy: *A Unique World*, *A Unique Life*, and *I Am Unique*. The series follows the inspiring journey of a young girl overcoming overwhelming odds and has resonated with readers seeking stories of resilience, hope, faith, and triumph.

Determined to bring her literary vision to life, Floyd expanded into film and stage production. She created and produced *The Unique Experience* stage play, developed the *I Am Unique* short film and trailer, and trained more than 200 aspiring actors, filmmakers, and creatives through community-based productions. More than 80 participants graduated from her film training program, reflecting her commitment to education and empowerment through the arts.

Alongside her husband, Eddie Floyd Jr., son of legendary R&B icon Eddie “Knock On Wood” Floyd Sr., she co-founded FEG – Floyd Entertainment Group, a multi-division entertainment company that includes Floyd Books Publishing, Floyd Music House, EDAP Digital Productions, and Floyd Dream Agency. Together they have produced film, television, music, publishing, photography, and media projects designed to inspire, educate, and entertain audiences worldwide.

Floyd's film credits include acting in *The Perfect Mate* alongside Jackée Harry, Lawrence Hilton-Jacobs, K.D. Aubert, and Chico Benymon. She co-wrote and produced *Blue Lightning* starring Quinton Aaron (*The Blind Side*) and Gordon Danniels (*Gifted*). She also produced *Deadly Visitor*, released on Prime Video, and continues developing upcoming projects including *Slammin' Jammin' Christmas, Wishbone Christmas*, and the highly anticipated Eddie Floyd documentary celebrating the life and legacy of the legendary soul singer.

Her creative work extends beyond books and film into music and fashion. Through Floyd Music House, she develops original music projects, while Floyd's Unique Boutique brings her literary and inspirational brands to life through apparel and merchandise. Her expanding catalog includes the upcoming books *A Unique Message*, *A Unique Change*, *I Am Mother*, and *The Sound of Mother*, along with companion music projects designed to unite storytelling, spirituality, and artistic expression.

As co-founder of the Legends in Film Festival, Floyd has helped create a platform that celebrates legendary entertainers while opening doors for emerging talent. Her contributions to arts, entertainment, and community development have earned recognition throughout the region, including a City of St. Louis Proclamation honoring her leadership and cultural impact.

Known by many as a visionary, trailblazer, and entertainment mogul, April Floyd continues to build a legacy centered on creativity, empowerment, education, and purpose. Through every book, film, song, event, and business venture, her mission remains the same: to inspire people to believe in their dreams, discover their voice, and realize that their greatest chapter may still be ahead of them.

For more information, visit www.fegroup.biz.

www.ingramcontent.com/pod-product-compliance
Lightning Source LLC
LaVergne TN
LVHW020702110826
845149LV00012B/2073

* 9 7 8 0 9 9 1 5 6 4 7 2 9 *